The Heraldic World of Lawrence Durrell

Also in the "Durrell Studies" Series:

1. *Borders and Borderlands: Explorations in Identity, Exile and Translation*
Edited by Richard Pine and Vera Konidari

2. *Lawrence Durrell's Woven Web of Guesses*
By Richard Pine

3. *The Eye of the Xenos: Letters about Greece*
By Richard Pine with Vera Konidari

4. *Nikolaos Mantzaros: Emergence of a Greek Composer*
by Konstantinos Kardamis (forthcoming)

5. *Mikis Theodorakis: Music and Politics*
by Gail Holst-Warhaft (forthcoming)

The Heraldic World of Lawrence Durrell:

The Man, His Circle, and His Art

(Durrell Studies 4)

By

Bruce Redwine

**Cambridge
Scholars**
Publishing

Dave, here's my book. During my 4 years in the Army, I carried a copy of Durrell's Quartet. And I recall that, in the old barracks of the 76th, someone had left a quote from Justine over the entrance. So, there you have it — or simply, "There it is!" GI jargon for Vietnam, which says it all. All the best,

Bruce   3 August 2022

The Heraldic World of Lawrence Durrell:
The Man, His Circle, and His Art
(Durrell Studies 4)

By Bruce Redwine

This book first published 2022

Cambridge Scholars Publishing

Lady Stephenson Library, Newcastle upon Tyne, NE6 2PA, UK

British Library Cataloguing in Publication Data
A catalogue record for this book is available from the British Library

ISBN (10): 1-5275-7798-8
ISBN (13): 978-1-5275-7798-5

For Kit Choy

I find art easy. I find life difficult.

— Lawrence Durrell, *The Paris Review* 22 (1960)

An artist's work and his private life are like a woman in childbed and her child. You may look at her child, but you may not lift up her chemise to see if there are any bloodstains on it, that would be indelicate on the occasion of a maternity visit.

— Vincent van Gogh, Letter to Theo, 11 March 1882

CONTENTS

Part Three: Durrell's Art

Coda: Durrell and Rilke

LIST OF ILLUSTRATIONS

I. Colour Plates

Plate 1: Alexandria, the White City (licenced by Alamy on 16 October 2021)

Plate 2: Ambron Tower (© Michael Haag, 2004)

Plate 3: David Green and Michael Haag (© Denise Tart, 2015)

Plate 4: Haag's Garden Mirror (© Denise Tart, 2015)

Plate 5: *Fowling in the Marshes* (British Museum EA 37977; reproduced by courtesy of the British Museum)

Plate 6: *Cleopatra on the Terraces of Philae* (1896) (Frederick Arthur Bridgman. Wikimedia Commons)

Plate 7: Tomb of the Diver, c. 470 BC (National Archaeological Museum of Paestum. © Michael Johanning, 2001. Wikimedia Commons)

II. Black and White Figures

FOREWORD

The trauma of birth has a special appeal for male artists. Otto Rank wrote a book on the subject with that same title. Both Freud and Jung wrote on the topic, and so did Lawrence Durrell. The connection between conception and creativity is long and obvious: women are naturally creative, and men must find a substitute. So it's not surprising that Van Gogh would choose birthing as being analogous to artistic creation. Van Gogh, however, emphasizes the "child" over the "bloodstained" sheets, and he advises his brother Theo not to lift the chemise of a woman on her maternity bed. Birthing considerations aside (Durrell actually believed he could recall his own birth), Lawrence Durrell and Vincent van Gogh had much in common besides artistic careers. Among other things, a type of creative madness included, they could have been neighbours, were the times right — both spent their last years in the south of France, and some of Durrell's landscape paintings resemble the Dutch painter's. Durrell may have approved of Van Gogh's advice to Theo, but I do not see that warning as relevant to the role of a literary critic. I understand that role to go beyond the printed page. I appreciate the need for privacy, but I will not follow Van Gogh's admonition to respect the proprieties. Instead, I shall take Durrell's own confession as a guide and offer some suggestions as to why he found "art easy" and "life difficult".

ACKNOWLEDGEMENTS AND INDULGENCES

Scholarship, or simply writing about writing, is a collaborative enterprise. I've found discussions among colleagues as a form of dialectic, as a way to test and refine my ideas. Over the years, I've been indebted to many people with whom I've had the pleasure of personal contact. This is especially true about the vast field of studies dealing with Lawrence Durrell. His literary genius and breadth of knowledge require the endeavours of many specialists to approach a rough understanding of his great achievement. On literary matters, I owe special thanks to Richard Pine for his support, advice, and innumerable insights into Lawrence Durrell. My friend Richard is today's premier scholar in Durrellian studies.

I have also benefited from exchanging ideas with the following people: Rony Alfandary, William Apt, Ciarán Benson, David S. Callahan, Candace Fertile, Pamela Francis, Kennedy Gammage, James Gifford, William Leigh Godshalk, David Green, Paul Herron, David Holdsworth, Benjamin Keatinge, Ian S. MacNiven, Ray Morrison, Sumantra Nag, C. Ravindran Nambiar, Nicholas Poburko, Charles L. Sligh, and, most importantly, Michael Haag. I have also benefited from the assistance of Andrew Stewart in the field of Classics and Anthony Durrell in psychoanalysis. In Egyptology, I have relied upon the published expertise of scholars I have not met. Those I have duly cited. None of the aforementioned individuals is responsible for any of my errors in whatever form they may take. All errors are mine.

Versions of these essays and reviews have appeared in the following publications: *Arion*, *C.20*, *A Café in Space*, *Islands of the Mind* and *Mosaic*. I have made minor corrections and revisions to these essays. Each of my chapters acknowledges the source of the original publication. I thank the editors of these journals and series for their willingness to publish my articles. My long essay, "Ancient Egypt and *The Alexandria Quartet*", makes its first appearance in this monograph. A short and preliminary version of this essay, "The Ancient Egyptian Context of *The Alexandria Quartet*", appeared in *Mosaic* 16.1 (2016). My final essay on Durrell and Rilke is new.

Finally, because this book is a collection of essays, published on many different occasions, some repetition of my argument is inevitable. I request the reader's indulgence in this regard.

REFERENCES AND ABBREVIATIONS

Primary references to Lawrence Durrell's works are cited in the main text and take a shortened form. They use the abbreviations listed below. Secondary sources are footnoted and also take a shortened form. Full citations to all works are listed in the bibliography.

Scholarly and governmental abbreviations conform to those in *The Chicago Manual of Style*, 17th edition (2017). For references to Classical literature, Greek and Roman, I use the abbreviations in *The Oxford Classical Dictionary*, 4th edition (2012). For Shakespeare's works, all my quotations from and citations to are derived from *The Norton Shakespeare*, 3rd edition (2016). All abbreviations to Shakespeare's plays are from C. T. Onions's *A Shakespeare Glossary*, 2nd edition (1969).

The following abbreviations will be used for Lawrence Durrell's works:

Bal	*Balthazar* [1958]
BB	*The Black Book*
BL	*Bitter Lemons*
BT	*Blue Thirst*
CP	*Collected Poems 1931-1974* [1980]
CVG	*Caesar's Vast Ghost*
DL	*The Dark Labyrinth*
DML	*The Durrell-Miller Letters*
EB	*From the Elephant's Back: Collected Essays & Travel Writings*
GI	*The Greek Islands*
Jus	*Justine* [1957]
Key	*A Key to Modern British Poetry*
MI	*The Magnetic Island*
PC	*Prospero's Cell*
Quartet	*The Alexandria Quartet* (*Justine, Balthazar, Mountolive, Clea*)
Quintet	*The Avignon Quintet* (*Monsieur, Livia, Constance, Sebastian, Quinx*)
RMV	*Reflections on a Marine Venus*
SC	*Sicilian Carousel*
Sel	*Selected Poems*
SME	*A Smile in the Mind's Eye*
SP	*Spirit of Place*
WES	*White Eagles over Serbia*

A word about dating. For dates associated with Lawrence Durrell's life, ancient Egyptian history, and classical studies, I rely upon the following sources: Brewster Chamberlin's *The Durrell Log* (2019), Toby Wilkinson's *The Thames & Hudson Dictionary of Ancient Egypt* (2008), and *The Oxford Classical Dictionary* (2012).

INTRODUCTION

Impressions and memories imprint themselves early in life. They endure and remain fresh through time. Some of mine began with readings in Egyptology and *The Alexandria Quartet*. When I was a teenager in the 1950s, I read histories such as James Henry Breasted's *History of Egypt* (1909) and John A. Wilson's *Burden of Egypt* (1951). Many years later, my interest in archaeology resulted in academic course work on the topic, and then, in 2000 and 2004, I participated in archaeological "digs" (excavations) at Tel Dor, Israel. But, at the beginning, Egypt came first. Hollywood films on ancient Egypt inspired my early adventures in these historical "realms of gold". Then, quite by accident, I came across Lawrence Durrell's *Quartet* in the late 1950s and assumed it too was about Egypt. I was initially wrong but was immediately drawn into a world of evocative experience. Durrell's Egyptian world, on the surface at least, has very little to do with ancient Egypt as such. His Alexandria — his "capital of Memory" — is largely an enclave of the imagination. The city is not unlike several of his island books: isolated geographically, poetic in its ambience, and entirely unique unto itself. It does not exist in the real world and cannot be found on any map. Durrell's claim in the note to *Justine* that "only the city is real" is highly misleading.

A short anecdote illustrates this point. In 2007, my wife and I attended the Durrell Celebration in Alexandria, Egypt, sponsored by the British Council. In *Balthazar*, Durrell uses the image: "flocks of spiring pigeons glittered like confetti as they turned their wings to the light" (*Bal* 45) (Note: "spiring" in the 1958 edition, replaced by "spring" in the 1962 edition.) We stayed at Durrell's Cecil Hotel on Durrell's "Grande Corniche". Late one afternoon, we went to the top floor of the Cecil and had drinks on a terrace overlooking the "White City". I longed to see Durrell's pigeons turning like confetti in the fading light. I didn't see any, however, nor do I remember seeing any such sight during our entire stay in Egypt. The image of flocks of pigeons recurs throughout the *Quartet* (*Quartet* 22, 234, 280, 670). Pigeons are a staple of the Egyptian diet, and "pigeon-tower[s]" or roosts dot the Delta countryside (*Quartet* 257). Nevertheless, Durrell's image, to my mind at least, remains odd and out of place. Then, in 2019, I believe I found Durrell's source. That year we went to Corfu, the Greek island where Durrell resided in the 1930s, and

xvi   Introduction

attended the Durrell Library of Corfu's symposium on "Islands of the Mind". There, in open-air restaurants, I watched huge flocks of swifts swooping and turning like confetti in the sky. The experience was overwhelming. Moreover, "spiring" aptly describes the flight of swifts — far more than does the bland adjective, "spring". And that emendation may be an indication of the image's original source. Most probably, Durrell's ubiquitous "mind's eye" conflates and transposes this and other such imagery onto other times and other places. His imagination creates its own reality — its own world — and that "reality" is what enthralls his readers.

So, around 1957, I began reading *Justine* for the first time, swallowed its opening "hot nude pearl" — which is not unlike the rich pearl Cleopatra swallows during her banquet with Antony — and awoke into another world. As a teenager, the power of Durrell's prose and poetry would cause me to lie awake late into the night and dream as though I were looking through a powerful lens into an immense sidereal universe. I no longer feel the same way, but I vividly recall the memory of those exhilarating experiences.

Durrell's world owes much to what he calls his "Heraldic Universe", a world of metaphor, poetry, and memory existing in some timeless and irrational dimension. In a strange and obscure way, "heraldic" characterizes Durrell's world. I seriously doubt that Durrell understood exactly what he meant by this concept. He says various things about it at various times and in various media. The Heraldic Universe can be transcendent, illogical, non-causal, timeless, symbolic, ideogrammatic, magical, or an "alchemical sigil". It can be a Buddhist mandala, Lao Tzu's *Tao*, or one of Durrell own poems. I prefer to interpret the concept — which is much like Plato's "Allegory of the Cave" in *The Republic*[1] — as an attempt to go beyond the mundane world of time, change, and causality and to reach some eternal and immutable realm beyond the dictates of rationality. A couple of my essays shall briefly explore Durrell's idea, but I basically stick to the Platonic analogy.

Durrell's Heraldic Universe is not an original idea. It is important as a stage in his own poetic development and personal philosophy, but his obscure concept is neither unique nor seminal. Alfred North Whitehead famously writes that "the European philosophical tradition" is "a series of footnotes to Plato".[2] I am lumping Durrell in with this Platonic tradition, although he would probably object strenuously to my presumptuousness. Durrell's thought processes were often Eastern. In his *Paris Review*

---

[1] Plato, *The Republic*, pp. 227-35 (VII. 514A-521B).
[2] Whitehead, *Process and Reality*, p. 39.

interview, he speaks of the "confluence" of "Eastern and Western metaphysics".[3] True. And so are some of Plato's ideas as they come under Eastern influences, particularly when he reverts to myth and allegory, much as Durrell himself does. Plato's use of myth is a way to avoid direct statements about matters not conducive to rational explanation, so he suggests in his "Seventh Letter".[4] And Durrell's use of obscurity serves a similar, albeit highly personal, function, especially in his poetry.

The pursuit of obscurity was one aspect of Lawrence Durrell, man and artist. His psychology was unusual but not unique. He had company in the pursuit of fame and anonymity. He was like another Lawrence, T. E. Lawrence (1888-1935), also known as Lawrence of Arabia. After his famous exploits, Colonel Lawrence of the British Army enlisted in the RAF under the pseudonym of Aircraftman John Hume Ross. He later joined the Tank Corps where he became Private T. E. Shaw.[5] Two years after Lawrence's death in 1935, Durrell published his second novel, *Panic Spring*, using the pseudonym of "Charles Norden". Creating pseudonyms became part of a pattern. In 1963, Durrell created the pseudonym of "Oscar Epfs", which he used to sign his paintings over the years. The pseudonymous artwork was exhibited and sold in several French venues.[6] Assuming false identities is another aspect of Lawrence Durrell. It is also called fabulation.

Durrell was a fabulator. He was not always the person he self-portrayed in his numerous interviews. This is a common human fault. Nevertheless, he misled his audience and threw up smoke screens to elude his interviewers. His public and private peronae did not always mesh. Two authors have presented controversial views of Durrell's private life — one is Joanna Hodgkin, daughter of Durrell's first wife Nancy Myers by her second marriage; another is Sappho Jane Durrell, his own daughter with his second wife, Yvette (Eve) Cohen. I have reviewed both of their writings and offered my opinions of how each adds something important to a portrait of a very complex man.

Durrell's circle included many fellow writers, acquaintances, and critics. He carried on an extensive correspondence with all of these, most notably Henry Miller. I shall, however, concentrate on only one of his followers, Michael Haag (1944-2020), whom I knew personally for a short period of time. Haag met Durrell at his home in Sommières, France and spent years working on a biography of the writer. The biography, which

---

[3] L. Durrell, "Art of Fiction", p. 57.
[4] Plato, *Complete Works*, p. 1659.
[5] J. Wilson, *Lawrence of Arabia*, pp. 681-82, 710.
[6] Chamberlin, *Durrell Log*, pp. 136, 138, 147, 157, 168, 186.

would have been his magnum opus, remained unfinished at his death. Haag was not an academic or a professional literary critic. He was educated and trained as an anthropologist. A polymath, he wrote books on a variety of subjects, historical and literary, and became an authority on Egyptian culture and history. Haag was also a practitioner of a type of biography that I will call a version of "field anthropology". To study his subject, like a good anthropologist, he went into the field, held interviews, and gathered information. He eschewed armchair scholarship in favour of first-hand experience. He was also interested in Durrell's use of obscurity and the way he used it to create "his own world". Haag saw obscurity as a dominant mode of Durrell's fiction and poetry, and he explained it in terms of Durrell's deep need to conceal — and yet to hint at — his private life and his anxieties. I shall explore the implications of Haag's analysis, as I understand his ideas and expand on them.

Finally, there is the matter of Durrell's art. I use *art* broadly. Lawrence Durrell was primarily a writer of prose and poetry. But his writings often had the descriptive qualities of paintings. He had the eye of an artist and was an evocative painter of people and landscapes, although he modestly called himself a "dauber" in *The Paris Review*.[7] Self-deprecation was one of Durrell's techniques to deflect attention from the mysterious workings of his art — and from himself. It had the opposite effect, of course. The simile of pigeons and confetti quoted above was immediately followed by the parenthetical jest of "(Fine writing!)", which makes a fine image seem too self-conscious. The poet making fun of himself falls flat.

Durrell was very self-conscious. As previously mentioned, he was a fabulator, and his primary subject of invention was his own multifarious identity. He was a master of creating *alter ego*s, such as Darley and Pursewarden in the *Quartet*. Another example is Count D. in *Prospero's Cell* and possibly the narrator himself. And nowhere is that clearer than in his travel book, *Sicilian Carousel*. The narrator of that book, purportedly Durrell himself, is another fabrication on a fabricated journey around Sicily.

Why? Why all the deception and misdirection? We must go back to the key concept of the psychological need for obscurity, Durrell's need to obscure his art and then, ultimately, himself. The need finally leads to a kind of self-extinction. I discuss this process in terms of Durrell's use of Virgilian pastoral and his suppression of indebtedness to ancient Egypt. I am not offering a solution to the problem of *why*. That would be far too

---

[7] L. Durrell, "Art of Fiction", p. 60.

presumptuous. I am simply suggesting some of its parameters.

My reading of Lawrence Durrell is personal, and my "I" will intrude in the following essays whenever appropriate. So this introduction ends where it began — in ancient Egypt and the profound effect Egypt had on Durrell — and on me. Another visitor to Egypt and its monuments was the great poet of the German language, Rainer Maria Rilke. Rilke's Egyptian experiences in 1911 were equally profound and lasting. They would later reappear in his landmark *Duino Elegies* and other poetry.[8] Durrell held the Bohemian-Austrian poet in high esteem and wrote an important comment, translated into German, on Rilke's only novel, *The Notebooks of Malte Laurids Brigge* (1910). I provide an English translation of Durrell's short essay as it appeared in a German newspaper. The two poets had much in common. As men, they were both exiles and rootless. As artists, they both dwelled within the confines of their own imaginations and listened to their own muses or angels. That sense of isolation (*"Islomania"* as Durrell reified it) or solitude (*"Einsamkeit"* as Rilke extolled it) was both real and symbolic. So Durrell emphasizes that Rilke's protagonist creates his art alone in a dark room, which is closed, shut off, and timeless. That imaginative space is similar to the Platonic dimension of Durrell's "Heraldic Universe", which also involves an attempt to transcend a cave-like experience.

---

[8] For Durrell's note on Rilke's *Duino Elegies*, see Vol. 2, pp. 279-80 of *Lawrence Durrell's Endpapers and Inklings 1933-1988.*

PART ONE:

LAWRENCE DURRELL: HIS FAME AND TRIALS

Introduction to Part One

When Lawrence Durrell told *The Paris Review* in 1960 that he found "art easy" and "life difficult", he was at the height of his literary fame. That statement was both accurate and prophetic. In 1960, he published *The Alexandria Quartet* as a single volume to the high acclaim of many literary critics. His fame, however, came at a price. Twenty years earlier, he had endured the trials of the Second World War while living and working in Egypt (1941-1945). That tumultuous experience was eventually followed by three fruitful but troublesome years on Cyprus (1953-1956). The island was then under British control and undergoing the Greek Cypriot struggle for *enosis* (union) with Greece itself. Subsequently, the author's own life was endangered because of his involvement with the British government as Director of Information Services. In 1960, Durrell was also on the verge of marrying Claude-Marie Vincendon, his third wife (1961-1967). His first two marriages to Nancy Myers (1935-1947) and Yvette (Eve) Cohen (1947-1957) had been stormy and traumatic. Then, in 1967, Durrell's beloved Claude died of cancer. More anguish would follow. In 1985, Sappho Jane, Durrell and Eve's daughter, committed suicide. Aspects of Durrell's literary fame and his personal trials are the subjects of the following three essays. The first of these essays reflects an event that will change over time, to wit, the fate of the Ambron Villa in Alexandria.

CHAPTER ONE

THE DURRELL CELEBRATION IN ALEXANDRIA[1]

I

The convocation had set up microphones in the audience to enable general participation, and after a little hesitation, a boy rose to speak in a large auditorium full of much older people. The topic of discussion was the preservation of the architectural heritage of the city of Alexandria, and a panel of experts sat on the stage and fielded questions. The meeting served as a call to civic action. The boy, maybe ten or twelve, followed a number of adults who had been commenting on the difficulties of involving the people of the city and the government of Egypt in the enterprise. As many observed, common folk and governments often have more pressing concerns than undertaking aesthetic projects without immediate or tangible returns.

      The young man spoke in Arabic, which required translation, and his comments were fluent, excited, and succinct. He agreed with the aims of the discussions and simply remarked that, if the work of the group was to succeed, the youth of Alexandria needed to be taught their history and the importance of preserving their heritage. It was a brave thing to do, for one so young to speak up before his elders and make such an eloquent and sensible plea. He deserved full credit for that, and the audience immediately applauded. It was a memorable moment. But credit also goes to the organizers and participants of the event that encouraged and facilitated his impassioned response: the Durrell Celebration in Alexandria.

II

The Durrell Celebration held in Alexandria, Egypt, in 2007 was the inspiration of Paul Smith, Director of the British Council and Cultural

---

[1] Originally published as "The Melting Mirage of Lawrence Durrell's White City: Impressions of the Durrell Celebration, Alexandria, Egypt, 29-30 November 2007" in *Arion* 16.1 (2008).

Counsellor to the British Embassy in Egypt, and it commemorated the fiftieth anniversary of the publication of Lawrence Durrell's *Justine,* the first novel of his great tetralogy, *The Alexandria Quartet.* Despite a little discord among some Egyptian observers, who apparently objected to the purpose of the event, I consider the conference a resounding success.

The celebration was primarily organized by the British Council, with the assistance of The Alexandria and Mediterranean Research Centre, under the direction of Dr. Mohamed Awad and his deputy Dr. Sahar Hamouda, and with the help of the Bibliotheca Alexandrina.

Other organizers included Smith's highly capable colleagues at the British Council, and here I must single out Cathy Costain, Manager of Knowledge and Information Services. She and her expert staff were gracious, accommodating, and made everything work smoothly. Michael Haag, author and historian of Durrell's Egypt, assisted in the selection and planning of the programme. Haag has written the best book on Durrell, *Alexandria: City of Memory*, and is working on his biography.

The two-day affair was open to the general public and took place in the conference centre adjacent to the Bibliotheca Alexandrina, a worthy successor to the great Ptolemaic library of Alexandria. The new and beautiful library faces the Mediterranean like an open oyster and contains all the electronic equipment and bibliographic treasures one would expect of a first class institution.

The Bibliotheca is located on the Eastern Harbour Corniche (or Sharia 26th July) at Chatby, about a mile east of the Cecil Hotel. Giuseppe Alessandro Loria, a prominent architect, designed that landmark in the Moorish-Venetian style of 1929, and Durrell used it as a centrepiece of activity in *Justine,* which he set during the years immediately preceding the Second World War. For admirers of the *Quartet,* it was obvious — the Cecil was the logical choice as the conference hub for social gatherings and functions. Inside the Art Deco hotel were mirrors, potted palms, a French elevator cage, a permanent resident in cashmere jacket and suede bedroom slippers, who always sat in a particular chair in the lobby and who was the scion of a Syro-Lebanese family, and outside before the Midan Saad Zaghloul were the waiting gharries and the clip-clop of horses, although no double-parked "great silver Rolls with the daffodil hubcaps", which might have been Justine's car (*Quartet* 29). All that to make any good Durrellian happy, notwithstanding the incongruity of a rooftop Chinese restaurant catering to a new global clientele.

Much jumbled history — political, architectural, literary — crowds this part of Alexandria on or near the sea, where names have changed to accommodate everchanging realities. Most recently, comparatively speaking,

Gamal Abdel Nasser's revolution of 26 July 1952 accounts for many of these resurgent sensibilities.

Until his death in 1933, the poet C. P. Cavafy lived in a nearby flat. His third-floor apartment, now a small museum on Sharia Sharm el Sheik, once known as Rue Lepsius, is a ten-minute walk away. The writer E. M. Forster came to Alexandria in 1915 and first stayed at the Majestic Hotel opposite the French Gardens. That hotel with its twin copulas is now a dreary office building, but it is also within walking distance of the Cecil. Durrell arrived on the scene in 1942, initially had a room in the Cecil, and later lived not far away on Rue Fuad, a street with a long history. During the Ptolemaic period, it was possibly called the Canopic Way, afterwards the Rue Rosette, then the Rue Fuad, and now the modern Egyptian Sharia Horreya ("Liberty Street"). Cab drivers, however, still know it as Rue Fuad. And today at the northwestern tip of the Corniche stands Fort Qaitbey. In 1480, the Ottoman conquerors constructed it on the granite and limestone ruins of one of the Seven Wonders of the Ancient World: the Pharos lighthouse. The exact dimensions of that Ptolemaic monument are unknown, but recent reconstructions have it towering over the present fortress by perhaps a hundred metres.[2] And so looms the mythos of Alexandria itself.

Alexandria makes one aware of things being in continual flux. It is a city of reused ruins and renamed streets. Conquerors and revolutions come and go, but as Cavafy says in his poem "Exiles": "It goes on being Alexandria still".[3] True. But that requires a little imagination. Another aspect of the city requires no imagination. Urban desolation is readily visible, especially as seen from Cavafy's balcony (**Figure 1**). That bleak prospect Cavafy could easily have lamented, or perhaps eulogized in "The City", as the "black ruins" of his life,[4] and that metaphor Durrell's narrator in *Justine* interprets as the "melancholy provinces" of an internal landscape (*Quartet* 18).

The proceedings were held in a large auditorium with a seating capacity for several hundred people. The turnout was remarkable and enthusiastic — almost all the seats were taken. The people responded with lively questions and sometimes lengthy expostulations. The audience itself

---

[2] Romer and Romer, *Seven Wonders of the World*, fig. 9.
[3] Cavafy, *Collected Poems*, p. 200.
[4] Cavafy, *Collected Poems*, p. 28.

Figure 1: Rue Lepsius from C. P. Cavafy's balcony (© Michael Haag, 2004)

was diverse: educators, students, citizens, reporters, and the stray foreign visitors, such as my wife and I, who had travelled from California. The students were mainly young women, most of whom wore the colourful *hijab*, the headscarf now widely favoured in Islam as a sign of piety. They either had an interest in Durrell and his legacy or were conscripts from the Department of English at Alexandria University. Dr. Sahar Hamouda, moderator and professor of English, joked about familiar faces and required attendance.

I was reminded of D. J. Enright's descriptions of English classes in his contemporaneous, but vastly different, novel about Alexandria, *Academic Year* (London 1955). His dyspeptic poem of that period, "Why the East is Inscrutable", first appearing in 1948, throws cold water on many of the oriental visions of his fellow countrymen. It proposes, "Sometimes the East is too hot / To be scrutable", rejects exoticism, and concludes, "Now friends are specious things. Wait for winter, / Mildly trying, meanwhile, not to make / Too many enemies".[5] Romantic Durrell and Augustan Enright would not have gotten along.

III

A literary conference devoted to a single author tends to define itself along predictable lines of academic inquiry. The focus will be on an author and his or her texts. A premium is normally placed on current or fashionable approaches to the study of literature. Happily, such was not the case with this conference, which was not really literary, rather an "event", in the sense of honouring a great writer and his vision of Alexandria, the "White City" of his novels.

As previously mentioned, the organizers of the event wanted the proceedings to appeal to a general audience, namely, whoever might walk off the street and be curious about Lawrence Durrell and his Egyptian preoccupations. The various speakers brought Durrell into focus, both as man and writer, and then transitioned into contemporary literature and the conservation of old Alexandria.

Michael Haag provided the historical context for Durrell in Egypt. Peter Porter assessed and analyzed Durrell's Mediterranean poetry. Penelope Hope Durrell presented family photographs of her father's life. Harry Tzalas and Ibrahim Abdel Meguid read from their own creative work. And Dr. Mohamed Awad discussed the attempt to save the Ambron Villa, the most important place where Durrell stayed in Alexandria.

---

[5] Enright, *Collected Poems*, p. 8.

I shall not attempt to summarize these talks and readings, rather I'll comment on one part of the discussions, which drew repeated criticism: Durrell's superficial portrayal of Alexandria and its Egyptian inhabitants.[6] Simplistic though his representation may be, I am not deeply troubled by it and do not expect writers of literature to write with the acumen of Alexis de Tocqueville when they visit foreign countries. I do expect a certain amount of honesty, however. In this regard, I find Durrell's life puzzling and contradictory and because of that, his art complex. I'll then connect this aspect of the writer's work to Alexandria and the Ambron Villa. This arc essentially follows the trajectory of the conference itself.

Honouring a writer's achievement does not necessarily mean agreeing with everything he has to say, and Durrell's poetic recreation of Alexandria as many-layered strata of memory, history, and ethnic diversity found few supporters among the discussants, in particular the Alexandrians and Egyptians themselves, who seemed to consider Durrell's work highly fanciful. Harry Tzalas, a Greek who was born in Alexandria and who is both writer and archaeologist, called Durrell's city "unreal" and said, "If you want to dream, [there's] nothing better than *The Alexandria Quartet*". Tzalas's comments may seem harsh, but Tzalas also defended Durrell's right to his own vision of the city, when someone in the audience attacked it as being unfair and unrealistic.

Durrell himself would probably not be much troubled by such personal criticism. In fact, he indulges in it himself. In his rousing assessment of Durrell's poetry, Peter Porter spoke of "On First Looking into Loeb's Horace" as Durrell's finest poem. Porter was himself a highly respected poet, and his judgment has to be taken very seriously. "Loeb's Horace" is indeed a marvellous tour de force in the tradition, as Porter noted, of Robert Browning's dramatic monologues ("Andrea del Sarto" comes to mind). Porter admires the poem for its artifice (*Sel* xv-xvii). I question its honesty.

In 1943, Durrell published "Loeb's Horace" in *Personal Landscape*, a Cairo publication that he helped to edit, along with his fellow editors, Robin Fedden and Bernard Spencer. They were all exiles who had met in Athens and then fled to Egypt before the German advance in 1941.[7]

---

[6] Negative appraisals of Durrell's portrayal of Alexandria, include Mahmoud Manzaloui's "Curate's Egg: An Alexandrian Opinion of Durrell's *Quartet*". It is reprinted in *Critical Essays on Lawrence Durrell,* ed. Alan Warren Friedman (Boston: G. K. Hall, 1987): 144-57. Another example is D. J. Enright's "Arabian Nights' Entertainment: Lawrence Durrell's 'Quartet.'" It is reprinted in Enright's *Conspirators and Poets* (London: Chatto & Windus, 1966): 111-20.

[7] Haag, *City of Memory*, p. 203.

Personal Landscape even called itself a magazine of "exile",[8] and as Haag notes, Durrell's contributions to the magazine "rarely had anything to do with Egypt".[9] During his years in Egypt, Durrell didn't like either the country itself or Alexandria in particular, although his attitude later changed. He made his antipathy clear in a letter to Henry Miller, when in May of 1944 he complained about Alexandria as "this smashed up broken down shabby Neapolitan town, with its Levantine mounds of houses peeling in the sun" (*DML* 168). Like a homesick exile from the Hellenic world, Durrell turned his eyes across the Mediterranean to Greece. The theme of exile or its variant, the self-imposed removal from society, plays a big role in "Loeb's Horace".

The poem is many-layered and develops through the complicated interplay of an unidentified speaker, probably male, his lost love, and the Latin poet Horace. The poem also glows with Keatsian splendour: imagery and diction that quietly allude to Keats's Great Odes, although they do so for other uses: negative in Durrell but positive in Keats. And here I'm thinking of Keats's vines and apples in "To Autumn" (cf. Durrell's "lover of vines" and "drying of the apples" [ll. 3, 10]); his "bride of quietness" in "Ode on a Grecian Urn" (cf. Durrell's "slave to quietness" [l. 3]); and his "Lethe-wards" in "Ode to a Nightingale" (cf. Durrell's "deathward" [l. 11]).

Despite these appealing qualities, "Loeb's Horace" is also unsettling. Durrell's twist on the title of Keats's famous sonnet, "On First Looking into Chapman's Homer", is not an act of homage, as the poem eventually reveals. Nor does Durrell appear to hold the poet John Keats in high regard. In the *Quartet*, Durrell will later create a character called John Keats, a nosy journalist, and have his narrator say this about him: "There was nothing wrong with John except the level on which he had chosen to live his life — but you could say the same about his famous namesake, could you not?" (*Quartet* 220). That snide remark, which I take as neither ironic nor playful, applies equally to Durrell's portrayal of Horace, for Durrell's poem is a severe critique of Horace the man, as he presents himself in his poetry.

The poem turns in a way similar to Horace's great Cleopatra ode (*Carm.* 1. 37), but in just the opposite manner. At the end of the ode, Cleopatra, the mad queen, the "regina dementes",[10] the enemy of the Roman empire, abruptly changes and becomes a proud, formidable woman, whom Horace allows a measure of triumph through juxtaposing "non humilis

[8] Thomas and Brigham, *Illustrated Checklist*, pp. 76-77.
[9] Haag, *City of Memory*, p. 203.
[10] Horace, *Odes and Epodes*, p. 98.

mulier" with the poem's final word, "triumpho".[11] Durrell, on the other hand, delivers Horace another kind of reversal. His poem begins in muted praise:

> I found your Horace with the writing in it;
> Out of time and context came upon
> This lover of vines and slave to quietness,
> Walking like a figure of smoke here, musing
> Among his high and lovely Tuscan pines.
>
> All the small-holder's ambitions, the yield
> Of wine-bearing grape, pruning and drainage
> Laid out by laws, almost like the austere
> Shell of his verses—a pattern of Latin thrift;
> Waiting so patiently in a library for
> Autumn and the drying of the apples;
> The betraying hour-glass and its deathward drift. (ll. 1-12)

The poem then ends in harsh criticism, which describes Horace as the man

> Who built in the Sabine hills this forgery
> Of completeness, an orchard with a view of Rome;
> Who studiously developed his sense of death
> Till it was all around him, walking at the circus,
> At the baths, playing dominoes in a shop—
> The escape from self-knowledge with its tragic
> Imperatives: *Seek, suffer, endure.* The Roman
> In him feared the Law and told him where to stop.
>
> So perfect a disguise for one who had
> Exhausted death in art—yet who could guess
> You would discern the liar by a line.
> The suffering hidden under gentleness
> And add upon the flyleaf in your tall
> Clear hand: 'Fat, human and unloved,
> And held from loving by a sort of wall,
> Laid down his books and lovers one by one,
> Indifference and success had crowned them all.' (ll. 53-69)

The condemnation is strong, total, and destructive: Horatian ode as Juvenalian satire. We probably see in Durrell's charge of "forgery / Of completeness" an effort to expunge Horace's "Exegi monumentum", the

---

[11] Horace, *Odes and Epodes*, p. 100. For Cleopatra's special triumph, see Commager, *Odes of Horace*, p. 93.

Latin poet's claim to immortality, his assertion that he has completed a
lasting monument (*Carm.* 3.30.1).

I suppose, were I to be critically correct about such matters, I
should differentiate between the "voice" of the speaker in a dramatic
monologue and the "voice" of the poet. They are usually not the same. But
I won't. For the voices I hear in "Loeb's Horace" are the same as Durrell's
own, and for this reason I hear the speaker as being male, though he need
not be. I see Durrell as basically a lyric poet. I don't see him as whimsically
creating various personae.

Now, Horace, is undoubtedly a very great poet, who also has a very
high opinion of himself. In the last ode of Book 3, he even thinks his poems
more imposing than the Pyramids of Giza ("regalique situ pyramidum
altius" [2]), and perhaps more enduring, although that race is too early to
call. As Porter rightly pointed out, Horace is a favourite among the British,
who consider him the "epitome of poets", and young Durrell, during his
days in an English public school, probably had a good dose of the Latin
poet. An older Durrell, however, strikes one of his anti-British poses and
takes Horace to task for various peccadilloes in his personality — those
foibles bear a suspiciously close resemblance to those of the stereotypic
English squire, perhaps a perverse version of Squire Allworthy in Henry
Fielding's *Tom Jones* (1749). So, Durrell describes Horace as a "landed
man" on his Sabine farm (l. 46), separated or walled off from society, a
country gentleman who was too prissy, too superficial, too sedentary, too
constrained, too complacent and easily satisfied, besides being fat and
obviously pompous, in sum, too full of himself — those sorts of thing. None
of which, by the way, detracts from Horace's greatness as a poet.

Durrell's criticism of Horace is, in short, petty, trivial, and unfair,
especially when measured against his own habits, for the pattern of Durrell's
living arrangements closely resembled Horace's. In 1943, he found a tower
in a quiet part of Alexandria and then, in a letter of May 1944, complained
to Miller about the city, "No, if one could write a single line of anything that
had a human smell to it here, one would be a genius" (*DML* 168). In 1953,
he changed his mind about Alexandria as a fit subject for a mature writer
or, possibly, a budding genius. In that year, he bought his own Sabine
retreat, a Turkish house in the beautiful village of Bellapaix, overlooking
the city of Kyrenia, Cyprus, and there, in a place whose very name
embodied peace and that was also "a testimony to the powers of
contemplation which rule our inner lives" (*BL* 78), he began writing *Justine*.
In 1958, he moved to the south of France and lived in Mazet Michel, a

farmhouse with "22 acres of garrigue and olive groves",[12] near Nîmes, and there he again looked back at Alexandria, his "capital of Memory" (*Quartet* 152), completed his *Quartet*, and found time to relax by building his own "dry-stone walls".[13] Durrell had much in common with the Latin poet he strenuously decried.

As Walt Whitman observes in *Song of Myself*, or nearly so, great poets don't have to worry about contradicting themselves, for they "contain multitudes". Durrell certainly had his full share of contradictions and even wrote twice in *Balthazar*, the second novel of the *Quartet*, that "Truth is what most contradicts itself" (*Quartet* 216, 277) — which is probably best understood as a subjective and not an objective statement. We don't read poets for consistency in their positions or not read them for flaws in their character. Rather, I think, we read them for their unique vision, which may be as elusive and tantalizing as Keats's summation at the end of his Grecian ode: "Beauty is truth, truth beauty". Durrell is entitled to his own complex vision of Alexandria, a city which he often describes as dirty and unappealing and in which he often portrays its Egyptian inhabitants unflatteringly.

Writers of fiction are conjurers. They create their own worlds, whether or not they really believe in them, and readers enter them at their own risk.

Let us not kid ourselves, Durrell's Alexandria is indeed a seductive depiction of a great city, unreal and yet real. Early in *Balthazar*, Pursewarden, the writer diplomat, provides a famous description of Alexandria, as it is approached from the sea:

> We were still almost a couple of hours' steaming distance before land could possibly come into sight when suddenly my companion shouted and pointed at the horizon. We saw, inverted in the sky, a full-scale mirage of the city, luminous and trembling, as if painted on dusty silk: yet in the nicest detail. From memory I could clearly make out its features, Ras El Tin Palace, the Nebi Daniel Mosque and so forth. The whole representation was as breath-taking as a masterpiece painted in fresh dew. It hung there in the sky for a considerable time, perhaps twenty-five minutes, before melting slowly into the horizon mist. An hour later, the *real* city appeared, swelling from a smudge to the size of its mirage. (*Quartet* 211)

Bewitching as this mirage may be, it is deliberately unsubstantial. The "melting" image dissolves into the *"real* city", and the two are difficult to

---

[12] Chamberlin, *Durrell Log*, p. 116.
[13] Chamberlin, *Durrell Log*, p. 118.

distinguish in Durrell's imagination.

Moreover, as William Leigh Godshalk has noted,[14] Durrell's evocation is itself a rendition of a passage from another source, R. Talbot Kelly's *Egypt: Painted and Described,* which reads,

> My first introduction to Egypt was in 1883, and was ushered in in [sic] rather a startling manner. We were still two or three hours' steaming distance before land could possibly be in sight, when suddenly we saw, inverted in the sky, a perfect miragic reproduction of Alexandria, in which Pharos Light, Ras-el-Tin Palace, and other prominent features were easily distinguishable. The illusion continued for a considerable time, and eventually as suddenly disappeared, when, an hour or two later, the *real* city slowly appeared above the horizon! A good augury, surely, of the wonders I hoped to discover on landing![15]

Durrell's version is superior. He is far better with words than Kelly, but he does not attribute his source, as he does elsewhere (*Quartet* 203, 390, 882-84). Instead, he passes off the mirage as his own invention, and he can be faulted for that, at least as severely as he faults Horace, whom he calls a "liar".

I like to think writers of fiction can get away with telling white lies. That's part of Coleridge's "willing suspension of disbelief" — how a reader enters poetry or fiction, not expecting things to be as they actually are. This submission tacitly acknowledges the misrepresentation of facts.

I used to think Durrell's "White City", one of his favourite epithets for Alexandria, was another one of those white lies (*Quartet* 57, 254, 280, 300, 314, 616). I wasn't sure if he was referring to a colour or an ethnicity, as implied in the official Roman designation for the city: *Alexandrea ad Aegyptum,* Alexandria *by* Egypt, not *in* Egypt.[16] And so, by extension, we have a white European city situated against the backdrop of a dark African continent. As one character in *Justine* says, "This city has been built like a dyke to hold back the flood of African darkness" (*Quartet* 59). That possibility would provide ammunition for those detractors eager to charge Durrell with racial prejudice (an argument, by the way, that I did *not* hear at the conference). Such an interpretation may still exist, but there is a simpler explanation. White means white. For the city is indeed white when seen from afar.

Stand on the Corniche (**Plate 1**), the esplanade stretching along the Eastern Harbour — which Durrell occasionally and inaccurately calls, the

---

[14] Godshalk, "Some Sources", p. 170, n. 57.

[15] Kelly, *Egypt*, p. 5.

[16] Fraser, *Ptolemaic Alexandria*, vol. 1, p. 107.

"Grande Corniche" (*Quartet* 209, 223, 301), thus making it his, artistically — stand there and view the city across the blue harbour and see its irrefutable whiteness. (Or, get a copy of Michael Haag's *Alexandria Illustrated* and see its beauty in photographs.) The quality of that light is not a hard, dazzling white, bright as enamel, rather it's chalky and friable, as though the substance could easily rub off. I assume the distinctive colour can be attributed to the limestone used in the plaster of its buildings. It's the same limestone which is found throughout Lower Egypt, which is the bedrock of Alexandria itself (**Figure 2**), and which went into the construction of the pyramids, whose outer casing of fine Tura limestone later got removed and recycled into plaster and other materials.

Figure 2: Limestone bedrock of Chatby necropolis (© Michael Haag, 2004)

Up close, however, the white surface of the buildings turns dingy, and its substance does rub off. Walk the crowded streets of Alexandria, and you see merchants continually washing their sidewalks. They're not simply rinsing off the dirt and pollution generated by a metropolis of over six million people. The cause is more subtle than that. It's the sand. It's the dust in the air. You feel that fine grit on your skin, in your hair, on your teeth, and after trudging through the streets, you too have the urge to wash.

At the beginning of *Justine,* the narrator speaks of Alexandria's "lime-laden dust" and "the taste of quicklime" (*Quartet* 17, 18). This is an accurate description of the residue left after the erosion of limestone. So, Durrell's poetic evocation of Alexandria, "painted in fresh dew", is not so farfetched. The city is, in a sense, literally melting away, but very slowly, like Horace's lofty pyramids, which are also being devoured by rain, the "imber edax" (*Carm.* 3.30.3). Durrell knows his Horace, although he doesn't seem to like the man, and maybe he doesn't because they were too similar.

IV

It gets cold in Alexandria during the winter. The morning was bright and chilly, and many people had on sweaters and jackets. Not a single woman in our group wore the *hijab*. We got in the first bus, found it packed with over sixty people, and had to find separate seats. A second bus carried the rest of the crowd. Across my aisle sat an older woman, who was exquisitely coifed and wrapped in a damask cape. She was carrying on multiple conversations: chatting with her young female companion in French, arguing with someone up front in Arabic, and answering her husband's questions in Italian. He sat next to me and answered my questions in English. I asked him where he was from, and he said Alexandria. He was born in the city. Casually dressed in slacks and Irish-knit pullover, he was retired and always welcomed new and diverting experiences.

The scene was surely not one Durrell would have noted and bothered to mention in his *Quartet*, but it was illustrative of a small, wealthy, cosmopolitan, and polyglot culture, although disconcertingly so. My wife and I felt at a definite disadvantage since we have only two languages between us, and all the other occupants in the bus had at least three or four at their command — Arabic, French, Italian, English, and quite possibly one or two more — and they easily switched among them, something done frequently. Fortunately, for the sake of visitors such as ourselves, the tour was being conducted in English.

On the second and last day of the conference, Gordon Smith, a member of the Bibliotheca Alexandrina, led a "walking tour", which was primarily a bus tour, through Durrell's favourite haunts in Alexandria. Voluble and energetic, Smith had the librarian's eagerness to impart information. He had painstakingly produced a beautiful brochure and map. He selected passages from *Justine* that identified places in the old city and illustrated some of these with Paul Hogarth's magnificent watercolours *(The Mediterranean Shore: Travels in Lawrence Durrell Country* [1988]).

I was surprised at the turnout and had thought the tour would appeal to only a few tourists, such as my wife and myself, neophytes completely unfamiliar with Alexandria. But I was wrong, and so were the planners of the Durrell event. The tour was a big hit. It was oversubscribed, required three buses, and had to be extended an additional day. As we soon discovered, many of the people eager to see what remained of Durrell's Alexandria were not wide-eyed, foreign sightseers, rather they were the Alexandrians themselves — or, more accurately, their remnants — who are perhaps the direct descendants of those inhabitants whose city once had "five races, five languages, a dozen creeds" (*Quartet* 17). But unlike Durrell's original "inquisitors of pleasure and pain" (*Quartet* 350), they rarely, if ever, visited some parts of their own city. They needed a foreign guide, another Englishman, no less, to explain things to them.

Smith proved to be an excellent architectural historian and was more informative than Durrell, whose descriptions of the city are usually poetic but sometimes careless:

> Streets that run back from the docks with their tattered rotten supercargo of houses, breathing into each others' mouths, keeling over. Shuttered balconies swarming with rats, and old women whose hair is full of the blood of ticks. Peeling walls leaning drunkenly to east and west of their true centre of gravity. (*Quartet* 26)

"Shuttered balconies" and "Peeling walls" are accurate, so too tottering structures, but a "supercargo of houses" is hard to visualize. Indeed, the metaphor doesn't make much sense, unless "supercargo", a person, perhaps a drunken sailor, is taken as an error for "cargo", a thing, immediately personified and sent reeling, open-mouthed, into back streets. Either option is odd. Unlike the poetry of Horace, Durrell's language does not always benefit from close scrutiny.

Nevertheless, Smith probably knew the city better than Durrell did and was able to point out features not mentioned in the *Quartet*: the Venetian and Moorish façades, decorated with ornate balconies and louvered shutters, usually painted green, or the zigzag of Arab buildings, designed to bring light into their interiors as the day progresses. He also mentioned the Italian Alexandrian architect of the city's greatest period of expansion along the Corniche: Giuseppe Alessandro Loria, architect of the Cecil Hotel and many other buildings of the 1920s and 1930s. Loria's name does not earn a spot in the *Quartet* among the city's "exemplars" (*Quartet* 22), its historical figures, such as the Greek poet C. P. Cavafy and the English author E. M. Forster, but it should have, for Durrell lived and worked in a house that was partly of his design, the Ambron Villa on Rue Al Maamoun, in the Moharrem Bey district of Alexandria.

V

The tour made its way slowly through the noisy city. After manoeuvring through the congested avenues, packed tight with clanking trams and honking cars, the bus pulled into a side street, lined with lush Egyptian sycamore (those same trees still visible in the ancient tombs along the Nile), and stopped halfway up the block. The area was quiet. The clamour of Alexandria had completely dissipated.

We all disembarked and stood around staring at the Ambron Villa and snapping photographs. The two-storey villa was a sad ruin, but still majestic, a dignified widow in tattered weeds the colour of café au lait. Ben Jonson's poem came to mind, the one about Penshurst Place, the home of the Sidney family in rural Kent. The Ambron mansion stood like an Alexandrian version of another "ancient pile" in a pastoral setting. The two places are by no means a close match — but close enough in terms of rusticity, peacefulness, and symbolism.

The villa's architecture was grand baroque, like a piece of Durrell's own prose, and recalled a great age of Alexandria's past: a palatial entrance with staircase, portico, balcony, balustrade, ornamental pilasters. At the corner was an octagonal tower (**Plate 2**) and in the back a detached atelier, the one which Loria designed and the artist Clea Badaro occupied. Blonde Clea Badaro would later appear as blonde Clea Montis in the *Quartet.*

Smith had cautioned everyone not to trespass onto the property. The new owners were very touchy about that. But, of course, one intrepid adventurer did, climbing up the rickety stairs and taking photos of the dark, empty interior. The attraction of history and its relics is too great: the impulse is always to touch, in spite of the signs warning not to.

As noted earlier, Durrell found this haven in 1943. He rented the top floor from the Ambrons, a wealthy Jewish family, and moved in with Eve Cohen, who would become his second wife and the model for Justine.[17] Durrell immediately took possession of the tower as a work area. "I have furnished myself a Tower", he writes to Miller on 8 February 1944 and emphasizes the fact with a small, idealized drawing of a bastion with crenellations (the Ambron tower has none). Then, on 23 May 1944, he again writes, "I am sharing a big flat with some nice people, and atop it I have a tower of my own from which the romantics can see Pompey's Pillar, Hadra Prison, and the wet reedy wastes of Lake Mareotis stretching away into the distance and blotting the sky" (*DML* 160, 171).

---

[17] Haag, *City of Memory*, pp. 261-64.

From his solitary tower, which good Romantics may discern as another Pharos with a lamp radiating seaward, Durrell could see more than some sights of Alexandria and the marshy lake separating the city from the rest of Lower Egypt. From that secluded spot, which recalls the Roman designation of *Alexandrea ad Aegyptum*, he also turned his back on Egypt, directed his brilliant "mind's eye" northwest (*Quartet* 17), and recollected his experiences on the island of Corfu. In that tower he wrote his memoir, *Prospero's Cell* (1945), which is his first and most celebrated travel book.

Prospero's Cell recounts his formative years on the Greek island with his first wife, Nancy Myers. It is magical, eerie, and unreal. It purports to describe the encounters of the young couple as they explore the Ionian coast and meet the people of the island. Right out of the pastoral tradition begun by Theocritus, another exile who probably lived in Alexandria for a while, the bucolic pair roam the countryside like carefree shepherds, although ones who also have a fondness for sailing and skinny-dipping. Corfu becomes an "Eden" (*PC* 19), a pleasance, a kind of *locus amoenus.*

Unlike the pastoral tradition, however, Durrell's Corfu is also an epiphany of strange light and blue water, as an opening passage announces:

> You enter Greece as one might enter a dark crystal; the form of things becomes irregular, refracted. Mirages suddenly swallow islands, and wherever you look the trembling curtain of the atmosphere deceives. (*PC* 11)

The image of Greece as a "dark crystal" recurs elsewhere. At the end of his book, Durrell again refers to Corfu as "the inner heart of a dark crystal" (*PC* 133), and three decades later he returns to the island and speaks of experiencing the light as "moving about in the heart of a dark crystal" (*GI* 21). The image is a peculiar variant of a common observation, indeed a *topos*, on the unique clarity of Greek light.[18] But Durrell finds darkness in the heart of clarity and gives the figure a subjective meaning, for in that

---

[18] In 1911, Sophie Atkinson remarks on "the absorbing loveliness of its [Corfu's] light and colour (Atkinson, *Artist in Corfu*, p. 2). In 1943, Dilys Powell describes Greece as "a land of cool brilliant colours and austere contours seen even through an atmosphere of miraculous clarity (Powell, *Traveller's Journey*, p. 33). And in 1957, C. M. Bowra has perhaps the fullest expression of this idea: "What matters above all is the quality of the light. Not only in the cloudless days of summer but even in winter the light is unlike that of any other European country, brighter, cleaner and stronger. [...] The beauty of the Greek landscape depends primarily on the light, and this had a powerful influence on the Greek vision of the world" (Bowra, *Greek Experience*, p. 11). I thank Michael Haag for providing the example of Powell's work.

luminous landscape he declares "Greece offers you something harder — the discovery of yourself" (*PC* 11).

The ringing sound of that imperial assertion, the characteristic voice of Romantic poets like Byron and Wordsworth, is precisely what is uncharacteristic of pastoral poetry. As Thomas G. Rosenmeyer notes, "detachment" is a "unique pastoral mood", that is, the poet usually suppresses or conceals himself, as Milton does in "Lycidas", and this process Rosenmeyer calls the "expunging of the ego".[19]

Durrell's ego, on the other hand, is anything but expunged. It dominates *Prospero's Cell*, even to the exclusion of his wife's. She is simply referred to as "N.", rarely speaks, and has little, if any, personality in the narrative. In a famous bathing scene at the shrine of Saint Arsenius, Nancy dives "like an otter" into a seaside pool and retrieves "in her lips" the cherries her husband drops into "two fathoms" of the limpid aquamarine (*PC* 16). The scene has great power: it transforms ordinary experience into something numinous and allows a glimpse into Durrell's private world of shimmering light and trembling images. That is one aspect. But there is another: Nancy is a trained seal, and Durrell is her master.

During her talk at the conference, Penelope Hope Durrell, the daughter of that first marriage, mentioned her mother's reaction to reading *Prospero's Cell.* Nancy said it was "all lies". Her anger was so great that she refused to read any more of her former husband's books.[20] Penelope did not elaborate on her mother's feelings. Perhaps Nancy felt some residual bitterness over the divorce, and that affected or clouded her judgment. Perhaps she resented being reduced to the letter N and the diminution of her role during their years on Corfu. Nevertheless, the charge remains emphatic, sweeping, and plain enough. So, the Horatian analogy persists, which Durrell, a great lover of irony, may or may not have enjoyed.

Like Horace, Durrell also had a need to withdraw and retreat into himself. They both sought out rural places. Durrell had his Greek islands and villas. Horace had his Sabine farm and enjoyed describing it, but, as Rosenmeyer again notes, Horace's pastoral descriptions do not make him a pastoral poet, for his "emphasis is on his own sensations, not on the responses of a small set of characters unrelated to himself".[21] Horace's ego stands out — and so does Durrell's. The "dark crystal" of *Prospero's Cell* is not the Greek landscape and its mysterious, refractive light; rather, it is

---

[19] Rosenmeyer, *Green Cabinet*, pp. 15, 63. See also Ransom, "Poem Nearly Anonymous", pp. 64-81.

[20] Richard Pine reports that Joanna Hodgkin told him that her mother, Nancy Hodgkin, Durrell's first wife, had in fact read his *Alexandria Quartet*.

[21] Rosenmeyer, *Green Cabinet*, p. 15.

Durrell's extraordinarily inventive imagination, where he recreates and expands himself.[22]

VI

The Ambron Villa is Durrell's "White City" in miniature, and it too is threatened with extinction. The villa now belongs to a land-development company, which bought the property in a "secret sale" from the Ambron family.[23] The company then planned to tear it down, build an apartment complex, and turn a good profit, which is a good tradition in a city where, as Durrell writes in May of 1944, "Even love is thought of in money terms" (*DML* 168). Those plans, however, have been forestalled by the efforts of a few dedicated citizens, who have appealed to the Egyptian Antiquities Organization and temporarily placed the property under its protection. Dr. Mohamed Awad, architect and academic, is a leader of those conservationists trying to preserve Alexandria's urban heritage.

The last meeting of the Durrell event focussed on the architectural conservation of the city that Durrell later came to describe so movingly. This is not an easy task, for as Awad has remarked elsewhere, Durrell's polyglot and cosmopolitan Alexandria no longer exists as he once envisioned it:

> Today Alexandria is a monoglot city: one race, one creed, fundamentally Islamic. The remains of cosmopolitanism are marginal, its society is extinct or on its way to extinction, and its physical heritage is hedged in and threatened. Yet something still remains. She is still recognizable, despite the circumstances and the effects of age.[24]

Alexandria is no longer *Alexandrea ad Aegyptum;* it has almost become *Alexandrea in Aegypto.*

On the face of it, the prospects of saving the villa are not sanguine, and the meeting served more as a forum to discuss problems than as a vehicle to initiate solutions. If the fate of the Ambron Villa can be taken as exemplary, then the larger situation is indeed tenuous, for the villa has been granted no more than a stay of execution. The company that bought the property has to be fairly compensated. And Awad has not yet been

---

[22] I am indebted to Michael Haag for numerous discussions on this aspect of Durrell's personality, as well as to other comments and corrections he has made throughout this essay.
[23] Awad, "House Revisited", p. 42.
[24] Awad, "House Revisited", p. 39.

successful in convincing the government that the villa deserves to be listed as a monument as worthy of preservation as those of Egypt's Islamic and Pharaonic past. Sadly, what is true of the villa is also true of the city.

I do see hope, however. The largely enthusiastic reception of the Durrell event itself demonstrates an increasing awareness of the need and desire to save Alexandria's historical character before it literally and figuratively "melts away". When a youth can stand up and speak up for his city, I am encouraged that there will be many others to carry on these struggles. A young Alexander of Macedon surely rose to similar occasions millennia ago.

As he would have readily acknowledged, Lawrence Durrell did not discover the mythos of Alexandria. The city has always been there as a source of inspiration for over twenty-three hundred years, and Cavafy and Forster had already begun to develop that potential long before Durrell arrived. Nor can he be credited with any particular foresight in the rediscovery of a forgotten or overlooked culture — which he may not have been so eager to admit — for he didn't immediately appreciate the city after his flight from Greece during the Second World War. In 1941, he didn't fully understand what he'd stumbled upon. His initial response was to reject the land in which he sought refuge. Durrell's friend, Robbin Fedden, shared this negative view of Egypt.[25] It took time for Durrell to reflect on his Egyptian experiences and to reshape his views about that environment.

Durrell likes to say in prominent passages of *Justine* that landscape or environment shapes and determines character. So, his narrator Darley can say, unflinchingly, in the novel's poetic preamble, "It is the city which should be judged though we, its children, must pay the price" (*Quartet* 17). Or he can also say, in a bit of philosophical discourse, "We are the children of our landscape; it dictates behaviour and even thought in the measure to which we are responsive to it" (*Quartet* 39-40).

How true is this? Does landscape or *deus loci,* the spirit of place, really have such a dominant role in the formation of character? I would think that the process is far more complicated than that, and I would argue that for many, and certainly for Durrell, it is actually the other way around: personality shapes place. The complexities of personality largely determine

---

[25] See Fedden's introduction to *Personal Landscape: An Anthology of Exile*, compiled by Robbin Fedden, et al. (London: Editions Poetry): 7-11. Fedden writes of Egypt, "Of a nightmarish unreality, the existence led by the wealthy Europeanized upper class epitomizes all that the word *Levantine* means: money and money values, a total absence of taste and tradition, and a pseudo-French culture" (p. 11). Fedden's introduction is reprinted in *Borders and Borderlands*, ed. Richard Pine and Vera Konidari (Newcastle-upon-Tyne: Cambridge Scholars Publishing, 2021).

how one responds to a given environment. Were it true that landscape shapes character, we should expect more homogeneity in artistic responses, but that is clearly not the case in Alexandria itself.

What Durrell really offers in *The Alexandria Quartet* is a highly poeticized and personalized vision of a city, and sometimes he even acknowledges that, albeit unobtrusively, for Darley also says "A city becomes a world when one loves one of its inhabitants" (*Quartet* 57). Durrell is probably at his best when he's least self-conscious, and that casual remark is closer to his big truth: the intensity of some strong emotion or need can turn a place into a highly-charged world of poetic beauty. And that is no mean accomplishment.

Durrell's vision of Alexandria is not the world of contemporary Alexandrian writers. Their voices are many, unique, and diverse. His vision of the "White City" is more like a mirage, an unsubstantial, distorted, and alluring depiction of something real. But beyond its intrinsic appeal, a mirage also has its usefulness, when it creates excitement and incites people to act. The city of Alexandria is real. It has a long history, and now many of its citizens are actively trying to protect and preserve that heritage. I cheer their efforts and hope they succeed.[26]

---

[26] In the case of the Ambron Villa, Lawrence Durrell's most important residence in Alexandria, such efforts at conservation were not successful. That architectural heritage of old Alexandria no longer exists. During 2017, the mansion was demolished and replaced.

CHAPTER TWO

WIFE AND HUSBAND ON CORFU[1]

Sometimes biographies end like eulogies: they emphasize the positive and offer a measure of uplift mixed with sadness. The impulse is understandable and works well for James Boswell's *Life of Samuel Johnson* (1791), Richard Ellmann's *James Joyce* (1959), and Kenneth S. Lynn's *Hemingway* (1987).[2] It does not succeed in Joanna Hodgkin's *Amateurs in Eden* (2012), which is primarily a depiction of the troubled marriage of "Nancy and Larry", formally known as Nancy Myers and Lawrence Durrell. However much Hodgkin, Myers's daughter by her second marriage, believes that the young couple on Corfu "had created a myth and a mystery that lived long after their laughter and their fights and their loving had faded to silence",[3] what persists, dismays, and does not fade away are the habitual insults, physical abuses, and public humiliations that a nascent artist inflicted on his vulnerable wife.

The life of Nancy Myers (1912-83) is only being published because she married the famous writer Lawrence Durrell (1912-1990). The circulation of her story depends on his reputation. But genius does not excuse bullying. Nor should anyone's fame impede anyone's right to be heard, and Hodgkin rightly presents her mother's side of a relationship between two "complex and mercurial" individuals.[4] Although flawed in its execution, this view is important and calls for the reassessment, if not the obliteration, of the Edenic "myth" and "mystery" of a couple living on a Greek island before the outbreak of the Second World War (1935-1939).

Hodgkin had access to her mother's unfinished memoir, spoken tapes, and private communications. Unfortunately, the author's documentation is poor or nonexistent. The book could greatly benefit from an index. Her

---

[1] Originally published as "Nancy and Larry", a review of Joanna Hodgkin's *Amateurs in Eden: The Story of a Bohemian Marriage: Nancy and Lawrence Durrell* in *A Café in Space: The Anaïs Nin Literary Journal* 10 (2013).
[2] Boswell, *Johnson*, pp. 1398-1402; Ellmann, *Joyce*, p. 744; Lynn, *Hemingway*, p. 593.
[3] Hodgkin, *Amateurs*, p. 328.
[4] Hodgkin, *Amateurs*, p. 326.

text is also marred by errors in fact and typography. Clea, not "Melissa", goes swimming with Darley near the end of Durrell's *Alexandria Quartet* (*Quartet* 846). Myers returned permanently to England in 1947, not "1937".[5] Moreover, Hodgkin's breezy prose suffers from an abundance of clichés: "None of the above", "End of story", "Move forward another ten years", "Game, set and match", and so on.[6] Durrell or Pursewarden, one of his fictional surrogates, might have referred to such narrative devices as throwbacks to the early English novel.

These imperfections aside, who was Nancy Myers, Lawrence Durrell's first wife (he had four), who often avoids the camera's eye and stares away, not unlike the elusive Greta Garbo, to whom she was compared?

Myers was English, born in Sussex. She grew up in a repressive home environment; from an early age, she was diffident and artistic, later statuesque and beautiful. The diffidence remained. She escaped from the provinces, moved to London, attended art schools, went bohemian, and eventually met Durrell, to whom she lost her virginity, and ended up marrying for uncertain reasons. It just happened, so Hodgkin quotes her mother, "in this odd, sideways way".[7] She apparently succumbed to Durrell's charm, brilliance, storytelling, and self-confidence — qualities she lacked.

The crux of the story occurred during the years on Corfu (the book derived its title from one of Durrell's poems), which is vividly related in Durrell's highly praised *Prospero's Cell* (1945). That period also included a stay in Paris, when they visited Anaïs Nin and Henry Miller at the Villa Seurat.

Myers's and Durrell's sojourn on the island began well, and Hodgkin writes of "the tenderness of their early years".[8] "Tenderness" is the *sine qua non;* its lack precipitates the breakup.[9] The idyll didn't last, for their experiences were fundamentally different. As Hodgkin emphasizes, Corfu was the place where Durrell found "his unique authorial voice", whereas for Myers "the island was, quite simply, a place to experience the joy of being".[10] The distinction is crucial and suggests what went wrong with their marriage. For Durrell, finding his voice meant undergoing the *"agon"* of writing *The Black Book* (1938) (*BB* 21), his first major novel,

---

[5] Hodgkin, *Amateurs*, p. 315.
[6] Hodgkin, *Amateurs*, pp. 100-01, 125, 211.
[7] Hodgkin, *Amateurs*, p. 97.
[8] Hodgkin, *Amateurs*, p. 181.
[9] Hodgkin, *Amateurs*, p. 276.
[10] Hodgkin, *Amateurs*, p. 161.

and living in what is called in *The Alexandria Quartet* "the kingdom of your imagination" (*Quartet* 877). His role was active and creative. For Myers, Corfu was an experience sufficient in itself: "She loved the sun, loved the warmth, loved the olive trees, loved everything about it".[11] Her role was passive and supportive. She loved Corfu existentially, honestly. Durrell loved it imaginatively, poetically.

Honesty is a key. It was an important aspect of Myers's personality, not so for Durrell, who stresses in the *Quartet*, "Truth is what most contradicts itself in time" (*Quartet* 216, 277). The aphorism could serve as Durrell's motto and as a licence to prevaricate. Hodgkin says of her mother, "She was unable to be dishonest in any fundamental way. It is a cruel irony that she had joined forces with a man for whom actual truth was less important than poetic truth".[12]

Dishonesty pervades the "myth" of Corfu and questions the extent to which Durrell's *Prospero's Cell* accurately reflects the couple's experiences. Little, it seems. The memoir is mostly fiction posing as fact. To be sure, it contains magnificent poetry; the deliberate deceptions, however, are troublesome. Here are three examples not mentioned by Hodgkin. One, *Prospero's Cell* is not a true travelogue of Corfu, although it pretends to be. Its misleading subtitle is *A guide to the landscape and manners of the island of Corcyra.* That's about as true as calling *The Alexandria Quartet* a "guide" to Alexandria. Two, it tricks the reader into thinking "Count D.", a prominent figure who's even listed in the dedication, is real, but he's actually the author himself in disguise. Three, plagiarism, a form of lying, is an issue. Durrell clearly stole some prose from Sophie Atkinson's *An Artist in Corfu* (1911).[13] Moreover, the most famous scene in the book — Myers diving nude for cherries near the shrine of Saint Arsenius — may well have been concocted. When Hodgkin asked if it happened, Myers "snort[ed]" derisively without further comment.[14] Hodgkin tactfully prefers to believe the myth; even so, she should have attended the Durrell Celebration in Alexandria in 2007. There she would have heard her sister Penelope report that their mother had called *Prospero's Cell* "all lies" (see Chapter One above).

Another aspect of dishonesty and living in "the kingdom of your imagination" is the need to control people and appearances. From August 1937 to April 1938, Myers and Durrell joined Nin and Miller in Paris and travelled elsewhere in Europe. Those months proved to be a "total disaster"

---

[11] Hodgkin, *Amateurs*, p. 152.
[12] Hodgkin, *Amateurs*, p. 186.
[13] I thank Michael Haag for pointing out this major example of plagiarism.
[14] Hodgkin, *Amateurs*, p. 155.

for their marriage.[15] According to Hodgkin, "Larry had morphed again";[16] this time he turned into a tyrant.

At the Villa Seurat, Durrell became the "star" and "main attraction" of the Nin-Miller circle.[17] His *Black Book* was a sensation. He dazzled his audience and developed an ego to match his elevated status. In this competitive environment, Myers was relegated to being a beautiful accoutrement. She served as cook and bedmate — the "helpmeet" (or possibly the "little helper") that Durrell's Pursewarden, another tortured artist, fantasizes about in the *Quartet* (*Quartet* 296). By nature shy and diffident, Myers was not encouraged to assert herself; instead, Durrell would tell her to "shut up" and humiliate her in public.[18] In private, he called her "whore" and "tart".[19] In a subsequent letter to Miller, he labelled her a "slut" (*DML* 107). The scurrilous charges were untrue, according to Myers.[20] Durrell himself, however, had an affair, attempted a seduction, and cavorted as a naked "Pan" with girls on a beach.[21] He also tried to control whom she could see. When she was disobedient, he gave her a black eye, and she ended up bruised at the bottom of a flight of stairs.[22] He would interrogate her like a Grand Inquisitor.

Nin's diary corroborates some of these scenes.[23] The pattern of abuse repeats itself in his later marriages to Yvette (Eve) Cohen, Claude-Marie Vincendon, and Ghislaine de Boysson.[24] On the whole, the incidents are repugnant and read like the abusive events in John Webster's *The Duchess of Malfi* (1613). Durrell was well versed in Elizabethan and Jacobean drama.[25] Coincidentally, the duchess comes under the insidious control of the cynical Bosola, whose behaviour recalls Durrell's interrogations. The analogy is not entirely gratuitous. As Hodgkin points out, Durrell had a great need to control people, which he did through the force of his personality and the determination of his will. And in one's imagination one has absolute control.

---

[15] Hodgkin, *Amateurs*, p. 188.

[16] Hodgkin, *Amateurs*, p. 189.

[17] Hodgkin, *Amateurs*, p. 203.

[18] Hodgkin, *Amateurs*, pp. 202-03.

[19] Hodgkin, *Amateurs*, pp. 204, 209.

[20] Hodgkin, *Amateurs*, p. 212.

[21] Hodgkin, *Amateurs*, pp. 218, 223, 235.

[22] Hodgkin, *Amateurs*, p. 210; cf. p. 278.

[23] Nin, *Diary*, vol. 2, pp. 233, 253, 262.

[24] Chamberlin, *Durrell Log*, p. 103 n. 13; possibly pp. 139, 167, respectively.

[25] Pine, *Mindscape*, pp. 45, 58-59.

Durrell's imagination meant literature, and Hodgkin's submerged metaphor is textuality. He controlled appearances through his writings. *Prospero's Cell* does this, so too his letters to Miller. Hodgkin says both writers depicted "private misery [. . .] as farce".[26] Life became a text for Durrell; his "personality" became "a carefully edited version of himself that he offered for public consumption".[27]

Four years later the marriage broke up. In 1941, the Durrells fled to Egypt before the German advance. They settled in Cairo, and Durrell found employment with the British Embassy. The following year, as Rommel's *Afrika Korps* invaded Egypt, British "non-essential personnel" were evacuated to Jerusalem. Myers left with her daughter Penelope and never returned. She began a new life. On at least two occasions, Durrell travelled to meet his wife and attempted a reconciliation. Myers adamantly refused his offers and refused to see him a second time.[28] Her intransigence suggests profound resentment. They were divorced in 1946; both remarried in 1947.

Hodgkin is fair and good at posing questions about the underlying problems of the marriage. Was Myers sexually repressed and unable to satisfy Durrell's physical needs? Was Durrell destructive towards those who came close to him? Was she, "as some of his admirers suggest", an unworthy mate "for the great man and should have understood his tortured needs better"?[29] Or, as the scholar Michael Haag once remarked in a personal communication, perhaps facetiously, that Nancy should have considered herself lucky to have been in Lawrence Durrell's presence, where she experienced the best years of her life. All possibilities. Durrell's apologists prefer the last two explanations.

On the other hand, why assume artists are privileged and deserve special dispensation? Why should the burden of maintaining a marriage fall on one partner, the one who is usually identified as the female "helpmeet"? Near the end of *Justine* (1957), Clea says about the deceased Pursewarden: "Underneath all his preoccupations with sex, society, religion [...] there is, quite simply, a man *tortured beyond endurance by the lack of tenderness in the world"* (*Quartet* 194; original italics). There's that word again. The Myers-Durrell marriage might have endured had Durrell shown Myers a little more "tenderness". But, as he himself admitted, "I find art easy. I find life difficult".[30]

---

[26] Hodgkin, *Amateurs*, p. 223.

[27] Hodgkin, *Amateurs*, p. 281.

[28] Chamberlin, *Durrell Log*, pp. 57, 62 n. 32.

[29] Hodgkin, *Amateurs*, p. 326.

[30] L. Durrell, "Art of Fiction", p. 61.

Literary criticism should pay more attention to what Durrell meant by "difficult". Thus far, the emphasis has been on "art". Joanna Hodgkin's *Amateurs in Eden* is an important step towards understanding Lawrence Durrell both as man and artist.

CHAPTER THREE

DAUGHTER AND FATHER IN LANGUEDOC[1]

I. Agon

In the autumn of 1991, *Granta*, a literary journal edited by Bill Buford, published a selection of Sappho Jane Durrell's diaries, poetry, and correspondence.[2] That issue of *Granta* was devoted to "The Family". Buford likes to shock. On the cover of the periodical, he announces his theme: "They fuck you up", a half line taken from the beginning of Philip Larkin's short poem, "This Be The Verse" (1971). The full line reads, "They fuck you up, your mum and dad". The final stanza (unquoted) ends with the message:

> Man hands on misery to man.
> It deepens like a coastal shelf.
> Get out as early as you can,
> And don't have any kids yourself.[3]

Larkin's poem was especially relevant to Sappho, although this is unclear from Buford's subsequent remarks.

Sappho's father was the famous writer Lawrence Durrell; her mother was his second wife, Yvette Cohen, a native of Alexandria, Egypt. They married in 1947; Sappho was born in 1951. Yvette had a history of mental illness and an episode of schizophrenia diagnosed in 1953. The parents separated in 1955 and divorced in 1957. Sappho was raised by her mother in London.[4] She affectionately signed her letters to her father as "Saph",[5] often sent him "lots of love",[6] frequently lived with him during holidays (**Figure 3**), and apparently had a "close relationship" with his third

---

[1] Originally published as "Tales of Incest: The Agony of Saph and Pa Durrell" in *A Café in Space: The Anaïs Nin Literary Journal* 11 (2014).
[2] S. Durrell, "Journals and Letters", pp. 55-92.
[3] Larkin, *Complete Poems*, p. 88.
[4] Chamberlin, *Durrell Log*, pp. 77, 90, 95, 102-03, 112.
[5] S. Durrell, "Journals and Letters", p. 74.
[6] S. Durrell, "Journals and Letters", pp. 88-89.

wife, Claude-Marie Vincendon.[7]

Lawrence Durrell and his daughter Sappho
at the *Mazet Michel* (circa 1963).

Figure 3: Saph and Pa Durrell at the Mazet Michel, c. 1963 (©William Skyvington, 1963)

The published materials date from about 22 March 1979 to 10 July 1982. Buford takes most of the excerpts from 1979. In these selections, Sappho relates a troubled relationship with her "Pa" or "pap"[8] — whom she describes as "an aggressive and demonic drunkard [who] has always lived on the edge of madness"[9] — and details her extensive therapy with Patrick Casement, a London psychoanalyst. Sappho's characterization of her father is entirely plausible. Biographers provide ample evidence that Durrell was in fact prone to violence and suffered from alcoholism in his later years.[10]

---

[7] S. Durrell, "Journals and Letters", p. 57.
[8] S. Durrell, "Journals and Letters", p. 73.
[9] S. Durrell, "Journals and Letters", p. 62.
[10] For a summary of Durrell's personality, see Bowker, *Through the Dark Labyrinth*, pp. 425-37. For Durrell's excessive drinking and violent behaviour, see Chamberlin, *Durrell Log*, pp. 103 n. 13, 159, 164-65, 184, 189, 191.

She also refers to Nabokov's *Lolita* (1955), a novel about incest and "nymphets", as though it has personal relevance, and she insinuates incestuous relations with her father, culminating perhaps "around the age of fifteen",[11] which would have been in 1967. During that year, she spent the Christmas holidays with her father at his home in Sommières, France. Durrell was then fifty-five and a recent widower. Claude-Marie had died of cancer on 1 January 1967.

The extracts of Sappho's diaries are often discursive, confused, and opaque. They do, however, tell a story of a distraught and lonely person on the way to self-destruction. In 1983, she attempts suicide with an overdose of sleeping pills; her mother Yvette intervenes, and doctors save her life. Then, on 1 February 1985, Sappho commits suicide by hanging herself. She was thirty-three.

Sappho's insinuations are serious and damaging. But how seriously should they be taken? Should they be ignored, as Candace Fertile does in her article on incest in Durrell's oeuvre?[12] Should they be dismissed as the ramblings of a neurotic or schizophrenic personality? This is the usual view of such cases. Disbelief has long been the reaction of legal and psychiatric authorities from John Henry Wigmore to Sigmund Freud, who referred to accounts of familial incest as largely "sexual fantasy".[13] And incredulity is the reaction of Bill Buford, Ian S. MacNiven, Durrell's authorized biographer, and other literary critics. They pay little attention to the complex relationship between Durrell and his daughter. Her side of the story, however approximate, deserves better treatment than being ignored, dismissed, or buried alive in a long footnote, as MacNiven does.[14]

Feminist scholars question the usual approach to incest. Judith Lewis Herman, M.D., is Clinical Professor of Psychiatry at Harvard Medical School. She conducted part of her research in a "clinical study" and forcefully argues that father-daughter incest is not a fantasy, rather a "common occurrence". She further argues that "the greater the domination of the father, and the more the caretaking is relegated to the mother, the

---

[11] S. Durrell, "Journals and Letters", p. 68.

[12] Fertile, "Meaning of Incest", pp. 105-23.

[13] For a discussion of the historical denial of incest, see Herman, *Father-Daughter Incest*, pp. 7-21. John Henry Wigmore, an American professor of law, wrote a major study on the law of evidence. Herman (*Father-Daughter Incest*, p. 11) writes, "John Henry Wigmore's *Treatise on Evidence* (1934), set forth a doctrine impeaching the credibility of any female, especially a child, who complained of a sex offense". On Freud's rejection of various accounts of incest, see Freud, *Letters to Fliess*, p. 264. Freud's letter is dated 21 September 1897.

[14] MacNiven, *Lawrence Durrell*, pp. 759-60, n. 218.

greater the likelihood of father-daughter incest".[15] Durrell's household fits this profile in its broad outline. Herman submits these definitions:

> Incest was defined to mean any sexual relationship between a child and an adult in a position of paternal authority. [...] We further defined a sexual relationship to mean any physical contact that had to be kept a secret.[16]

She also examines two types of incest: one in which the father commits "overt" incest and another in which he exhibits seductive behaviour or "covert incest". Herman defines "seductiveness on the part of fathers to mean behavior that was clearly sexually motivated, but which did not involve physical contact or a requirement for secrecy".[17] Durrell seems closest to the latter type.

In 1979, Sappho read Herman's early article on incest, published by the New York Academy of Sciences, and wrote to the psychiatrist a perfectly sane and professional letter requesting further information on the subject.[18] In 1981, Herman published her full study on incest. Sappho may have read this book, and the extent of its influence is open to debate and awaits further research. Given Herman's work on the subject, however, it is hard not to conclude that outright dismissal is outright negligence. The matter deserves serious consideration. I therefore propose that Lawrence Durrell's literary treatment of incest, that is, his obsession with the issue, be examined closely as an insight into his and his daughter's motivations.

The problem baffles and teases. On the one hand, we have a talented but unstable daughter whose insinuations of paternal incest are provocative but unverifiable; on the other, we have a mercurial and authoritarian father whose writings wallow in incest and suicide. Sappho appears to play out her father's fantasies — with disastrous consequences. In a perverted sense, what might be said of her is what Ben Jonson said of his son Benjamin: "his best piece of poetry".[19] Daughter Sappho might be called Lawrence Durrell's best (or worst) creation. I shall argue that Sappho Jane Durrell may have been a victim of her father's weird obsessions, sexual and thanatological, which include such curiosities as quoting the Marquis de Sade in the epigraphs to each of his novels comprising *The Alexandria Quartet* (*Quartet* 15, 208, 396, 656).

---

[15] Herman, *Father-Daughter Incest*, pp. viii, 7, 63.
[16] Herman, *Father-Daughter Incest*, p. 70.
[17] Herman, *Father-Daughter Incest*, p. 109.
[18] S. Durrell, "Journals and Letters", p. 82.
[19] Jonson, *Ben Jonson*, p. 8.

II. A Story

The first thing to keep in mind about Sappho Durrell's "Journals and Letters", only thirty-one pages of which appear in *Granta*, including commentary, is that they represent Bill Buford's edited version of a much larger corpus, which filled "several carrier-bags".[20] Buford arranges this material to present one view of Sappho Jane's personality. Although enthralling, the retelling of her story cannot be anything more than a scrapbook of snapshots and miscellanea. In his preface, he simply presents the facts of Sappho's life and doesn't comment on the quality or accuracy of her writings.[21] Then in a later interview with *The New York Times* in 1991, he describes Sappho's manuscripts as "a large and largely incoherent body of work" and observes, "It was certainly Sappho's fantasy and belief that there was an incestuous relationship with her father". That statement probably pleased Yvette Durrell, who unsuccessfully "sought an injunction" to stop the publication of her daughter's writings.[22] But it is questionable whose fantasies are most relevant to this discussion — Sappho's or her father's.

Although Buford does not believe the sensational implications of Sappho's journals, he nevertheless makes her materials coherent and turns them into a story of paternal abuse illustrating his stated theme, however ironic and appropriate: "They fuck you up". Which is not surprising. For Buford, author of books and essays, specializes in storytelling. He revived and edited *Granta* for sixteen years (1978-1994) and later worked for eight years at *The New Yorker* as the fiction and literary editor (1994-2002). Buford attaches great importance to storytelling as an essential aspect of human experience. In a 1996 manifesto appearing in the magazine, he describes a return to the old way of telling stories and rejects the postmodern variety of narration:

> There were stories about stories, there were stories about writing stories, and there were stories about searches for the writers to write the stories. It was art! It was modern! And, finally, it disappeared![23]

One date Buford provides for the waning of postmodernism is 1985, coincidentally or not, the same year as Sappho's suicide and the same year her father published *Quinx*, the last novel of his *Avignon Quintet* (1974-1985).

---

[20] S. Durrell, "Journals and Letters", p. 57.
[21] Ibid.
[22] Cohen, "Daughter's Intimations", 14 August 1991.
[23] Buford, "Seduction of Storytelling", p. 12.

Buford then defines his idea of good stories. In his "simplest" definition, they "[make] the reader want to find out what happens next". They are also restorative:

> [They] protect us from chaos, and maybe that's what we, unblinkered at the end of the twentieth century, find ourselves craving. Implicit in the extraordinary revival of storytelling is the possibility that we need stories—that they are a fundamental unit of knowledge, the foundation of memory, essential to the way we make sense of our lives: the beginning, middle, and end of our personal and collective trajectories.[24]

Buford's good stories are therapeutic because they have a particular form, and that form ultimately derives, as he well knows, from Ralph W. Rader's model of the "full Aristotelian action". As Rader explains,

> [The Aristotelian action] follows the predicament of a central character from a beginning which defines the terms of that predicament, through a middle which develops and complicates it and our reactions to the full, to an end which resolves the complications and brings our emotional participation to satisfactory discharge and close.[25]

I am not opposed to Buford's aims, but we should assess their relevance to Sappho Durrell, whose writings, like her father's, do not conform to the conventional mold as Buford and Rader define it. Most conspicuously, Sappho's "action", Buford's representation of her life, does not end in a "satisfactory discharge and close".

Storytelling can be a form of therapy for both writer and reader; it can give structure to the turmoil of anxiety. If Sappho's writings appear incoherent, if she cannot make sense of her life, then Buford brings coherence and meaning to her work through his editorial skills. There she struggles against a tyrannical father: "I want to play around with the idea of parricide — not in general but in specific. Vis à vis my father".[26] She fights to win his affection and overcome his influence: "Love him but don't trust him (Father)" and "If I can swim clear of the wreck of my father".[27] And

[24] Ibid.
[25] Rader, "Literary Form", p. 22. Ralph W. Rader (1930-2007) was a professor of English at the University of California, Berkeley (1956-1997). During the fall and winter quarters of 1976-1977, Bill Buford and I attended Professor Rader's graduate seminar on the English novel: from its origins with Samuel Richardson (1689-1761) to its culmination with James Joyce (1882-1941).
[26] S. Durrell, "Journals and Letters", p. 58.
[27] S. Durrell, "Journals and Letters", pp. 75, 77.

she finally succumbs to her own inescapable loneliness: her suicide note (paraphrased) mentions abortions, a possible nervous breakdown, and "*asks that certain relatives be kept at a distance from her writings and her belongings*".[28] A beginning, a middle, and an end — the classic narrative sequence. Buford heightens the drama by interspersing Casement's invoices for psychotherapy, which increase in frequency as her death nears.[29] This is indeed a compelling story, but does this make it less true? Has Sappho's voice been altered and diminished? Has she become more deranged and less reliable?

Evidently only a few people have read Sappho Jane's unexpurgated manuscripts. I am not one of them, so my comments are necessarily speculative.

To understand Sappho we need to read everything she wrote, and even then we may fall far short. Truth is elusive, but one fact stands out — her writings often read like a warped version of her father's own writings. And Lawrence Durrell's novels, in particular those of *The Avignon Quintet*, fit well Buford's characterization of the postmodern novel as "stories about searches for the writers to write the stories". In *Livia* (1978), the second novel of the *Quintet*, we find a fictional character (Sutcliffe) talking to his fictional author (Blanford): "What would you give me if I wrote a book to prove that the great Blanford is simply the fiction of one of his fictions?" (*Quintet* 351). Durrell was deeply concerned about such problems, and Sappho apparently took him seriously. When she refers to herself as "Saph" and to her father as "Pa" or "pap", she absorbs her father's identity. She creates nominal twins, nouns similar in sound and spelling, that suggest both familial and literary intimacy, the very kind that Lawrence Durrell exploits in his *Quintet* (e.g., Blanford/Bloshford, Akkad/Affad, Constance/Constanza).

What follows is a comparative analysis of father's and daughter's writings — an indirect way to catch a glimpse of Sappho's kaleidoscopic mind. This is an alternative narrative to Bill Buford's story of a delusional woman on a downward spiral to dissolution and suicide.

III. Another Story

From early childhood, when her parents lived together, Sappho Durrell began to assume aspects of her father's personality. In her journals, she recalls her mother saying that "I [Sappho] would suddenly come out with a cutting remark about my mother, speaking as though I were my father and

---

[28] S. Durrell, "Journals and Letters", p. 71; Buford's italics and commentary.
[29] S. Durrell, "Journals and Letters", pp. 61, 72, 79, *et passim*.

fully adult [...] that it was as if I were mirroring the worst aspects of my father and just coughed them up".[30]

Sappho also mirrors some of her father's most famous prose. Early in her journals, after she contemplates "parricide", she describes a David Hockney painting, *A Bigger Splash* (1967) and a film of the same title (1973):

> Some fortuitous things happened today. That film which had such an effect on me—probably quite out of proportion with its true merit—*A Bigger Splash*. The pool in the final picture haunted me. [...] Florence took me to her house—very California—and from the balcony we looked down the mountainside past the two or three turquoise patches of swimming pools. [...] It was like looking down on a myth—this tiny slip of blue three kilometers down—was the very scene which held so much imaginative meaning for me. [...] Something that Peter Adams had said earlier in the day came back to me like a perfume: 'Nothing is real outside the head; all is illusionary except what is in the mind.' When one's world is polluted to the soles of the shoes—then the mind must recreate a liveable world. Hockney for me was one of those starting points for imagining a world one can taste again.[31]

Hockney's painting depicts a splash of water in a California swimming pool of cobalt blue. Compare this with the pool scene in her father's early success, *Prospero's Cell* (1945):

> Causality is this dividing floor which falls away each morning when I am back on the warm rocks, lying with my face less than a foot above the dark Ionian. All morning we lie under the red brick shrine to Saint Arsenius, dropping cherries into the pool—clear down two fathoms to the sandy floor where they loom like drops of blood. N. has been going in for them like an otter and bringing them up in her lips. The Shrine is our private bathing-pool; four puffs of cypress, deep clean-cut diving ledges above two fathoms of blue water, and a floor of clean pebbles. (*PC* 16)

"N." is Nancy Myers, Durrell's first wife. Sappho's "myth" of the swimming pool is a gloss on the myth of the "bathing-pool" that her father invented in his book on Corfu. There he reworked some painful experiences into an idyllic description of his early years on Corfu with Nancy.

As Sappho restates in her own way, one of her father's basic themes is the power of the imagination to recreate its own world. That world eschews his "causality" and relies on her "some fortuitous things". The

[30] S. Durrell, "Journals and Letters", p. 72.
[31] S. Durrell, "Journals and Letters", pp. 58-59.

sunny aspect of this process appears at the end of *The Alexandria Quartet*, when Clea tells Darley "I have a feeling that you too perhaps have stepped across the threshold into the kingdom of your imagination" (*Quartet* 877). Pools of blue water are on the edge of such thresholds; they are, as young Durrell implies, on the other side of the "dividing floor".

But there is another side, one not so bright. Sappho describes the darkness of this vision when she visits Claude-Marie's grave with her father:

> We went to visit the tomb and found dogroses and Venus' mirror on Claude's grave. On the way back, in the strange light, he began to improvise a Poe-like story very badly to demonstrate how the Languedoc lent itself to this, but more generally to show how the world was inside, waiting for its spring to be tapped, for the story-teller to tap it. I understood all this, tacitly, rationally, but in me I felt so dead: like a gourd with a good shape, but dry. I know that, *rationally*, he would like me to stand up and create, but that there is something in him which would 'kill' me if I did— would knock what I did. I will always have his ego between me and the world, and my surroundings will be as dry as dust.[32]

Sappho does not relate her father's "Poe-like story", but Edgar Allan Poe was famous for his macabre tales of decay, doubling, death, and hints of incest. One of those is "The Fall of the House of Usher" (1839); the story contains a ramshackle mansion in a "dreary tract of country", a twin brother and sister, a live burial of the sister, and a suggestion of incest between the siblings.[33] All these elements could readily fit into Durrell's *Avignon Quintet*, which is set in the Languedoc region of France and which "lent itself to this".

The second novel of the series is aptly titled *Livia or Buried Alive* (1978). Sappho's metaphor of the self as a dry "gourd" echoes, negatively, a figure of speech in *Livia*: "Blanford wanted [...] to let his thought of Livia ripen like some huge gourd" (*Quintet* 452). Blanford, the *Quintet*'s main narrator, is infatuated with Livia, the twin of Constance, and his simile is ironic, for Livia turns out to be a bad seed, perhaps as "dry" and barren as Sappho felt. According to Buford, Sappho thought she was the "inspiration" for Livia,[34] who has an incestuous relationship with her brother Hilary and who commits suicide by hanging herself (*Quintet* 1285, 819).

Durrell's inner reality is dark and morbid, and his daughter struggles against his lifelong obsessions. In the *Quartet* of the late 1950s,

---

[32] S. Durrell, "Journals and Letters", p. 58.
[33] Poe, *Poetry and Tales*, pp. 317, 329, 334-45.
[34] S. Durrell, "Journals and Letters", p. 57.

Pursewarden, a major character, commits incest with his sister Liza, and this relationship contributes to his suicide. Durrell partly models Pursewarden's character on the Romantic poet George Gordon, Lord Byron, who reputedly had an incestuous relationship with his half-sister, Augusta Leigh.[35] The similarities between the two poets are not coincidental. After Byron's death, his "Memoirs" were burned;[36] after Pursewarden's death, his "letters" are burned (*Quartet* 801-04). The correspondences are striking and compelling.

Twenty years later in the *Quintet*, Durrell creates another world permeated with aberrant behaviour. A major component of the plot involves a suicide cult which seeks to preempt death and "counter the laws of entropy" (*Quintet* 1119). This is a very weird idea, even when expressed under the guise of literary fiction.

In July of 1979, Sappho calls her father "suicidal"[37] and a month earlier cries out, "I'm terrified. He's going to commit suicide and he's trying to take me with him. *Livia, or Buried Alive.* Suttee/puttee".[38]

Like Shakespeare's Hamlet, Sappho's madness, if such, has method. "Suttee" is the Hindu practice of a widow throwing herself on her husband's funeral pyre. On other occasions, Sappho refers to herself as her father's "wife".[39] "Puttee" (Hindi: cloth wrapped around the lower leg) may be simply a childish rhyme, or it may be a pun on French *pute* (whore, tart), which is highly pejorative.[40] Sappho knew French well. She says in an earlier entry that her father thinks of a wife as a "*whore*".[41] In any case, the usage of "Suttee/puttee" implies both suicide and incest. Another of Poe's tales, "A Descent into the Maelström" (1841), has some relevance. Sappho may have fought against being sucked into the vortex of her father's "monstrous ego"[42] and crazy obsessions, just as she fears being dragged down by "the wreck of my father".[43]

Incest takes many forms in Durrell's *Quintet.* It need not mean actual intercourse, so it's not farfetched when Sappho accuses him of "mental incest":

---

[35] Marchand, *Byron*, pp. 403-04: "Byron's correspondence with Lady Melbourne hints very strongly that he had become involved in a liaison with his half-sister, Augusta".

[36] Marchand, *Byron*, pp. 1248-50.

[37] S. Durrell, "Journals and Letters", p. 79.

[38] S. Durrell, "Journals and Letters", p. 75.

[39] S. Durrell, "Journals and Letters", pp. 76, 78.

[40] Robert Collins, *French English Dictionary*, s.v. *pute*.

[41] S. Durrell, "Journals and Letters", p. 61.

[42] S. Durrell, "Journals and Letters", p. 75.

[43] S. Durrell, "Journals and Letters", p. 77.

> I feel very threatened by the fact that my father is sleeping with women
> who are my age or younger. I feel he is committing a kind of mental incest
> and that it is a message to me as his favourite daughter.[44]

A subsequent scene in *Constance* (1982) illustrates this kind of activity. It
occurs in chapter two: "The Nazi". Candace Fertile does not include the
episode among her examples of incest in Durrell's oeuvre. Given the
subtitle, Durrell may have intended incest to demonstrate the evils of Nazi
culture, similar to the theme of decadence in Poe's "Fall of the House of
Usher". This analysis, however, is muddled and runs into two problems.
First, Von Esslin, "the Nazi", has dubious credentials as a member of the
Nazi party. Aside from an admiration for Hitler's military strategy (*Quintet*
602), he reveals few Nazi sympathies. He is a *Junker*, a Prussian aristocrat,[45]
and a general in the *Wehrmacht*. German officers were not normally
members of Hitler's party.[46] Second, if evil breeds incest, then Durrell's
world is saturated with evil, for some form of incest touches many of the
families in his *Quintet* and elsewhere.

So, during the Second World War, Major General Von Esslin
returns home and visits his mother. Son and mother are very close; he
lovingly calls her "Katzen-Mutter" (cat-mother) because of her "passion"
for cats (*Quintet* 600-01). That night the son sleeps with the maid, who
remains nameless and who is described as a "spindly Polish girl", possibly
young and certainly docile (*Quintet* 604; cf. 601). As the pair make love,
the mother lies in bed and listens:

> Two storeys above them his mother lay with open eyes, staring into the
> darkness and thinking as she listened with furious concentration to the
> silence which from time to time blurred into the small sounds of congress
> which they made. A chimney-flue conveyed whatever sound there was up
> to her room; but that was little enough, so she must supplement it with
> guesswork to imagine clearly what she had already imagined so often in
> the last years of his father. Then silence came. (*Quintet* 608)

Durrell's scene ostensibly enables Von Esslin's mother to reimagine her
deceased husband's habitual rape of the Polish maid. But the mother is

---

[44] S. Durrell, "Journals and Letters", p. 70.

[45] German *von* (from) is a nobiliary particle (e.g., Wolfgang von Goethe). It always
appears in the lower case, unless beginning a sentence. Durrell consistently
capitalizes *von*, as in "Von Esslin", which is either a careless error or a deliberate
mistake. If the latter, he further questions the authenticity of "the Nazi".

[46] M. Mann, "Contradictions", p. 150: "Only a minority of officers and men were
Nazi members".

"clearly" indulging in a kind of voyeurism or, in Sappho's words, "a kind of mental incest".

Voyeurism is a prominent activity in the *Quintet*. It sometimes takes the form of child pornography and is possibly related to Sappho's anxiety that her father is sleeping with "younger" women. In *Livia*, two characters turn into peeping Toms, look through a "lavatory" window in Avignon, and observe an Egyptian prince in a brothel, "surrounded by children" (*Quintet* 444, 449). The theme of pedophilia occurs earlier in *Mountolive* (1958), when David Mountolive, the British ambassador to Egypt, undertakes a nighttime adventure in Alexandria and "stumble[s] into a house of child prostitutes" (*Quartet* 628). No stumbling around in *Livia*, no chance encounters with illicit sex, the Egyptian prince deliberately seeks out pedophiliac experiences. What is dark and latent in the *Quartet* becomes clear and explicit in the *Quintet* as a general coarsening of sexuality. One half expects Durrell to turn into another Henry Miller, a close friend. In a letter dated 5 September 1949, Durrell excoriates Miller's novel *Sexus* (1949) as a "shower of lavatory filth" (*DML* 233).

In *Constance*, Durrell suggests that voyeurism is an aspect of suppressed sexuality. Von Esslin's mother is reserved, possibly frigid, and has timid gestures, a "bird-like nod" (*Quintet* 601). Then, in what may be a dream or an example of psychic powers, a bird-like hand, presumably the mother's, awakens and summons her son to the maid's room (*Quintet* 607), where she listens in and exercises her imagination. Indeed, the entire Von Esslin household reeks of suppressed incest and intertwined relationships. The deceased father, another German general, "worshipped" and "pined" for his deceased daughter Constanza (*Quintet* 600), just as the mother loves and worships her son, the twin of his dead sister.

A few questions arise regarding the composition of this scene. Why so much suppression? What is Durrell concealing? Was he aware of his own motivations? If he was unaware, then his daughter appears to have understood them better than he did.

Durrell drops other hints which offer alternative motives, conscious or not. Earlier in the chapter he notes that the Von Esslin family is distantly related to "the Kleists" and specifically alludes to the suicide of Heinrich von Kleist (*Quintet* 604-05). The Kleist family was Prussian nobility with a long military tradition. Heinrich von Kleist (1777-1811) was a German writer of Romantic tendencies, who committed suicide at the age of thirty-four (Sappho dies at thirty-three) and whose famous short story, "The Marquise of O", contains a notorious scene which strongly suggests father-daughter incest.[47] Moreover, like Von Esslin's beloved *Katzen-Mutter*, Sappho was also fond of cats and kept several of them at her home in London.[48] The many similarities are suspicious — a "passion" for cats, a young maid, an older lecher, Kleist's age, his suicide, his incest theme — these coincidences are easily open to reinterpretation by someone as susceptible as Sappho. She was, after all, her father's daughter, a graduate in English literature, and trained in the art of literary allusion. After reading this chapter in *Constance*, she could have easily thought her father was sending her "a message" about the varieties of familial incest.

 Solitary Practices is the subtitle of *Constance*, and it presents a conundrum. What and whose "solitary practices"? The novel suggests two types of such behaviour: existential and abnormal. The first stresses how one lives in society. Durrell names the novel after its principal character, Constance. Her lover Affad has a wife, Lily, whom he describes redundantly as a "solitary hermit" (*Quintet* 864) living in a Coptic monastery at Wady Natrun, Egypt. As we learn later in *Sebastian* (1983), Lily lives in solitude and silence on the edge of the western desert (*Quintet* 1021). Her solitary practice is existential; she chooses to remove herself from society. In 1980, Sappho received a letter from the secretary of a Carmelite monastery in Kent; the letter confirmed her attendance for a weekend retreat at the monastery.[49] The Carmelites are a contemplative order of Catholic nuns who live in seclusion and who have taken the vow of silence. Sappho did not join the Carmelites, but her last years were an erratic but steady withdrawal from society.

 The second type pertains to abnormal behaviour. In this context, incest may be considered a "solitary practice". Blanford, Durrell's primary narrator, makes this comment on lovers: "Secret practices — lovers sharpened by slavery" (*Quintet* 931). Substitute *incest* for *slavery* and note the similar usage. One reason paternal incest is considered abhorrent is because it involves a figure of authority enforcing his will on a weaker person. Secrecy, it will be recalled, is an essential part of Herman's definition of father-daughter incest, which is just another way to look at slavery. The Polish maid in the Von Esslin household is a sexual slave. Two generations of Von Esslins rape her, while the *Katzen-Mutter* observes surreptitiously. The maid later commits suicide by stabbing herself in the heart with Von Esslin's ceremonial "dirk" and leaves a note: "I do not wish

---

[47] Kleist, "Marquise of O", p. 107. For the German, see Kleist, *Sämtliche Werke*, vol. 2, p. 138. The wife observes her husband passionately ("heiße und lechzende") kissing their daughter "just like a lover" ("gerade wie ein Verliebter").

[48] S. Durrell, "Journals and Letters", pp. 69, 87.

[49] S. Durrell, "Journals and Letters", p. 83.

to be a slave" (*Quintet* 750). The phallic pun on "dirk" (viz. *dick* or *dork*) is obvious and not unlike Sappho's pun on "Suttee/puttee".

There is, of course, the danger of reading too much into Durrell's life and art and seeing too many connections and coincidences. Frederick Crews endorses the warning about the "elementary misunderstanding of the difference between an author and his created characters".[50] A point well taken but not a hard and fast rule. I don't see much distance between Durrell and his main characters, as the narrator asks at the beginning of *Quinx*, "Perhaps they [the principals] could also be the various actors which, in their sum, made up one whole single personality" (*Quintet* 1177)? Whose personality? Durrell's, I would argue. Gordon Bowker adjudicates the issue of incest: "On the charge of incest with his daughter, Durrell must be declared innocent until proved guilty".[51] This is fair but should not prohibit discussion. The psychiatrist, Anthony Durrell, M.D., of Sydney, Australia, also reminds me about the Electra complex and Sappho Jane's intense competition with her father, which could have resulted in incestuous fantasies.[52] Her dream of making love to her mother Yvette could well be interpreted as one aspect of Oedipal desires,[53] a situation where the daughter assumes her father's role. Another well-founded consideration.

These caveats acknowledged, I still find room for much doubt concerning father-daughter incest in Durrell's household, and I would argue for suspended judgment rather than complete absolution. The circumstantial evidence is substantial. As mentioned before, the psychiatrist and scholar Judith Herman includes within her definition of father-daughter incest the category of the "seductive father", who does not engage in intercourse but whose favouritism betrays sexual motivations. Herman further argues that such behaviour has harmful consequences for a woman's psychological development.[54]

Sappho calls herself Durrell's "favourite daughter".[55] It's not hard to see why. She was beautiful, intelligent, and creative. Daughter and father also complement one another — not only artistically but also behaviourally. Her behaviour conforms to much of Herman's profile of "incestuous abuse": victimization, low self-esteem, guilt, depression, and promiscuity. His fits the general pattern of the "seductive father": violence, withdrawal,

---

[50] Crews, *Memory Wars*, p. 43.

[51] Bowker, *Through the Dark Labyrinth*, p. 429.

[52] Personal communication from Anthony Durrell on 21 August 2013. Dr. Durrell's genetic relationship to Lawrence Durrell is unknown.

[53] S. Durrell, "Journals and Letters", p. 60.

[54] Herman, *Father-Daughter Incest*, pp. 119-23.

[55] S. Durrell, "Journals and Letters", p. 70.

excessive drinking, favouritism, and jealousy.[56] The pair are "regular correspondent[s]". He gives her fatherly advice on psychotherapy, comments on her "*rat-like super-ego*", says she may have a "*phobic thing underneath*", and signs a letter "*Lover*".[57] Sappho responds by thanking him for the "lovely letter" but takes offense at the reference to her rodent inhibitions.[58] Her "phobic thing" may refer to what Durrell calls, in another letter, her problems with "trying to grow a prick in the wrong place".[59] In a previous entry in her journal, she writes, "When I look in a mirror I see a rat. Which is my internalized image of my father's image of me".[60]

On 15 November 1981, she replies to "Dear Pa" and mentions a package he has sent. Buford reports that the package ("like many previous ones") contained

> a large collection of press clippings and reviews about his work, correspondence, some of it intimate, from friends and other members of the family, and a number of love letters from admirers.[61]

Thus, the "favourite daughter" gets privileged access to the father's successes and secrets. But his motivation is puzzling. Why would a father invite his daughter to share the details of his fame and his love life, especially when he knows she is emotionally unstable? Was he baiting her? The parcel begs the question — was Durrell trying to dominate, to put Sappho in her place, and, above all, to make her jealous of her rivals, who were, quite possibly, younger women? As Sappho says about her own affairs, she too engages in flirtation: "Flirtation is the only way I have of keeping my sane sexuality (and it *is* positive) alive".[62]

Lawrence Durrell had an active and extensive love life. In a letter dated 4 June 1978, he told Henry Miller that he was being chased by a "beautiful young Alexandrian", whom he described as "pleasant target practice" (*DML* 496). He later rejected her, and she threatened suicide.[63] Durrell had no dearth of young female admirers during 1978-1984. MacNiven mentions three; there were others, no doubt, and those were only

---

[56] Herman, *Father-Daughter Incest*, pp. 29-31, 111-16.
[57] S. Durrell, "Journals and Letters", p. 72, 74. Buford summation, p. 72.
[58] S. Durrell, "Journals and Letters", p. 73.
[59] S. Durrell, "Journals and Letters", p. 80.
[60] S. Durrell, "Journals and Letters", p. 69.
[61] S. Durrell, "Journals and Letters", p. 89.
[62] S. Durrell, "Journals and Letters", p. 69; original italics.
[63] MacNiven, *Lawrence Durrell*, p. 634.

the young ones.[64] In accord with his many conquests, Durrell's characterization of an affair as "target practice" displays a fine male bravado, ultimately calling into question his own truthfulness. Nevertheless, the comment betrays a callousness which could have easily extended to his daughter Sappho. She, on the other hand, "bait[s]" him and "flaunt[s] her feminism".[65]

Buford's selection of Sappho's materials clearly shows an intense competition between father and daughter. They're locked in a "power struggle", as Sappho later describes:

> He [Durrell] has been placing more and more of the wife's role on me and he is *always* aggressive towards wives. They can't do anything right except be sweet and kind and giving. Before, when I withdrew, he would accept that I was different. Now he is aggressive, using the psychology of hostile silences or bitchiness. He is a master in the art of psychological destruction. He knows just where to hit. [...] I am frightened of him physically and mentally.[66]

Sappho's struggles recall her mother's and father's, as Yvette must have reported in graphic detail about the breakup of their marriage:

> He [Durrell] started to argue but when he saw that her [Yvette's] ring was gone, the breath went out of him. He wheezed with shock and started to throw her around. Instead of fighting back, as she usually did, she submitted because he couldn't hurt her. Three days three nights they played cat and mouse. He became the devil. He refused to believe she had the will to leave him. She peed on the bed. It was a pure power struggle. At the end of the three days he was frightened of her. She was frightened of herself. She was having hallucinations.[67]

This powerful scene resonates. "Cat and mouse" also describes Sappho's perspective on the game she and her father are playing. Their letters sound like quarrelling lovers.

In a letter of 14 June 1979, she responds to his comment about her "*rat-like super-ego*" and writes, "I shall cross swords with you for that you old fart!" In an earlier draft of that letter, she annotates her response with "CALLING HIS CARD". Other annotations include: "HIS BLUFF CALLED", "I AM PUTTING FEAR IN HIM", and "ME TRYING TO SAY I FORGAVE HIM. HE'S NOT SURE I HAVE THOUGH BECAUSE HE

---

[64] MacNiven, *Lawrence Durrell*, pp. 637, 638, 662-63.
[65] MacNiven, *Lawrence Durrell*, p. 640.
[66] S. Durrell, "Journals and Letters", p. 61.
[67] S. Durrell, "Journals and Letters", p. 63.

CAN'T CONCEIVE OF ANYBODY EVER FORGIVING HIM. HE'D BREAK UNDER THE STRAIN".[68] The letter and its drafts have bipolar swings in mood. The annotations are vicious, but the final letter itself is affectionate. It begins with "Dearest Pa" and ends with "LOTSA LOVE, AS ALWAYS Saph".

Sappho's three-way dialogue between her two selves and her father resembles the kind of multiple dialogue Durrell sets up in the *Quintet* between Durrell himself, his main character Aubrey Blanford, and Blanford's *alter ego* Robin Sutcliffe. In *Livia*, these long exchanges revolve around some of Durrell's pet theories: the unstable ego, androgyny, and wounded sexuality.[69] The accounts of these oddball ideas strain credulity. Blanford asks, "What always bothered me was the question of a stable ego — did such a thing exist" (*Quintet* 335)? No, he answers and says, "The human psyche is almost infinitely various" — and "contradictory". Androgyny prompts a comparison to the male organ: "The head [of the penis] lends itself particularly well to the expression of bisexual conflicts, and can cunningly represent both male and female genitalia" (*Quintet* 320). And sexual trauma occurs early in life, as Blanford explains, "Childhood, with its gross sexual and psychological damage to the psyche — what a terrible thing to be forced to undergo" (*Quintet* 320).

The idea of wounded sexuality, figurative and literal, appears at the beginning of *The Alexandria Quartet.* The narrator dresses it up as part of a metaphor, when he famously quotes another source: "Alexandria was the great winepress of love; those who emerged from it were the sick men, the solitaries, the prophets — I mean all who have been deeply wounded in their sex" (*Quartet* 18). Durrell's usage is unclear; he could be referring to "sex" as sexuality, as the sex act, or as a sexual organ. He soon reifies the disability: "I found Melissa, washed up like a half-drowned bird, on the dreary littorals of Alexandria, with her sex broken" (*Quartet* 26). Then an extreme manifestation of this condition occurs in the *Quintet*: Blanford suffers a spinal injury resulting in impotence. A Greek female nurse revives him through intense physical therapy, and she, in effect, "rape[s]" him (*Quintet* 668-69). You might say, the nurse delivers "tough love": a wound heals a wound. Although Durrell's version of tough love works in his fiction, it does not work on his daughter Sappho and her "*rat-like super-ego*".

Sappho embodies some of her father's crackpot theories. Like the best of Durrell's characters, she has an unstable ego or personality. She is

---

[68] S. Durrell, "Journals and Letters", pp. 73-74; original capitalization.
[69] My thanks to Sumantra Nag, Kennedy Gammage, and David Green. I have greatly benefited from our discussions on "wounded sex".

probably bipolar, undergoes psychotherapy, and suffers a "*nervous breakdown*".[70] She professes androgyny: "Androgyny is the only way I can survive and not be the object of retribution".[71] And she exemplifies a woman with "her sex broken". It begins with her given name, which she finds a curse, extends to her experiments in lesbianism and heterosexuality, and ends renouncing both.[72] In sum, she lives her father's fiction, especially the trope of "wounded sex", and so states, "I'm attracted to anyone who's really traumatized by sexuality as I am".[73] Like Livia, Von Esslin's mother, and Affad's wife, all of whom end up as solitaries or lonely figures, Sappho slowly withdraws from the world and disappears into her own private darkness.

IV. Aporia

Lawrence Durrell wrote three plays. His first was *Sappho* (1950), "a play in verse" about the Greek poet of the seventh century BC. Sappho Jane Durrell also had aspirations as a playwright and was working on a drama about another famous poet, Emily Brontë. Sappho was apparently continuing the project her father had discussed in a letter to Diana Gould in 1944: "I have a plan for a play called EMILY about Miss Bronte [sic]".[74] He later abandoned the proposal. Buford mentions Sappho's manuscript but does not provide any excerpts, although Sappho refers twice to the play and seems to consider it her major work.[75] In her letter of 14 June 1979, she writes,

> I'm having fun welding my Brontë sketches together. Branwell is something of a tough nut because he comes across so much (in researches) as a joke figure. But then there are two versions of him (of course) and in EJB's mind something else rather interesting is going on.[76]

"EJB" is, of course, Emily Jane Brontë, and Branwell was her older brother, Patrick Branwell Brontë. What was "going on" in Emily's mind? What was that "something else rather interesting"?

---

[70] S. Durrell, "Journals and Letters", p. 87. Buford commentary.

[71] S. Durrell, "Journals and Letters", p. 78.

[72] S. Durrell, "Journals and Letters", pp. 70, 69.

[73] S. Durrell, "Journals and Letters", p. 75.

[74] See Fertile, "Meaning of Incest", p. 107. Fertile quotes from a letter Durrell wrote to Diana Gould on 7 August 1944. The letter is located in Special Collections, Morris Library, Southern Illinois University, Carbondale.

[75] S. Durrell, "Journals and Letters", pp. 57, 73, 88.

[76] S. Durrell, "Journals and Letters", p. 73.

The answer to those questions probably involves incest. Durrell himself had no doubt that some kind of incest characterised Emily's relationship with Branwell. In his letter to Gould, he writes, "[Emily was] in love with her brother but having no sort of real sex: it [had] gone too far underground by cerebration".[77]

Sappho and Emily shared *Jane* as their middle name. Which is surely no coincidence. Durrell was a poet, and he named his second daughter after two renowned poets. Sappho calls Emily one of her "female literary models".[78] Aside from her fine poetry, Emily's great achievement was *Wuthering Heights* (1847), and that extraordinary novel undoubtedly had special appeal to Sappho and her Romantic sensibilities. The story focuses on the tormented love affair of the changeable Catherine and the demonic Heathcliff. Although Heathcliff is a foundling, the two are raised as siblings. Eric Solomon argues that Heathcliff was possibly the "illegitimate offspring" of Catherine's father, "old Earnshaw", so the pair may be half brother and sister. Solomon summarizes: "There can be no doubt that Emily Brontë casts a vague incestuous aura over the entire plot of *Wuthering Heights*".[79]

Emily's "vague incestuous aura" includes Heathcliff's bizarre death wish. In Chapter 29, late in the novel, Heathcliff has the village sexton dig up Catherine's grave. Then he stares at her corpse, still recognizable, leaves her reluctantly, and wishes to be buried next to her. Catherine's coffin has a loose side. His coffin will also have one, so that their remains, over time, will intermingle and people will not be able to tell "which is which".[80] The grave becomes a bed of incest, consummation, and necrophilia. All very good themes in Romantic and Victorian literature.

On 6 July 1981, Sappho added a codicil to her will, which reads in part:

> I should like, if possible, to be buried in Steep churchyard. [...] In the event that my father should request to be buried with me—my wish is that the

---

[77] Fertile, "Meaning of Incest", p. 107.
[78] S. Durrell, "Journals and Letters", p. 77.
[79] Solomon, "Incest Theme", p. 82. See also Knoepflmacher, *Emily Brontë*, pp. 46, 87, 91-92. Knoepflmacher suggests an aberrant relationship between Catherine and Heathcliff: "Something resembling the transgression that brought ruin to King David's children may lurk at the Heights. The irrational patriarch who imports an alien child may well be guilty of some dire offense, as I have suggested. If so, however, the name of the sin that no Christian need pardon will stay veiled" (p. 91). I take the unpardonable "sin" to be "veiled" incest.
[80] Brontë, *Wuthering Heights*, p. 218-19.

request be refused.[81]

This is indeed a strange "wish". It is highly improbable that Lawrence Durrell would have ever made such a "request", for his apparent plan (later honoured) was for some of his ashes to be buried with the ashes of his beloved third wife, Claude-Marie Vincendon, in the cemetery of Saint-Julien de Montredon, Salinelles, France.[82] But this doesn't matter. What matters are Sappho's perceptions, the depth of her feelings, and the reason for her refusal. Her codicil makes a clear statement of her belief that her father harboured strong emotions for her, possibly erotic, and perhaps they were similar to Heathcliff's love of Catherine. She sees herself as her father's lover, and Durrell, like Heathcliff, was given to "diabolical violence".[83] Whether or not that physical relationship actually existed is moot and unresolved. Sappho's writings and her father's, however, suggest that something did happen in some indeterminate form.

In his discussion of the baroque novel, George Steiner places Durrell's *Alexandria Quartet* just below Brontë's *Wuthering Heights* in importance.[84] Steiner's apt comparison has relevance which goes beyond the literary and inadvertently touches upon the biographical. For Durrell's comment in 1944 about Emily Brontë having incestuous desires for her brother Patrick Branwell could also foretell his own personal situation with his second daughter: Durrell and Sappho have (quite possibly) incestuous feelings but "no sort of real sex: it gone too far underground by cerebration". And then Durrell elaborated his comment: "so that [their] love degenerates at all points into pity and weakness". In Aristotle's definition of tragedy, pity and fear result in the purgation of emotions. Sappho and her father had a tragic relationship — but no catharsis. This is also the ending to *Wuthering Heights*, albeit ironically, where Lockwood, an obtuse narrator, stares at the graves of the lovers and "wondered how any one could ever imagine unquiet slumbers for the sleepers in that quiet earth". The careful reader knows better. Such "slumbers" are deeply "unquiet".

---

[81] S. Durrell, "Journals and Letters", p. 81.
[82] Hogarth, *Mediterranean Shore*, p. 139; MacNiven, *Lawrence Durrell*, pp. 688-89.
[83] Brontë, *Wuthering Heights*, p. 206.
[84] Steiner, "Baroque Novel", p. 23.

PART TWO:

DURRELL'S CIRCLE

Introduction to Part Two

Lawrence Durrell's circle, which I define broadly, includes many prominent scholars, most noteworthy are Ian S. MacNiven, his authorized biographer, and Richard Pine, his chief advocate, promoter, and interpreter. Both of these men knew Durrell, met him on various occasions, and had a personal relationship with him. I also include in this group Michael Haag, now deceased, who spent much of his life following in Durrell's footsteps around the Mediterranean and elsewhere. He also knew Durrell.

Haag was both historian and biographer, and his publications on Durrell are perceptive and innovative. They often break new ground and attempt to make a biographical connection between the man and his work. He unfortunately died in 2020 before the completion of his projected biography of Lawrence Durrell. My first two essays in this section eagerly anticipated Haag's future biography, and they reflect my positive expectations at the time I wrote them.

Haag's biographical method of interpreting a literary figure and his writings is not popular in today's literary criticism and is sometimes called a "biographical heresy". It is, however, in my opinion, entirely relevant to the study of Lawrence Durrell, who used his writings both as a way to explore himself and as a way to develop a personal philosophy. On a literary level, Haag changed the way I read and understood Durrell. On a personal level, I briefly knew Haag and observed him both socially and professionally. Lawrence Durrell became Michael Haag's obsession, and I believe that obsession had both positive and negative consequences.

CHAPTER FOUR

HAAG'S CITY[1]

I

Michael Haag knows Egypt. Both writer and photographer, his many books include *Egypt: Cadogan Guides* (London 2004), *The Timeline History of Egypt* (New York 2005), *The Rough Guide to Tutankhamun* (London 2005), and *Cairo Illustrated* (Cairo 2006). The first three are good to read because they have a point of view. They're handbooks written by an opinionated guide with a sharp eye, who's sometimes acerbic, always acute. You may not agree with everything he says; nevertheless, he's compelling, you like listening to his voice. These books are also handy references, good places to get facts, but, as everyone knows, or should know, facts can be deceiving. Somewhere, well east of Suez, Marlow says, during the "official Inquiry" at the beginning of *Lord Jim*, "They demanded facts from him [Jim], as if facts could explain anything".[2] Joseph Conrad knew that facts explain little about human experience, and his presentation of facts often serves to deepen mystery. That is a big aspect of Conrad's art.

    Haag's other works have a similar effect. They read like literature. The products of a cultural and literary historian, they elucidate the past, uncover the background of people and events, and then deepen the mystery that Conrad cherished. Unlike Conrad, however, whose disdain of facts leaves the port of Singapore unidentified as the probable location of Jim's inquest,[3] Haag situates himself squarely and unambiguously in a real port. His major interest focusses on the Mediterranean city of Alexandria, as the following titles indicate: *Alexandria: City of Memory* (New Haven 2004), *Alexandria Illustrated* (Cairo 2004), and *Vintage Alexandria: Photographs of the City, 1860-1960* (Cairo 2008). He is presently working on a new biography of Lawrence Durrell, also to be published by Yale, and, once it

---

[1] Originally published as "Haag's Many Alexandrias" a review of *Alexandria: City of Memory* and *Vintage Alexandria: Photographs of the City, 1860-1960* by Michael Haag, in *Arion: A Journal of the Humanities and the Classics* 17.3 (2010).
[2] Conrad, *Lord Jim*, p. 27.
[3] Sherry, *Conrad's Eastern World*, p. 59.

is completed, Haag will have his Alexandrian *Quartet*, as Durrell had his *Alexandria Quartet* (1962), consisting of the novels *Justine, Balthazar, Mountolive*, and *Clea*. Moreover, as Durrell has done, Haag emphasizes Alexandria's Mediterranean heritage, not its Islamic, and *Mediterranean* refers to ethnic diversity, inhabitants often fluent in Arabic, English, French, Greek, Italian, and Ladino.

II

Alexandria City of Memory concentrates on C. P. Cavafy, E. M. Forster, and Lawrence Durrell. To this tradition should now be added Michael Haag.[4] One muse, one city, many views. The grouping, however, does not include someone like André Aciman. He is not in this lineage. His highly praised *Out of Egypt: A Memoir* (1994) is an exquisite and wonderful story of a Sephardic family and its relations, as they live in Alexandria prior to the diaspora of the early 1960s. (The family's flight was an eventual consequence of Gamal Abdel Nasser's Revolution of 1952.) Like Haag's books, Aciman's narrative is compelling, but it is not what I would call Alexandrian.

The contrast helps to define the category. Writers in the Alexandrian tradition make the city paramount or, at the very least, give it special prominence, but Aciman's subject is not Alexandria — it's his family and Sephardic roots. His city is marginal and without a vivid identity. It doesn't have, in Durrell's preferred term, a *"deus loci"*, a spirit of place. Although Aciman's blue Mediterranean dazzles supreme — "that color blue lining the limitless horizon, quiet, serene, and forever beckoning: the sea"[5] — the city itself shrinks to a pleasing corniche, a seaside resort, where fascinating people converge, a Levantine *Magic Mountain*, with a French, Italian, and Jewish milieu. Nor does he acknowledge his Alexandrian predecessors, and he makes only two slight references to Cavafy and none at all to either Forster or Durrell.[6] The omissions are telling and suggest a desire to disassociate himself from that famous threesome.

The proposed lineage requires some explanation. Durrell calls Alexandria his "capital of Memory" (*Quartet* 152), and Haag chooses a

---

[4] See P. Green, "Alexander's Alexandria", p. 3. Green alludes to the "myth" of modern Alexandria as "evok[ing] memories of E. M. Forster, Constantine Cavafy, and Lawrence Durrell". Green's linkage of these three authors identifies a literary tradition, as previously described by Jane Lagoudis Pinchin in *Alexandria Still: Forster, Durrell, and Cavafy* (1977).

[5] Aciman, *Out of Egypt*, p. 107. Similar descriptions appear on pp. 119, 125, 264, 284, 306.

[6] Aciman, *Out of Egypt*, pp. 290, 292.

variant of this phrase as his subtitle, *City of Memory*. The choice is apt and
complex, for Alexandria has many strata of memory: Hellenistic, Roman,
Islamic, Mediterranean. The Greek poet C. P. Cavafy, of course, began the
whole approach of mining the city as a source of historical memory, but he
largely went unnoticed until E. M. Forster shone a spotlight on him in his
seminal *Alexandria: A History and a Guide* (1922) and then in *Pharos and
Pharillon* (1923). In 1986, Haag published a new edition of Forster's
Alexandria, and in an afterword, "The City of Words", he recounts his first
visit to Alexandria in 1973. He then acknowledges his debt to Cavafy and
adds "In Alexandria the poet [Cavafy] created a world in which later Forster
and Durrell would build many possible Alexandrias".[7]

Remembering can be mythmaking. Although Cavafy died in 1933,
his memory becomes incorporated in the *Quartet*. Durrell makes him the
presiding genius of those novels, where Cavafy is reverentially referred to
as "the old poet of the city" (*Quartet* 18, 203). What Cavafy began has been
amply and ably described by Edmund Keeley in *Cavafy's Alexandria: Study
of a Myth in Progress* (1976) and by Pinchin in *Alexandria Still: Forster,
Durrell, and Cavafy* (1977). Cavafy's eminent position as poet is secure, as
attested by Daniel Mendelsohn's recently published "Constantine Cavafy:
'As Good as Great Poetry Gets'".[8]

However great Cavafy's poetry, the contrast remains between the
shabbiness of the city itself and the richness of its past. Forster emphasizes
this point in *Pharos and Pharillon*. He ruefully describes Rue Rosette (the
splendid Canopic Way of the Hellenistic Period) as one of the city's
"premier thoroughfare[s]" and then exclaims, as though the street were now
something out of Pope's *Dunciad*, "Oh it is so dull! Its dullness is really
indescribable".[9] Fifty-three years later Keeley bluntly writes, "Today's
Alexandria strikes one first of all as squalid".[10] Little evidence of the city's
former grandeur is visible, for those ruins are either destroyed, buried, or
underwater — or in the case of Alexander's lost tomb, possibly all three.

There are exceptions, naturally. Jean-Yves Empereur's heroic
efforts in marine archaeology are recovering Ptolemaic statuary and
artifacts (see his *Alexandria Rediscovered* [1998]), and plans are underway
for an underwater museum in the Eastern Harbour, where ruins would be
viewed *in situ*. This impressive project has many obstacles to overcome, not
least of which is the murkiness of a harbour without adequate sewage
treatment. If successfully completed, the museum would invite comparison

---

[7] Haag, "City of Words", p. 239.
[8] Mendelsohn, "Constantine Cavafy", p. 55.
[9] Forster, *Alexandria*, p. 243.
[10] Keeley, *Cavafy's Alexandria*, p. 4.

with the Monterey Bay Aquarium in California, where visitors stroll among towering glass tanks of marine life. The idea is appealing but probably fanciful. Regardless, it highlights the difficulties in making accessible what is left of the material culture of Alexandria's glorious past.

In *Pharos and Pharillon*, Forster succeeds in imagining aspects of ancient Alexandria, his "city of the soul",[11] but his outright rejection of the modern city begins and ends two prominent essays. These sentiments are the alpha and omega of his coda on Alexandria. Forster's flat assertion, "Modern Alexandria is scarcely a city of the soul", opens the famous piece, "The Poetry of C. P. Cavafy", and, in the conclusion to *Pharos and Pharillon*, he compares the city to a historical pageant, one which ends badly:

> But unlike a pageant it would have to conclude dully. Alas! The modern city calls for no enthusiastic comment. [...] Menelaus accordingly leads the Alexandrian pageant with solid tread; cotton brokers conclude it; the *intermediate space* is thronged with phantoms, noiseless, insubstantial, innumerable, but not without interest for the historian.[12]

But does his harsh critique of modern Alexandria really do justice to the city? Isn't his dull city the very one that inspired others? In a subtle way, Cavafy, Durrell, and Haag all demur. The critique does not do Alexandria justice.

Love — sensual and spiritual, expressed or suppressed or diverted — defines the relationship of these four authors to Alexandria, the city that Haag calls a "cosmopolis" and that Forster says once clung "to the idea of Love".[13] In "The God Abandons Antony", Cavafy's speaker bids Mark Antony to "say your last goodbyes / To Alexandria as she is leaving" (*Quartet* 202);[14] Durrell has his own "beloved Alexandria!" (*Quartet* 17); and Haag's selection of period photographs in *Vintage Alexandria* betrays an equal infatuation with the modern city. Unlike Forster, who conceals his feelings, the tone among these three writers is elegiac. They share a sense of loss and sadness, and you cannot bereave what you do not love.

---

[11] Forster, *Alexandria*, p. 244.

[12] Forster, *Alexandria*, pp. 245, 250. My italics.

[13] Haag, *City of Memory*, p. 84, 85; Forster, *Alexandria*, p. 68.

[14] See Cavafy, *Collected Poems*, p. 226. In Edmund Keeley's note to this poem, he comments, "The poem's anonymous protagonist is not a historical figure". On the contrary, I have always taken the unidentified figure as the Mark Antony of Plutarch's biography, the source for Dionysius abandoning Antony (*Plut. Ant.* 75.3-4). I assume Lawrence Durrell did too.

Cavafy and Durrell have similar approaches, if not similar methods, as they invest the city with their own kinds of erotic memories. Again, Cavafy shows the way. He confines his Alexandria to small rooms and quiet streets. "In the Evening" begins ambiguously in what may be a bedroom, as a speaker recollects a transient love affair, and concludes on a balcony, a definite balcony, perhaps Cavafy's own balcony at 10 Rue Lepsius, as he observes dusk descend,

> Then, sad, I went out on to the balcony,
> went out to change my thoughts at least by seeing
> something of this city I love,
> a little movement in the street and the shops.[15]

Cavafy's erotic eye casts a soft glow, perhaps a post-coital glow, on mundane things. Durrell's wanton eye, on the other hand, tends to pick out squalor or depravity. At the beginning of *Justine*, he visualizes Alexandria from afar, from a promontory on some island, perhaps Cyprus or one of the Cyclades, and says, "Flies and beggars own it today — and those who enjoy an *intermediate existence* between either"(*Quartet* 17; my italics).

I would stress the word *enjoy* in this bewitching description. Forster's "intermediate space" is not Durrell's "intermediate existence", and — in a way that Forster wouldn't or couldn't — Durrell is taking his full pleasure in the sights of modern Alexandria. Like Cavafy, he too stands on a balcony — a remote promontory in this case — reflects on the past, and enjoys the moment.

Michael Wood, in a recent reassessment of the *Quartet*, calls attention to Durrell's "adventive moment".[16] The phrase "adventive minute" appears in *Justine* (1957; *Quartet* 31) and later in Durrell's poem "Cavafy" (1960) as "adventive / Minute" (*CP* 253). Wood is unsure of Durrell's meaning, but he takes it as an attempt to capture small moments of experience, perhaps as Cavafy does. In this attempt, he sees the *Quartet* as ultimately failing. Wood has it wrong, I think, on both counts. "Adventive" means something extraneous, and applying that idea to time suggests something foreign to the moment. I think Durrell preferred to exist somewhere outside the here and now. That was the "world" he created and preferred to live in.

Many Egyptians fault Durrell for an unfair, grubby caricature of their country. Perhaps as many Western critics fault him for a romanticized portrait of that same place. At heart, however, Durrell is a Romantic, and

[15] Cavafy, *Collected Poems*, p. 73.
[16] M. Wood, "Sink or Skim", pp. 11-12

the Romantics just loved contradictions and delighted in the imagination, where they could indeed *enjoy* that "intermediate existence".

III

"Imagined cities", to use Robert Alter's term, is the underlying subject here, the subjective recreation of a place.[17] Another concern is the relationship between literature and factual works. Ralph W. Rader argues persuasively for elevating some narratives beyond their usual classification as purveyors of fact.[18] Few histories and biographies, as Rader notes, ever merit consideration as literature, but I believe Haag's recent books on Alexandria do. Why?

Rader reminds us that "literature in general is, in Coleridge's phrase, that species of composition which proposes pleasure rather than truth as its immediate object".[19] Coleridge explains that the enjoyment of literature also derives from the "part", in effect, reflecting the "whole". Works of literature, then, should be able to withstand the scrutiny of both their details and their overall form, so that the former increases the pleasure of the latter. This is true of *City of Memory*.

I myself prefer parts over wholes, which is to say I like fragments, and perhaps Coleridge did too. The poet himself declares "Kubla Khan", one of his great poems, a fragment, and his entire poetic career, brilliant as it was, broke off early and itself became a fragment. This is all Romantic Hellenism: the love of fragments, ruins, and a shattered classical past. Friedrich von Schlegel (1772-1829) provides a philosophical basis for this genre in the *Athenaeum Fragments*, where he offers a pithy, if odd, definition: "A fragment, like a miniature work of art, has to be entirely isolated from the surrounding world and be complete in itself like a

---

[17] Alter, *Imagined Cities*, p. x: "To write a novel, after all, is to re-create the world from a highly colored point of view—inevitably, that of the novelist, and, often, that of the principal character as well". Alter's "imagined cities" include Flaubert's Paris, Dickens's London, Bely's Petersburg, Woolf's London, Joyce's Dublin, and Kafka's Prague. Not included, unfortunately, is Durrell's Alexandria.

[18] Rader, "Literary Form", pp. 3-42.

[19] Rader condenses S. T. Coleridge, whose original definition reads: "A poem is that species of composition, which is opposed to works of science, by proposing for its *immediate* object pleasure, not truth; and from all other species (having *this* object in common with it) it is discriminated by proposing to itself such delight from the *whole*, as is compatible with a distinct gratification from each component *part*". Original italics. See Coleridge, *Collected Works*, vol. 2 of vol. 7, p. 13.

porcupine".[20] A porcupine? A metaphor for something compact and solitary? Not entirely. Schlegel's idea of a fragment also contains the notion of prickliness. A fragment goads the onlooker and excites the imagination.

Michael Haag, a meticulous historian, may object to the proposition that he prefers "pleasure" over "truth", and he may not like the idea of an attempt to fragmentize his narrative. *City of Memory*, however, is indubitably a history of parts, composed with parts. It recounts parts of the lives of three great writers and recreates a small part of Alexandrian history during the twentieth century, recovering part of a lost culture in a once-cosmopolitan city on the Mediterranean littoral.

Haag's narration flows — but deceptively. It is in fact a skillful compilation of many sources, whose fragments coalesce like tesserae in a Hellenistic mosaic. Haag uses comparatively few secondary sources and relies on primary materials, like personal interviews and unpublished diaries and letters. The narrative becomes like a chorus with the author as conductor. Haag selects, modulates, and yet allows these voices to speak for themselves, as he gathers together sources from far and wide: various libraries, residences, and private collections in Alexandria, Cairo, Athens, Mani, Paris, Sommières, Burgundy, London, Sussex, Cambridge, and Oxfordshire. What unifies all these parts is Alexandria as a trove of the imagination, that is, its rich history and culture as a source of inspiration. And what sustains this sense of Alexandria is the voice and judgment of the historian himself: thorough, judicious, pointed, and, above all, ironic. Like Schlegel's porcupine, Michael Haag is also prickly.

The reader hears this voice in the Prologue to *City of Memory*. It is the voice of the visitor to Cavafy's flat at 10 Rue Lepsius, now a museum, who observes a representation of the famous poet, and remarks, "His death mask, like a prize cabbage at a farmers' fair, is propped upon a cushion".[21] Cavafy would surely have been delighted. It is also the voice of an author who knows when to be silent and let his subjects speak and reveal themselves. In 1977, an old and tired Lawrence Durrell returns to his "capital of Memory", sits in the bar of the Cecil Hotel, and admits, "It sounds silly [...] but I am extremely incurious, and my real life seems to pass either in books or in dreams".[22] The genesis of *The Alexandria Quartet* encapsulated in one casual sentence. Acid, mordant, terse, funny — in short,

---

[20] Schlegel, *Fragments*, p. 45, no. 206. Schlegel's phrase is "wie ein Igel". The German normally translates as "like a hedgehog". The animals are similar in shape. Porcupines are larger, but both have protective quills or spines. See Schlegel, *Fragmente und andere Schriften*, p. 99.

[21] Haag, *City of Memory*, p. 4.

[22] Haag, *City of Memory*, p. 2.

ironic — these are the distinctive qualities of Haag's voice.

Early in *Justine*, Darley, one of Durrell's stand-ins, gives a talk on Cavafy the "ironist". Darley reflects on the irony of his situation — how he finds himself lecturing on the poet of the city's lowlife to a "dignified semi-circle of society ladies" (*Quartet* 31). Justine attends the lecture and says nothing. Darley leaves. She follows and corners him in a grocer's shop, where he's eating Orvieto olives. Then she demands to know what he meant by "the antinomian nature of irony"; he notes "her dark thrilling face" (*Quartet* 32). Darley claims to have forgotten, rudely returns to his olives, and so begins their great love affair, on a note of irony. Enjoyment of *City of Memory* begins a little like that: irony mixed with Mediterranean olives and mysterious beauty.

Love affairs comprise much of *City of Memory*. One of the greatest of these is the strange relationship between E. M. Forster and Mohammed el Adl, an Arab tram conductor, whose role in the author's life Haag describes fully. Haag's handling of this romance demonstrates tact, restraint, impartiality, and yet — implies judgment.

This unlikely relationship was sporadic, punctuated by numerous separations, and lasted six intense years. Adl died in 1922, Forster in 1970. For forty-eight years Forster kept the affair private and revealed it only to a few friends. As Haag points out, Forster cleverly dedicates *Pharos and Pharillon* to "Hermes Psychopompos". The meaning is complex, a cryptic allusion to Adl the tram conductor, for the Greek attribute means "conductor of souls", and Hermes has phallic associations, as represented in ithyphallic herms.[23]

The affair poses a problem. If Forster's love of Adl is "one of the two most cherished events in his personal life",[24] why does he disparage the environment in which it occurred? Why does he call modern Alexandria soulless and "dull" in *Pharos and Pharillon*? Why doesn't he say, as Darley does twice, with minor variation, "A city becomes a world when one loves one of its inhabitants" (*Quartet* 57, 832)?

Was Forster seeking safety through obfuscation? Was he making "dull" and insensate what in fact had not been? Could Forster's emphatic denial of the modern city have been a subterfuge, an act intended to divert attention away from or, possibly, to cover up, a homosexual affair? Haag quotes Forster as calling Octavian, later Augustus, "one of the most odious of the world's successful men", especially because "vice, in his opinion,

---

[23] Haag, *City of Memory*, p. 109.
[24] See Forster, *Alexandria*, pp. xx and 252, n. 6. Allott, as editor, deduces that the other "cherished event" is Forster's love for the policeman, Robert Buckingham.

should be furtive".[25] The irony is all too human. As Haag shows, Forster keeps his affair with Adl "furtive", and homosexuality during Forster's time was indeed considered a "vice". It was a crime punishable under British law, as the imprisonment of Oscar Wilde illustrates, even if Forster was not subject to that law in Egypt.

The affair ends with Adl's death and two letters. He dies of tuberculosis in Egypt, and his last letter, dated 6 May 1922, ends with the valediction, "My love to you", repeated twice.[26] Forster's last written words to Adl appear in "The Letter to Mohammed el Adl", written after Adl's death, a letter begun on 5 August 1922 and finished on 27 December 1929.[27] Haag quotes the last sentences: "I did love you and if love is eternal I may start again. Only it's for you to start me and to beckon. So much has happened to me since that I may not recognise you and am pretty certain not to think of you when I die. I knew how it would be from the first, yet shouldn't have been so happy in Egypt this autumn but for you, Mohammed el Adl [—] my love, Morgan".[28]

The letter must be sincere; it has no audience other than Forster himself. It's a private apology. But the farewell also sounds like a "Dear John letter", and Haag makes the phrase, "if love is eternal", as the title of this chapter. It is ironic. He offers no comment but ends their story with three dry sentences: "Four months later in London Forster met Bob Buckingham, a policeman. Not long afterwards, Bob married, and after some initial stormy scenes by his wife the three settled into a lifetime of mutual devotion. Forster died at their home in 1970".[29]

Haag leaves the final judgment to the reader, but the implication lingers: Mohammed el Adl got shortchanged — unavoidably so, but shortchanged nonetheless. The affair recalls "Tonio Kröger" and Mann's dictum about the penalty of unequal and impossible relationships: "He who loves the more is the inferior and must suffer".[30]

IV

Although Haag tells love stories and other personal histories, he never strays far from his major subject — Alexandria. So, Forster's London gets short shrift, and nearby Cairo earns scant mention and little description. Moreover,

---

[25] Haag, *City of Memory*, p. 77.

[26] Haag, *City of Memory*, p. 108.

[27] Forster, *Alexandria*, pp. 329-34.

[28] Haag, *City of Memory*, p. 118.

[29] Ibid.

[30] T. Mann, *Short Stories*, p. 86.

odd details about the city pop up. They have little bearing on the story but have major importance for the background, which is really the foreground.

Forster's first rendezvous with Adl occurs at the Municipal Gardens in eastern Alexandria. Adl tells Forster to meet him at "the column". Haag is too subtle to make a cheap comment on phallic possibilities, proleptic or otherwise. Instead, he prefaces the story of this first meeting by giving a short history of the column itself, officially known as the Khartoum Column, which is a colonial war memorial. His narration is bland and straight-faced. The reader learns of the column's Ptolemaic origins, "a monolithic shaft of pink Aswan granite", of sphinxes and Sekhmet, the ancient Egyptian "lion-headed goddess of war", of the Mahdi and the death of General Gordon in 1885, and of the exact date of General Kitchener's victory near Khartoum, on 2 September 1898.[31]

This may be Haag at his funniest. It is also the voice of Haag the tourist guide, the author of the lavish guidebook *Egypt* (1993), the informed person who suddenly stops the tour bus on its journey elsewhere, points out the window, and then explains some landmark by the side of the road. Very interesting, you say, but is it relevant to the main story? Yes, absolutely, if the purpose of your narrative is to imbue a place with history and spirit, to give it an emotional archaeology — to do with modern Alexandria what Forster does not do with the "dull" city of his day, instead, following in the footsteps of Durrell, who gives the city of his experiences a soul. Now, with Haag's retelling of a love affair, the column has a bit of literary history added to its significance. You might say that it has another (figurative) carving on its granite surface, like those left by Greeks and Romans on numerous Egyptian monuments, a kind of lover's graffito.

Another part of this reimagining of Alexandria is the adverb *now*, one of Haag's favourite words (as in *now* Sharia Horreya, formerly Rue Fuad). It's the signal of an emotive time shift: the contrast between the present and the past, usually to the detriment of the latter. He uses it continually to update events, name changes, and other facts in Alexandria's everchanging landscape.[32]

Other techniques contribute to this effect. Catalogues enrich the city's modern history. The long list of wealthy Greek families has a Homeric ring — "They were the remnants of Byzantium" — and the enumeration of flowers around Lake Mariut creates a garden like one out of Theocritus's pastoral lyrics.[33] The description of Mariut and the Delta is another

---

[31] Haag, *City of Memory*, p. 38.
[32] Haag, *City of Memory*, pp. 1, 3, and 5 *et passim*.
[33] Haag, *City of Memory*, pp. 72-73, 78.

example.[34] It traces the history of the region back to the origin of ancient Egypt, starting with Narmer and the Harpoon Kingdom, and brings to mind Durrell's poetry at the beginning of *Balthazar* (1958): "Taposiris is dead among its tumbling columns and seamarks, vanished the Harpoon Men" (*Quartet* 209).

And then there are the maps. Both *City of Memory* and *Vintage Alexandria* have the same detailed maps: one of Alexandria and its environs, one of Cavafy's city, and one of Durrell's. These are overlays of time as well as precise visual aids. On these maps is to be found virtually every important place mentioned in the text (thus the Khartoum Column gets plotted), and it is here that Haag follows the paths of Cavafy, Forster, and Durrell.

The overall effect is at times Jamesian, not in stylistic convolution but rather in terms of sensation, atmosphere, and density: James's genius at making small things bear the heavy weight of the past. Houses are major vehicles for creating this impression. Here, for example, is James's Spencer Brydon in "The Jolly Corner" (1908), relating his nostalgia for a childhood home in a wealthy part of New York City:

> He spoke of the value of all he read into it, into the mere sight of the walls, mere shapes of the rooms, mere sound of the floor, mere feel, in his hand, of the old silverplated knobs of the several mahogany doors, which suggested the pressure of the palms of the dead; the seventy years of the past in fine that these things represented, the annals of nearly three generations, counting his grandfather's, the one that had ended there, and the impalpable ashes of his long-extinct youth, afloat in the very air like microscopic motes.[35]

Haag redirects this kind of focus on Alexandria. For example:

> Brinton was thinking in particular of Baron Felix de Menasce's great rambling house on the corner of the Rue Menasce and the Rue Rassafa in Moharrem Bey. Baron George de Menasce, Felix's son by his first wife, lived there too and was a more than competent classical pianist whose Tuesday afternoon concerts, in which he was often accompanied by like-minded friends, became an Alexandrian institution. His half-brother Jean, Felix's son by his second wife Rosette, was that friend of Cavafy's and promoter of his poetry whom Forster had met at Lady Ottoline Morrell's. Whenever he returned from Europe to stay with his family in Alexandria Jean would speak of his friendships with a wide variety of literary figures,

---

[34] Haag, *City of Memory*, pp. 76-77.
[35] James, *Complete Stories,* p. 704.

among them T. S. Eliot, who called him my 'best translator': he translated *The Waste Land* and later *Ash-Wednesday,* 'East Coker' and other of Eliot's works into French. Felix and Rosette's two daughters lived in the house as well, Denise until she married Alfred Mawas, who practiced at the Mixed Courts, and Claire for several years after her marriage to Jacques Vincendon, who was secretary-general of the Land Bank of Egypt, of which her father was director. Claire's Vincendon's passion was the theatre, which was how Brinton and most other people got to know her; she acted in and designed costumes for the entertainments she staged for guests at the great house in the Rue Rassafa, where her daughter Claude was born in 1925.[36]

The passage is an evocation of weight and scope, an era in microcosm. Geographically it ranges from Rue Rassafa in Alexandria to a country estate in England. Biographically it reprises the rich culture of Alexandrian society between the two wars: three generations of Jewish high society; the arts of music, poetry, and drama; the artists Cavafy and Forster. Eliot, a founder of high modernism, also makes a brief but grand appearance. He was Durrell's mentor at the London publishing house of Faber and Faber. The introduction of Jean de Menasce suggests the literary scene in Paris, and the reference to Lady Morrell's manor in Oxfordshire further broadens the geographical sweep to include the literary landscape of rural England in the 1920s.

Here Haag does not specifically mention Durrell, who arrives in Alexandria almost two decades later, but his hidden presence hangs in the air, much like Brydon's "microscopic motes", especially at the opening and close of the description. To achieve this effect, the historian turns novelist and enters the mind of Jasper Yeates Brinton, an actual jurist in the Alexandrian Mixed Courts. Haag uses Brinton as a kind of Darley figure, unlikely as this role may be, for Brinton was a very proper American lawyer. The judge mirrors the main narrator of the *Quartet*, who is far from proper, and acts as a guide into the city's complicated world. When the lawyer "thinks" of "Menasce's great rambling house", he sounds like Darley when he visits Justine's mansion on Rue Fuad and says "That was the first time I saw the great house of Nessim" (*Quartet* 32). "Great" appears at the beginning and the end of the paragraph. This signature adjective is possibly Durrell's favourite intensifier.[37] It serves as an entirely suitable tribute that

---

[36] Haag, *City of Memory*, p. 137.
[37] This habit, which some consider highly pretentious, has received scathing criticism as "the insistent meaningless dramatization of everything—theatricalization". See M. Green, "Minority Report", p. 135. This objection I take as a serious misunderstanding of Durrell's "world". See my brief discussion of Durrell's "adventive minute" above. Durrell's "world" is to be more fully discussed below in "Michael Haag: A

honours both the house and the occupant named last, Claude Vincendon. She later became Claude Durrell, Lawrence Durrell's third wife, his favourite and most beloved.

Quietly and without introduction, Haag has snuck Durrell into the social setting of the Menasce mansion and household — and probably much to the dismay of Jasper Yeates Brinton, had he ever been aware of this sly irony and his unknowing complicity. For Judge Brinton clearly disapproved of Durrell, and Haag uses one of Brinton's published remarks as a preface to this chapter:

> [Alexandria] was a very European city, very cultivated, artistic and musical. I don't want to pick an argument with that gentleman [Lawrence Durrell], but I thought it very wrong of him to describe it as a degenerate city. The people were aristocrats, behaved themselves; just as well behaved as the elegant society of old Philadelphia.[38]

On occasion, Haag has a wicked sense of humour. Old Philadelphia undoubtedly has many things in common with old Alexandria — protecting the virtue of its young women, being one of them, as he points out[39] — but the Mediterranean city does not appear as staid or proper as the judge from Philly would have it.

V

Vintage Alexandria: Photographs of the City, 1860-1960 is both companion and supplement to *Alexandria: City of Memory*. The collection of photographs can be studied and enjoyed on its own merits as a historical document or in conjunction with the previous history, which is by far the richer of the two experiences. It also helps to keep Durrell's *Quartet* well in mind. Like the maps, the old photographs elaborate on, and give greater substance to, Haag's main text, suggesting new ways to look at old things.

As the subtitle indicates, the collection covers the years 1860 through 1960. This is roughly the period of Cavafy, Forster, and Durrell. Cavafy was born in Alexandria in 1863 and lived there continuously from 1885 until his death in 1933; Forster resided there during the First World War, from 1915 to 1919; and Durrell during the Second, when he worked in the city, between 1942 and 1945. That leaves fifteen years to round out the century and allows the emphasis to end on Alexandria, Haag's cosmopolis,

---

Memoir".

[38] Haag, *City of Memory*, p. 119.
[39] Haag, *City of Memory*, p. 184.

the main subject, after all, of these photographs.

Many of them record the development of the city over the century, the way things were and are now, the changes in the social and urban environment. These are always fascinating as they reveal shifting styles and landscapes. Some of the photographs, however, also have an erotic component — erotic in the sense of enticement. They are a sensual apprehension of a culture and a place, even as they provide an insight into the imaginative processes and the urgings of desire that possessed Cavafy, Forster, and Durrell. I would like to pick out a few of these.

The frontispiece is a photograph of Rose de Menasce, née Tuby (**Figure 4**). She was married to Baron Edmund de Menasce, a cousin of Baron Felix de Menasce, both prominent members of Alexandrian society. She was a friend of Cavafy and Durrell.[40]

Figure 4: Rose de Menasce at the Sporting Club, Alexandria, c. 1914 (*Vintage Alexandria* [2008], with kind permission of Michael Haag)

---

[40] Haag, *Vintage Alexandria*, p. 46.

The legend tells us Rose is attending an event at the Sporting Club in 1914, whose location we ascertain by glancing at a map on page viii. She is standing in front of a small group of men and women in sporty attire, wearing a black feathery hat and long black dress, which highlight her pale face. She is aloof, standing apart from her group and turned slightly to address the camera. All the other faces are obscured; she alone looks directly at the viewer. She neither smiles nor beckons; hers is not aristocratic hauteur. Her gaze seems to say, in her customary French, "*Vous pouvez regarder — mais ne plus*". Or she may have shrugged and said, in equally proficient English, "I am here, and this is my world". We are neither invited inside nor prohibited from entering, but we may stay and look awhile.

Rose de Menasce appears in four other photographs, five in total and more than any other figure. She may be Haag's heroine; she is certainly his favourite, with a place reserved at the forefront. (As it happens, Haag did not choose this picture for his frontispiece. It was the inspiration of the designer, Fatiha Bouzidi, who grasped something crucial about the book.) The Baroness poses for two formal portraits, taken outside her home.[41] The rest are either informal or spontaneous, either an impromptu gathering or two shots caught at a moment's notice, as the one at the Sporting Club appears to be. Her character changes between the two types of pictures. In the formal portraits she strikes a pose of feminine submissiveness. She's demure, looks down, and avoids eye contact. She's what Judge Brinton would probably call aristocratic and "well behaved". In the informal photographs, she displays her assertive side. She's confident, bold, and looks into the eye of the camera. She has the look Durrell ascribes to Justine when Darley first describes her demeanour as "mannish" and having an "air of authority" (*Quartet* 31, 32).

The model for Justine was Yvette (Eve) Cohen, an Alexandrian and Durrell's second wife. Haag includes one of her early photographs (**Figure 5**), when she's about twelve. Even then Eve has something of that look, although she's a schoolgirl and slightly tentative. She's a little sad around the eyes — perhaps because of the dark shading or perhaps because she's been forced to take a school picture — but put a hat on her and isolate that face and you have Rose's self-assertion beginning to form. Other Alexandrian women have this gaze, both aristocrats and common folk: Irène Valassopoulos, Argine Salvagos, Claire Vincendon, Safinaz Zulfikar, the Greek girls in a cigarette factory.[42] It is caught also in some of the men, like Cavafy and Adl.[43]

---

[41] Haag, *Vintage Alexandria*, p. 47.
[42] Haag, *Vintage Alexandria*, pp. 47, 50, 52, 64, 69.
[43] Haag, *Vintage Alexandria*, p. 49; Haag, *City of Memory*, p. 29.

Figure 5:   Eve Cohen at St Andrew's School Alexandria, c. 1930 (*Vintage Alexandria* [2008], with kind permission of Michael Haag)

The expression on these faces is always unsmiling, the stare directed at the camera or fastened on some distant elsewhere. That fixed gaze makes the viewer feel like an intruder — someone who's irrelevant, insignificant, unwelcome, and only tolerated for the moment. It's very old and very Egyptian. Art historians sometimes describe this attitude as facing eternity or "gazing into eternity".[44] It certainly goes back a long way, to the Old Kingdom, at least. Look at the Great Sphinx. It's there; even time cannot erode or obliterate it. The paradox of this gaze is that what rejects also attracts. We see this confirmed in Rose de Menasce's photographs. The irony of her pictures is that she's most alluring when least feminine, and the converse is also true: she's least appealing when most feminine. Durrell knew something when he gave Justine "mannish" characteristics.

Another photograph of Rose shows her on a beach (**Figure 6**). *Vintage Alexandria* has many photographs of Alexandria's citizens enjoying themselves at the seashore — relaxing, strolling, showing off. These snapshots are innocent, amusing, and uncomplicated. But the same cannot be said of Rose and her beach party.

The camera captures a scene of eight people, three men and five women, sitting or kneeling on the sand. Their dress is curious but typical of the formality of the period. Two of the men are in formal or semi-formal attire, one in a white tuxedo, his homburg tossed before him, and the other in homburg and tie but without a coat. These styles mix and become confused. Two of the women wear hats and dresses. Rose and another woman are in swimming costumes. A third man also wears a swimming outfit, but his face is outside the frame. The picture appears unposed, but the arrangement is as suggestive as one of those *tableaux vivants* or costume photographs which Alexandrians were fond of staging.[45] It's also reminiscent of that "faded photograph" Darley pores over in *Balthazar*, when he studies a barbershop scene and reconstructs the interconnecting lives of his friends and acquaintances (*Quartet* 218-21).

As in the frontispiece, Rose dominates the scene. She presides in the centre of the group and is taller than everyone else. She and two other women stare into the lens, but the others are less intimidating: one smiles and opens her lips; a shadow obscures the eyes of the other. Rose, confident and unsmiling, alone confronts the intruder.

---

[44] See W. Smith, *Art and Architecture of Ancient Egypt*, p. 113. Smith was a prominent Egyptologist (1907-1969). In this classic study on ancient Egyptian art, he comments on one of the treasures of Old Kingdom statuary (c. 2500 BC): the graywacke dyad of King Menkaure and his Queen Khamerernebty in the Boston Museum of Fine Arts. Smith writes, "There is something infinitely appealing about the confident way in which this pair faces eternity, the wife placing her arm about her husband's waist".

[45] Haag, *City of Memory*, p. 167, fig. 45.

Figure 6: Rose de Menasce at the beach, c. 1928 (*Vintage Alexandria* [2008], with kind permission of Michael Haag)

Haag identifies only two people in this photograph, Rose and her husband Edmund, the man in the homburg. The identities of the others, I suspect, are deliberately withheld. The man in the tuxedo may be Baron Felix de Menasce,[46] whose mansion we've seen previously. The young woman resting on Edmund's arm could be his daughter or relative, and the woman in a white dress next to Rose may be her sister, since they strongly resemble one another. Rose raises her arm to adjust her hair, just as a breeze disturbs it and her (possible) sister's scarf. Thus, the photograph seems to present an innocent and tranquil scene of an extended family on an outing at the beach.

But that is not certain. The context is obscure. I'm reminded of a scene in *Justine*, when Darley and Justine are in bed at her home. They hear footsteps on the staircase and fear they're about to be discovered by her husband Nessim. Darley relates, "Looking over Justine's shoulder I saw developing on the glass panel of the frosted door, the head and shoulders of a tall slim man, with a soft felt hat pulled down over his eyes. He developed like a print in a photographer's developing-bowl" (*Quartet* 123). Although probably Nessim, the man does not enter, and his identity is not ascertained.

---

[46] Cf. Haag, *City of Memory*, p. 138, fig. 35.

This photograph has the quality of images on frosted glass. It is also like a primal scene in a Freudian manual. Obscuring the identities of people injects uncertainty into an innocuous situation and casts a sinister light on the setting. Another scenario unfolds: A shadow covers Rose's left eye, like a pirate's eye patch, and she raises her right arm, exposing an underarm in what could be a hostile or sexual gesture. The group activity acquires sexual connotations. Her husband appears to be caressing a young woman, who is about to stroke the ear of an older man, who is courting another young woman. All rather strange but not impossible in this city, Alexandria. Through the silence of the photograph, its withholding information even as it offers it, Haag has created a scene as ambiguous, complicated, and bizarre as the love affairs in the *Quartet*, and he has done this through understatement, which is just another form of irony.

Such photographic understatement is not unique. In another photograph, Rhona Haszard, an artist, appears in her rooftop garden tending flowers (**Figure 7**).[47] Haag provides a little information about the artist and her husband but goes no further and provides no context. He then concludes with a kind of non sequitur:

> On the day after the opening of her second exhibition at Claridge's in 1931, she mysteriously fell to her death from the tower rising behind her in this photograph, where she had been sketching.[48]

The tower of her death has what appears to be a sturdy parapet. It's reasonable to conclude that Rhona Haszard didn't just fall. She would have had to climb over the balustrade and then leap to her death. Haag, the meticulous historian, gives no background, offers no suggestions, and her death remains mysterious. Why include such a photograph? What is Rhona's connection to other people in the collection? Does suicide have a hidden and pervasive presence in Alexandrian society? Keep in mind that a major event in Durrell's *Quartet* is the suicide of the artist Ludwig Pursewarden. His suicide is never adequately explained and variously attributed to politics, incest, or ennui. It remains a mystery, and Durrell clearly wanted it kept that way. He wanted to puzzle his reader and provoke the imagination. Haag does the same.

---

[47] The faded handwritten note reads: "[illegible word] Rhona Haszard in her roof garden. Tower on right from which she fell".
[48] Haag, *Vintage Alexandria*, p. 94.

Figure 7: Rhona Haszard in her rooftop garden, Alexandria, c. 1931 (*Vintage Alexandria* [2008], with kind permission of Michael Haag)

VI

Haag's farewell to Alexandria is a photograph of wealthy Greeks celebrating the end of 1957. Three men in suits and an attractive woman toast the New Year.[49] The dark lady and her companion smile at the camera. The occasion is an appropriate but sad example of dramatic irony. The smiling couple may not know it, but it's the end of an era. Nasser has nationalized the canal; the Israelis have fought Egypt on behalf of the British and French; and the USA and USSR are now the superpowers of the modern world. Greeks founded this cosmopolis, and now they conclude a tradition. The restaurant is Pastroudis on Rue Fuad. It was one of Durrell's favourite meeting places and appears several times in the *Quartet*. This photograph, however, brings us back to still another valediction, even more evocative and certainly more sensual, six pages earlier.

Anna Bajocchi leans on her balcony over Rue Fuad and looks at the city below (**Figure 8**). It's 1952, the year of Nasser's revolution, but Anna has other things on her mind. She is young, blonde, and pretty. In the Alexandria of the imagination, she resembles Clea Badaro, the artist who becomes Clea Montis in the *Quartet*. Anna wears a light, checkered dress. It might be a "new summer frock" (*Quartet* 54). Melissa Artemis wears one in *Justine*, and she is one of Durrell's most appealing and sympathetic women. The caption traces Anna's lineage back to "an Italian doctor in the service of Muhammad Ali and Ibrahim Pasha". Here Haag leaves no doubt about identity: Anna is an Alexandrian of long and good standing.

Anna's vision is unfocussed. Her gaze wanders left. It's not clear what, if anything, she's looking at. She could be lost in reverie, or observing the people and traffic on Rue Fuad, or she could be dreaming of Alexandria's Eastern Harbour and Corniche. For if we glance outside the frame of the picture, which the layout clearly encourages us to do, we see that she is really focussed on the facing page, which is a view of the harbour at night.[50] Haag has given her another option: Anna dreams of her city and its enduring beauty. Durrell's term for this dreamy state is "abstracted" (*Quartet* 77, 166, 274, *et passim*). The condition occurs often in the *Quartet*; it's chronic and suggests an authorial predisposition for such idle activity.

---

[49] Haag, *Vintage Alexandria*, p. 135.
[50] Haag, *Vintage Alexandria*, p. 128.

Figure 8: Anna Bajocchi on a balcony, Alexandria, 1952 (*Vintage Alexandria* [2008], with kind permission of Michael Haag)

So Anna leans on a balcony, one of those prominent fixtures in Cavafy and Durrell — promontories, platforms, springboards, windows, enablers of immersion in the moment or in memory. They are like those "magic casements" in Keats's "Nightingale", those entrances into the imagination. Or, since we are in Egypt, they may be like that balcony in Amarna where Nefertiti and Akhenaten stood over three thousand years ago.[51] On the other hand, perhaps Anna doesn't dream — perhaps she listens intently, as Antony once listened from an "open window", when the Rue Fuad was known as the Canopic Way. In "The God Abandons Antony", Cavafy's speaker says that the Roman general heard in the streets of Alexandria beautiful music, which Durrell freely translates as the "ravishing music of invisible choirs" (*Quartet* 202). Or perhaps Anna hears the music that Keats calls, in "Grecian Urn", the "ditties of no tone". We have many possibilities. Which is surely the way Haag would want it.

---

[51] The royal balcony in Tell el-Amarna, Upper Egypt, is also known as "the Window of Appearance". See Kemp, *Akhenaten and Nefertiti*, pp. 22 (fig. 1.1) and 42 (fig. 1.13). The depictions appear in the Tomb of Ay at Amarna (c. 1322 BC). For a detailed line drawing of the balcony scene, see Norman de Garis Davies, *Rock Tombs of El Amarna*, pl. XXIX.

There is one other possibility to consider. On a balcony, Anna Bajocchi rises, steps out of her frame, and joins those other beautiful blonde women who inhabit Haag's and Durrell's worlds: Clea Badaro, Clea Montis, Claude Vincendon.

Michael Haag offers many Alexandrias — Cavafy's, Forster's, and Durrell's — but his special contribution to this tradition may be his recovery and preservation of a great city's past, before it becomes completely lost and forgotten. He has rescued what ought to be saved. He tells the story of artists, individuals, and families in the mix and flux of events. His great theme is modern Alexandria. His achievement is both history and art.[52]

---

[52] My special thanks to Nicholas Poburko for his keen eye and sharp knife.

CHAPTER FIVE

HAAG'S DURRELLS[1]

Potboilers are not necessarily a bad thing. Professional writers have to make a living, so they occasionally turn out books which are below their own standards. Lawrence Durrell's early fame was in part attributed to his excellent book on Corfu — *Prospero's Cell* (1945) — and to his equally fine one on Cyprus — *Bitter Lemons* (1957). (Keep in mind the transition from Shakespearean romance to Modernist pessimism.) But, by his own admission, he called his later travel piece, *Sicilian Carousel* (1977), a potboiler, although I strongly disagree with that assessment and still have a special fondness for his largely fictional memoir of a journey around Sicily. As D. H. Lawrence once observed: "Never trust the artist. Trust the tale. The proper function of a critic is to save the tale from the artist who created it".[2] Lawrence Durrell and Michael Haag share a common trait when it comes to self-criticism — either they are poor judges of their own work or they conceal their own intentions, deliberately or not.

In *The Durrells of Corfu,* Michael Haag describes the family's origins in colonial India and then traces its journey to England, Corfu, and beyond. His stated aim is "[to shed] new light on old stories and [to uncover] fresh stories".[3] He occasionally accomplishes this, but he also has another goal, implicit in the task itself, that is, to provide background material for a television series of the same title. Haag has undoubtedly written a potboiler which capitalizes on the production's popularity. British Independent Television (ITV) will produce four seasons of installments. The show is a hit. The book's blurb characterizes the series as an "adaptation" of Gerald Durrell's highly successful *My Family and Other Animals* (1956), which, as the blurb gushes, "immortalised" the Durrell family. In today's popular culture of "selfies" and social networking, immortality or notoriety — however fleeting either may be — has financial rewards for those who can market it.

---

[1] Originally published as "Haag's Durrells: The One or the Many?", a review of *The Durrells of Corfu* by Michael Haag (London: Profile Books, 2017) in *A Café in Space: The Anaïs Nin Literary Journal* 15 (2018).
[2] Lawrence, *Classic American Literature*, p. 2.
[3] Haag, *Durrells of Corfu*, p. xi.

Haag was apparently hired to write a book which satisfies the hunger of those devoted fans who crave more information about the Durrells and their travelling circus: materfamilias and dipsomaniac Louisa, great writer-in-the-making and elder brother Lawrence (Larry), gun-toting and ne'er-do-well brother Leslie, oversexed and underrated sister Margaret (Margo), and youngest brother Gerald (Gerry), child prodigy and lover of all creatures great and small. Their very weirdness assures success. Haag's task is to elaborate on these characters, to correct misconceptions, and to provide new and interesting material. The task is basically an old one — to teach and to delight — or to tell "Tales of best sentence and moost solaas", as Chaucer puts it (A 798).

As potboilers go, Haag's book is nowhere near the same quality as Lawrence Durrell's money-making enterprises. Nor does it even remotely approach the excellence of Haag's previous works: *Alexandria: City of Memory* (2004) and *Vintage Alexandria: Photographs of the City, 1860-1960* (2008).[4] Perhaps we should not expect the same degree of high quality, given the nature of his assignment, for the book is clearly not intended for the specialist. What makes it worthwhile, nevertheless, is the insight it provides (inadvertently no doubt) into Haag's considerable abilities as a writer and his obsession with the life and work of Lawrence Durrell, the author who has become his lifelong passion. The exposé of those many Durrells tends to meander (as they themselves did), but it is most affecting about one Durrell in particular, that is, brother Larry, especially as Haag's treatment resembles a Platonic argument, as Aristotle describes in the *Metaphysics* — "the one over many".[5] Plato argues for the primacy of a "Form" over a set of particulars.[6]

As Plato's argument loosely applies to Haag's book, the question arises — is the book really about many persons, as the title indicates, or is it secretly about one person who incorporates, to some extent, all the others? And who is that protagonist? In the plot of Gerry's book about his family, as well as that of the television series, a child of insatiable curiosity (Gerry himself) dominates the action at the expense of an adult of overweening literary ambitions (brother Larry). So, Gerald Durrell's many fans (undoubtedly far more than Lawrence's) may think Haag's book is primarily about Gerry, whose mother and siblings make up a supporting cast, but I think that when

---

[4] For an analysis of Haag's formidable talents, see my review of these two books in Chapter Four above.

[5] Aristotle, *Complete Works*, p. 1566 (991a).

[6] I am indebted to Gareth B. Matthews and S. Marc Cohen for an explanation of these issues regarding Platonic Forms. See their "The One and the Many", *The Review of Metaphysics,* 21.4 (1968): 630-55.

Haag speaks of "Durrells", he really has Larry at the back of his mind and cannot resist the pull of his personality.

Haag's real story is about Lawrence Durrell the artist and his rise and decline. A Gibbon could tell this story — a very big exaggeration, of course — although the Roman analogy holds, for Durrell's last book is titled *Caesar's Vast Ghost: Aspects of Provence* (1990). Durrell lived in Provence for over the last thirty years of his life, and his "vast ghost" haunts Haag's book.

Unfortunately, Haag's *Durrells of Corfu* has problems of execution and of documentation, both probably resulting from the publisher's restrictions on timeliness and readability. Haag's *Alexandria: City of Memory* is a beautiful work of scholarship, meticulously written, convincingly argued, and accurately documented. It is not a commercial product hastily thrown together to meet a deadline. The same cannot be said of his latest endeavour. One oversight is inexcusable. Haag knows that Lawrence Durrell was born in 1912, but early on he implies that Larry was born in 1911.[7] A careful proofing or a good editor would have found the error and any subsequent slips. One assumes neither occurred. Haag's method of narration is to incorporate his own research, which includes many personal interviews. These are of great value and point to his future work, a forthcoming biography of Lawrence Durrell to be published by Yale University Press, which will build upon this important research. His current text, however, sometimes lacks a clear identification of its sources and a clear differentiation of Haag's own commentary, which has the breeziness of fictional narration.[8] He does not use footnotes or endnotes — probably at his publisher's insistence — and as a consequence his narrative occasionally slides in and out of various voices and sources. These sources must be taken on faith. The casual reader would not object; a careful reader would find this method frustrating, inadequate, and annoying.

Despite these objections, Haag's book has many delights. These involve revealing secrets or telling untold stories about the Durrell family. One family "secret" pertains to Louisa Durrell, the matriarch, who had a nervous breakdown and was prone to alcoholism.[9] While in England, she tried to return to India, booked a passage on a liner, but failed to show up. Haag speculates that Louisa was attempting "to return to the land of her ghosts"; he also speculates that "possibly Larry" prevented her from taking the voyage.[10] It should be kept in mind that Lawrence Durrell himself was

---

[7] Haag, *Durrells of Corfu*, p. 3.
[8] Haag, *Durrells of Corfu*, pp. 42, 71, 91, 95.
[9] Haag, *Durrells of Corfu*, p. 36.
[10] Ibid.

an alcoholic and subject to bouts of depression. Mother and son mirror one another. Although Haag's "ghosts" have multiple images, they seem to collapse into one image — Larry's.

Another of those untold stories is Haag's sketch of Margaret Durrell. Margo does not come off well in either the first of the ITV versions, nor in Gerald's *My Family and Other Animals*, nor does she even merit a mention in Lawrence's *Prospero's Cell*. Gerry treats her as a nonentity, as "something of an airhead", according to Haag.[11] But through his interviews, Haag shows her to have been a woman of courage and acumen. Unlike her brothers, Margo did not flee when the German army threatened Corfu in 1940. "Margo was going nowhere", Haag reports.[12] She wanted to stay on and blend in with the local peasantry, no matter how impractical that would have been. She remained loyal to Corfu and its people and had to be convinced to flee. Moreover, she was not taken in by her bothers' bewitching rhetoric. Haag quotes her as saying that Lawrence and Gerald wrote books which were untrustworthy and embellished: "I do not trust writers" and "I never know what's fact and what's fiction in my family".[13]

Margo is a unique figure in her own right, but Haag also treats her as an ironic surrogate for her elder brother. Her refrain of being unable to distinguish fact from fiction is also an enduring theme throughout Lawrence Durrell's oeuvre. It occurs at the end of *The Alexandria Quartet*, where Darley, Durrell's *alter ego*, is advised to live within "the kingdom of your imagination" (*Quartet* 877), and it gets mentioned in *Sicilian Carousel*, where a fictional character writes a letter to Durrell himself and says, "We have been brought up to believe that facts are not dreams—and of course they are" (*SC* 36). By emphasizing this recurrent theme, Haag keeps the ghostly presence of Lawrence Durrell alive in his text, even when discussing other members or friends of the family. Here is another instance. Why does he relate a conversation about the best way to commit suicide — "[to hold] a revolver in the mouth at a forty-five degree angle"[14] — if not because suicide is another persistent theme in Durrell's corpus? So, we have the prime example of Pursewarden's suicide in the *Quartet* (*Quartet* 310). In Haag's text, Lawrence becomes like the ghost of Hamlet's father — his voice echoes, he haunts, he will not go away.

Besides being a fine writer and historian, Michael Haag is also a professional photographer of distinction. Egypt is one of his specialties, and he has published lavish studies of two Egyptian cities: *Alexandria Illustrated*

---

[11] Haag, *Durrells of Corfu*, p. 192.

[12] Haag, *Durrells of Corfu*, p. 160.

[13] Haag, *Durrells of Corfu*, pp. 130; xi, 160.

[14] Haag, *Durrells of Corfu*, p. 126.

(2003) and *Cairo Illustrated* (2006). At its best, his work is characterized by lush images of place and a sharp eye for the telling detail. Haag and Durrell have similar sensibilities, an acute sensitivity to what the latter calls "the spirit of place", and Haag sometimes achieves in photography what Durrell accomplishes in prose. *The Alexandria Quartet* could be read with a copy of *Alexandria Illustrated* nearby. This exercise is surely intended. The art of making beautiful images aside, Haag's use of photography has a strong narrative aspect. In *Vintage Alexandria*, his selection of old photographs tells a story: a city and its cosmopolitan past flourish and then abruptly terminate at the onset of a new cultural era. Haag has also selected the photographs for his *Durrells of Corfu*, and they too tell a story, although possibly not the one he intends.

Haag selects over eighty photographs and illustrations for his little book. They complement his text with photos of the Durrell family, its associates, and the places and things encountered. The book's cover is a marketing ploy and is probably the publisher's idea — a glossy illustration of "the Durrells of Corfu". It represents the television series and shows a composite of the main cast of actors as they portray real-life people. A smiling Gerry sits with his animals at the centre of the family photo; he is flanked by his mother and siblings in characteristic poses.

The question returns, however. What is the primary focus of Haag's book? Is it Gerald Durrell of *My Family and Other Animals*, or is it Lawrence Durrell of *The Alexandria Quartet* and *The Avignon Quintet*? Gerry has twenty photos, either solitary or in a group, showing him as he grows and develops. Larry has seventeen. Advantage Gerry. Still, their poses and demeanours differ markedly. Gerry often smiles, stares inquisitively at the camera, and shares space with his beloved animals. His personality remains unchanged over the years. Gerry at two is essentially the same as Gerry at fifty-two.[15] In contrast, from an early age, Larry typically assumes a posture of bold self-assurance. His persona dominates, but, as he ages, it changes profoundly. It slowly shifts from haughty self-confidence to dark gloom. Durrell's career as writer follows the same path: a journey from the dazzling light of *Prospero's Cell* to the morbid darkness of *The Avignon Quintet* (1974-1985), his final fictional sequence.[16]

Nowhere is Lawrence Durrell's evolving personality more evident than in three photos Haag has chosen as stages in a literary career. The first serves as the book's frontispiece, the second as a prelude to Durrell in Egypt,

---

[15] Haag, *Durrells of Corfu*, pp. 18, 197.
[16] For a personal exploration of Durrell's psychic landscapes, see David Green, "Out in the Midi Sun—Adventures in Lawrence Durrell country", *A Café in Space: The Anaïs Nin Literary Journal,* 14 (2017): 85-95.

and the last as a final portrait of the famous author.

In the frontispiece, the Durrell family poses on a veranda at the "Daffodil-Yellow Villa" on Corfu. The year is 1936. Leslie Durrell presumably took the group portrait. They all face the camera, including Larry's wife Nancy. Margo stands off to the side, as her brothers portrayed her. Gerry scales the railing like the unruly boy he is. Louisa looks serious. All are vertical except Lawrence, who grins and dominates the scene by sprawling across the railing. His right hand may hold a quill, possibly an emblem of his aspirations, and his diagonal posture disrupts the geometry of the composition, much like a transversal in Euclid's final postulate. The Fifth Postulate of the third century BC was unprovable and led to non-Euclidean geometry of the nineteenth century.[17] Lawrence Durrell was equally intractable and, if not "unprovable", then at least inexplicable. He is jaunty, rebellious, and mischievously arrogant.

In a photo taken in 1939,[18] Lawrence strolls in Athens with George Katsimbalis, a giant of Greek letters, whom Henry Miller calls "the Colossus of Maroussi".[19] It is winter. Both men wear heavy suits. A long wool scarf trails from Lawrence's neck, and he clutches a book or file of papers in his left hand. He could pass for an academic in the peripatetic mode, as he strides a step ahead of the older man, who looks down attentively at his young companion. Lawrence appears self-absorbed and caught in the act of explaining some point about literature. Katsimbalis was a head taller than Durrell, who was short, about five foot two. But in this photo Durrell dominates the scene like a colossus.

The final photo is the penultimate one in Haag's book.[20] There an old and aged Lawrence Durrell stares morosely at the camera. The year is 1984 when he was working on the conclusion to the *Quintet*. Haag locates "the acclaimed novelist" as posing somewhere in Paris.[21] Haag is being coy, for look closely at the backdrop, which is obscured and slightly out of focus. Durrell stands in a cemetery, possibly Père Lachaise, the most famous cemetery in Paris and the resting places of many famous writers, Oscar Wilde and Marcel Proust among them. In 1984, Durrell was seventy-two and had six more years to live. His sad and heavily lined face shows that he was fully aware of his own mortality. The background suggests that he was also aware of his posthumous fame.

---

[17] Kline, *Mathematical Thought*, pp. 59-60, 873.

[18] Haag, *Durrells of Corfu*, p. 162.

[19] Miller, *Colossus*, p. 40.

[20] Haag, *Durrells of Corfu*, p. 198.

[21] Ibid.

Haag does not conclude his book with Lawrence Durrell's photo, rather with a much earlier photo taken on Corfu,[22] where a twelve-year-old Gerry and his Greek friend Spiro Halikiopoulos cook an eel near the seashore. Behind them, Spiro's old Dodge car sits at the water's edge. In 1947, Lawrence sent the photo to Henry Miller and inscribed the following: "Just after this was taken the car was nearly carried away by the sea and we had to stand up to our waists in water and dig it out".[23] So, Haag lets the elder brother have the last word of his main text. This final emphasis suggests that Lawrence Durrell is the real subject of Haag's book. He is the prime storyteller and encapsulates all the other members of the family. He tells a good story, in keeping with the many adventures of the Durrells of Corfu, but it is also highly improbable that a few people could extricate a large and weighty vehicle stuck in the sand at high tide. As Haag himself says, "The Durrells themselves were masters of fabulation".[24] And Lawrence was the master fabulator.

At the end of his book, Michael Haag's selection of photographs reveals a problem with focus and conception. Is the book about Gerald and his supporting cast, or is it about Lawrence and his wayward career? There is no doubt which of the two brothers is the more interesting. The final photo of Gerald and the Dodge, along with the story of its unlikely rescue from the sea, suggests that Haag felt compelled to end on a note about the Durrells of Corfu and their often fabulous exploits. After all, this is surely what he was paid to do. But the final inscription and the graveyard photo of Lawrence Durrell points to Haag's real obsession — the secrets lurking behind the life of one of the great and most perplexing artists of the twentieth century. That mystery still awaits unravelling, although it is undoubtedly resistant to any definitive solution.

---

[22] Haag, *Durrells of Corfu*, p. 201.
[23] Ibid.
[24] Haag, *Durrells of Corfu*, p. xi.

CHAPTER SIX

MICHAEL HAAG[1]

I. Haag and I

Michael Haag was born in Manhattan in 1943 and died in London on 5 January 2020. I knew him from 2006 until 2010; during which time we exchanged hundreds of emails related to Lawrence Durrell (1912-1990) and other literary matters. Haag wrote many books on various historical subjects, but he intended his biography of the British poet to be his major achievement. He worked many years doing his research on Durrell, possibly as many as twenty or more, but he never finished his biography, and that sad fact has to be considered a great loss. I have not read any parts of his incomplete manuscript, but I believe our extensive exchanges provide a rough map of how he read and interpreted Durrell, both man and poet.

　　This memoir attempts to sketch some of Haag's important ideas as I understand them. In a small way, it attempts to compensate for the loss of Haag's unfinished biography. It also treats some aspects of Haag's personality as they pertain to his biographical and literary methodology. Furthermore, I want to make my method plain and upfront, even at the expense of obviousness. All memoirs are subject to the vagaries of memory, and mine is certainly no exception. I do not claim to be factually accurate all the time. This is especially true in recalling conversations and the places where they occurred, but I try to be fair and just to those distant circumstances as best I can. I indulge in a small amount of invention — under the assumption or misconception that sometimes a faulty memory has to be enhanced. And by that I mean that a dim recollection lends itself to repair and touch-up. As Haag himself suggested about Durrell's approach to life and art, invention is not necessarily a bad thing.

---

[1] Originally published as "Michael Haag: A Memoir" in *C.20: an International Journal*, Issue 4, 2021. https://durrelllibrarycorfu.wordpress.com.

II. The Meetings in Canada and Egypt

Haag and I met on four occasions: twice in 2006 at Victoria, British Columbia and twice in 2007 at Alexandria and Cairo, Egypt. The meetings in Victoria and Alexandria occurred during literary conferences on Lawrence Durrell. At the one in Canada, I had flown up from my home in the San Francisco Bay Area. I am an American. Our introductory meeting was brief, but it became the basis for our future correspondence and eventual reunion in Egypt. "Michael", I said, "I enjoyed your talk on the *Quartet*". We were at one of those wine and cheese gatherings. The room was crowded with "Durrellians", and he was standing alone and off to the side. He was startled and jerked around. "Sorry, I didn't catch your name", he replied. He expected a formal introduction; that expectation was an essential part of his British formality. In public situations, he was always polite and always "proper" (in the very British sense of the word).

He was tall and wore a sports jacket, a tieless shirt underneath. His English accent was rich and upper class, his diction quaint. He referred to the restroom as the "loo". I assumed he was British and educated at an Oxbridge university. At that time, I didn't know his origin was American. He had an odd way of looking at you, not directly but slightly askance, at an angle. His eyes looked down a lot and focussed on the floor.

On another occasion at the same conference, he signed my copy of his *Alexandria Illustrated* (2004). He used his own fountain pen and added a warm inscription. The ink was green, like Darley's "green ink" in *Justine* (1957; *Quartet* 35)*,* and his handwriting flowed easily, much as Durrell's did when he signed his books. Now, looking back, the two artistic hands seem to resemble one another.

In Egypt, Haag was very generous with his time and hospitality, but our meetings were memorable because of their settings, not because of what was spoken. In person, he was curiously quiet, subdued, retiring, and perhaps even secretive. He was always an exemplar of British courtesy and restraint. I can recall, however, only odd fragments of our conversations. What I vividly remember are the situations, the places where we spoke.

Egypt was the backdrop. Haag's beautiful wife came from a wealthy Alexandrian family, perhaps members of the elite of their society. Like Haag, his wife and her family were paragons of courtesy. Her first language was French; she also spoke Arabic, English, and Italian. Her mother had a spacious flat not far from the harbour and the Corniche; it was inside an old Art Deco building with an elevator cage similar to the one in the Cecil Hotel where my wife and I were then staying. The Cecil of Alexandria figures prominently in Durrell's *Alexandria Quartet*.

The apartment building could have provided a baroque scene in the *Quartet*. One night at the flat, we had an elegant dinner with Haag, his Egyptian wife, and her mother, a most gracious hostess, who was also a native Alexandrian. Others, whose identities I've regretfully forgotten, were also at the dinner table. In deference to my monolingualism, our conversation was carried on in English, but it could have been in French, the language of choice.

I only remember the ambience of antique furnishings and some large brass vessels, which struck me as Islamic, spare like the interior of a mosque. No animate images, just geometric designs and arabesques. I stood in the living room admiring the oriental rugs; some hung on the walls like paintings. I was afraid to step on the ones on the floor. "That's all right", Haag explained. "These are meant to be walked on. The rugs on the walls are rare, mostly Turkoman and Persian. The Persian are very old, from Kerman and Isfahan". Aside from that comment, I recall very little of the conversation.

Another vivid occasion occurred in Cairo. It was night. Haag and I were standing on a balcony overlooking the dark Nile and the twinkling lights of Cairo in the distance. Again, my wife and I were attending a late dinner hosted by Haag's charming mother-in-law, who also owned an upper-storey flat in the Zamalek district of Gezira island. Zamalek and its residences also had an Art Deco appeal. The interior of the flat was like the one in Alexandria: dark antique furniture; no artwork other than shiny brass objects, rugs on walls and floor; books in bookcases with glass doors. All the titles were in French and Arabic. The tile floor had geometric patterns.

We were on the balcony. A cool night, a breeze off the river. The Pleiades a bright necklace. The refuge of Zamalek was quiet and fresh and very different from our hotel near the Egyptian Museum. During the day, the centre of Cairo was overwhelming — noisy, chaotic, and dusty. Now the night was calm and peaceful.

Haag had recently located Durrell's residence in Zamalek during August of 1941. He was pleased and remarked, "Durrell always chose the best places to live". Indeed. Haag seemed to be living in one of Durrell's Alexandrian novels, and he later reported that his Egyptian wife told him, in effect, that he really belonged in that lost Alexandrian world. That too pleased him. Not having his sense of nostalgia, she seemed to find his benign obsession amusing. She knew better; she was raised in Egypt. How can you be nostalgic about something you never experienced as a child? That vanished past was Haag's true habitat, and one might even say that he adapted the modern world to accommodate the vanished.

Houses and their furnishings reflect their owners' personalities. This universal commonplace was especially true of Haag's home in London. It was a small ground-floor flat located at Belsize Park, Hampstead Heath. He made many references to it in our correspondence and seemed most proud of its backyard: a small, unkept garden with geraniums and an olive tree. I later confirmed that the ambience was Mediterranean, the associations clearly Durrellian. Durrell also had an unruly garden at his Gothic mansion outside the medieval town of Sommières, in the south of France. The town is situated in what was once a Roman province (*Gallia Narbonensis*). Its roots remain Roman. A Roman bridge still crosses the Vidourle River near Durrell's home.

I never visited Haag's residence. But David Green and Denise Tart, my good Australian friends, spent an afternoon with Haag in July 2015 (**Plate 3**). I've seen Denise's photographs of Haag's home and garden and read David's comments on the occasion. Against a garden wall of brick, amidst vines and creepers, Haag had propped a tall antique mirror set in what looked like an ornate frame of Ionic columns and acanthus leaves (**Plate 4**). Its design and location evoke Roman ruins in a pastoral scene. Within the frame's pediment was a small androgynous face staring at the viewer as the viewer stared back.

Mirrors proliferate throughout Durrell's *Alexandria Quartet* (*Quartet* 25, 28, 32, *et passim*); they have symbolic importance and suggest various possibilities such as multiple perspectives or the self-referential gaze. Velázquez's *Las Meninas* (1656) comes to mind with its mirror, reflections, and multiple perspectives. Had Durrell visited Haag, he might have said that the classical face above the mirror represented the *deus loci*, the spirit of place, the term which Durrell made famous. Haag might have enjoyed that comparison. On that warm afternoon, many years ago, Haag and my Australian friends relaxed in the shade of his Roman garden and shared refreshments of olives and wine. They discussed the virtues of grapes from various locations. David advocated Australian Chardonnay. Haag declared that he only drank wine from "the Roman Empire".

I believe that Haag felt at home in the Roman Empire and wouldn't have minded living in one of the cities of the eastern provinces, from *Antiochia* to *Alexandrea ad Aegyptum*. As Mark Antony says, "I'th' East my pleasure lies" (*Ant.* 2.3.39).

III. Haag's Worldliness

Haag got around. He seemed to have been everywhere and to have read everything. He knew Egypt historically, sociologically, and geographically.

His *Timeline History of Egypt* (2003) is a very handy compendium of useful facts and observations. Well connected and with many contacts, he knew important people in Egypt: Jean-Yves Empereur and Harry Tzalas, authors and marine archaeologists, Mohamed Awad, lecturer and prominent architect, and Hisham Kassem, publisher and activist for democracy. He also knew the heads of institutes, local writers, and many others of note. To know these people and to call at least one of them "a very good friend" (as he did Kassem) was to be at their level of discourse and standing. In 2007, Hisham Kassem was the recipient of the Democracy Award, an American honour given by the National Endowment for Democracy.

Haag was like Darley in the *Quartet* — he too had numerous connections to the elite of Egyptian society, to many of its intelligentsia. Of course Haag met Lawrence Durrell at his home in Sommières, France. And, when he met Durrell, he said "Thank you", and by that he probably meant that he thanked the man who had opened his eyes to a new world.

Haag's historical knowledge of the Middle East was vast. He could comment authoritatively on the Trojans and their relationship to the Hittites (they were not siblings, maybe distant cousins), or he could explain what happened to the Great Library at Alexandria (it was neither burned by the Roman nor pillaged by the Arabs, rather it simply "fell apart"). He was also a film critic. He severely criticized Ridley Scott's *The Kingdom of Heaven* (2005), a film about the Crusades. He was horrified at Scott's portrayal of Guy de Lusignan and Raynald of Châtillon, supposed Templar Knights, and said that they were not Templars and that the film was historically inaccurate.[2] True, his criticisms were valid, but what does that matter when creating a work of fiction?

Haag had strong opinions, sometimes contradictory opinions. At times, the meticulous historian got in the way of the perceptive literary critic. He stumbled over his own feet. What he abhorred in Ridley Scott, he admired in Lawrence Durrell. But he was not unaware of his own prejudices. He admitted that some of his judgments had the effect of turning on a "blowtorch". Not in public, however. The blowtorch could get turned on when he engaged in written communications. Public and authorial Michael Haag were two different persons. This is not unusual for many people, but it is noteworthy.

I once had a question about an ancient Egyptian exhibit in London's British Museum. Haag didn't know the answer; instead, he asked, "Did you ask a curator behind one of those closed doors leading to the back offices?" I said no. I was too timid. "Well, you should knock on doors —

---

[2] Haag, *Templars*, p. 344.

you'd be surprised". Well, Haag knocked on doors, and they opened to him. That was a source of his impressive knowledge. But Haag's worldliness also betrayed a weakness. He occasionally made sweeping pronouncements — simultaneously pompous, acute, and witty. I think he enjoyed being wicked. It was part of his act. He had an Oscar Wilde quality.

In an early letter to Henry Miller, Lawrence Durrell remarked, "In order to destroy time I use the historic present a great deal — not to mention the gnomic aorist" (*DML* 55). The gnomic aorist is a past tense in ancient Greek; it is used to express, as Herbert Weir Smyth comments, "a general truth".[3] Whatever his rationale for the gnomic aorist, Durrell was fond of maxims and aphorisms. They added spice. He admired the aphorist François de La Rochefoucauld and even titled one of his poems "La Rochefoucauld". In *Mountolive* (1958), Durrell speaks through Pursewarden, another of his *alter ego*s, and equates "gnomic phrases" to "oracular thoughts" (*Quartet* 524-25).

Similarly, Haag had a penchant for formulating maxims or cultural aphorisms, which are a species of Durrell's "gnomic" utterances. So, a Coptic patriarch in *Mountolive* proclaims, "*Gins Pharoony*. Yes, we are *genus Pharaonicus* — the true descendants of the ancients, the true marrow of Egypt. We call ourselves *Gypt* — ancient Egyptians" (*Quartet* 421-22). Haag echoes this sentiment in his pronouncement: "Nobody can out-Arab an Arab, out-Muslim a Muslim, or out-Egyptian an Egyptian more than a Copt".

Another species of these gnomic tendencies is a concise observation on character, a cryptic image, what Durrell calls "Character-Squeezes" in *Justine* (*Quartet* 197), such as, "Justine Hosnani: arrow in darkness" or "Clea Montis: still waters of pain". So, I once asked Haag if Durrell had ever visited the Siwa Oasis in the western desert. I was curious about Durrell's vanity — if he had deliberately followed in the footsteps of Alexander, whose hubris had led him to seek the advice of the famous oracle of Ammon. Haag's pithy response: "Durrell never got as far as Siwa. He was auto-oracular". In some ways, Haag's pithy prose also has an "auto-oracular" tone.

---

[3] Smyth, *Greek Grammar*, p. 431 (sec. 1931).

IV. The Correspondence

Aside from his remark on that balcony in Cairo overlooking the Nile, telling in its reference to Lawrence Durrell and his preferred habitat, what I find most memorable about Haag is his correspondence, not only as it relates to Durrell but also as it is indicative of Haag's own personality.

Undoubtedly, Haag's public and authorial personae differed greatly. Nevertheless, Michael Haag was a gifted writer of eloquent, authoritative, and compelling prose. He resembles Henry Miller's depiction of the Greek writer George Katsimbalis as the "Colossus of Maroussi". In his writings, published and epistolary, Haag was a giant, and like a giant he had the attributes and bad habits of giants. He could tower over a literary landscape, and he could also trample on peoples' toes. *What* he said as opposed to *how* he said it — content versus form — are both important in talking about Haag. I have some things to say about the latter, but I shall focus on his main quality — his ideas.

Our correspondence was extensive and comprised over hundreds of emails. I have copies of these exchanges in print and digital formats. I take all my direct quotations either from that correspondence or from his publications. I will occasionally date an important email, but it is inconvenient to date or cite every one of his comments.

What I primarily rely upon is what he told me in our written exchanges. I accept his statements as true, and I make no attempt at the verification of facts, nor do I have dates for many of the events I will be discussing. As we all do, Haag was fully aware that his ideas would change over time as he acquired new information. As he said about his important article — "Only the City Is Real: Lawrence Durrell's Journey to Alexandria"[4] — "I will have to read it again to be sure what I said, and furthermore to see if I agree with it". I do not have his subsequent response, but the article still holds true. I am not attempting to present Haag's ideas as he might have finalized them — rather, I shall discuss his ideas as how they strike me as true and important.

V. Haag's Background

Haag led an extraordinary life. He was born and raised in America but chose to reside in London, where he also received his university education. Although he held three passports — American, British, and Irish — he identified himself as British. In 1992, he told Richard Pine that he once lived

---

[4] Haag, "Durrell's Journey", pp. 39-47.

in Dublin.[5] Haag called London his "paradise" and lived for much of his life in Belsize Park, which is within the London Borough of Camden. Belsize Park is close to the natural areas of Hampstead Heath, replete with greens, woods, and ponds. Haag was an avid and frequent walker. Walking was a way for him to collect his thoughts and solve problems. His visitors, so I'm told, were sometimes treated to arduous walks around the Heath. Those long excursions were not to everyone's liking.

Although London was his home and base, the Mediterranean was his field of study. He travelled throughout Israel and Syria, but Greece and Egypt were his special areas of interest, Alexandria in particular. The city was his special love, and he called himself a "one-man unfunded industry for the recording of Alexandria's past". And he proved himself worthy of that task by writing two superb books: *Alexandria: City of Memory* (2004) and *Vintage Alexandria: Photographs of the City, 1860-1960* (2008).[6] His unfinished biography of Lawrence Durrell would have been his magnum opus.

I say "field of study" deliberately, for Haag obtained a degree in anthropology from University College London (UCL). His "tutor" was the anthropologist Mary Douglas (1921-2007), who was known for her work on symbolism in such works as *Purity and Danger: An Analysis of Concept of Pollution and Taboo* (1966). Another of his professors was Phyllis Kaberry (1910-1977), a specialist in Aboriginal kinship and author of *Aboriginal Women: Sacred and Profane* (1939). Haag worked closely with these two famous anthropologists. They seemed to serve as his role models. He admired them for what they did — they went into the field, underwent hardships, and endured difficult circumstances. Douglas was known for her "fieldwork" in the jungles of the Congo, Kaberry for hers in the outback of Australia. At UCL, Haag specialized in "West Africa as region" and the "Nuer of the Sudan". He did not go into the field to study these peoples. Rather, his chosen fields lay elsewhere.

Like Durrell the skilled painter, Haag was an excellent photographer. He had a sharp eye and knew how to organize his material for stunning effects. This rare ability is especially true in his compilation and arrangement of photographs in his *Vintage Alexandria*. While at UCL, he studied film at the Slade School of Fine Art. In the field, not only did he record his findings and observations in notebooks, he also photographed the places he visited and the people he encountered (the cover of *Alexandria: City Memory* has one of his photographs).

---

[5] Personal communication from Richard Pine on 29 August 2021.
[6] See my review of these two books: "Haag's Many Alexandrias" in Chapter Four above.

VI. Haag's Methodology

Haag's methodology owes much to cultural anthropology. Some of its methods and issues were also Haag's in his approach to research and biography. Three such anthropological issues include:

(1) the necessity of working in the field,
(2) the need to consolidate facts into principles, and
(3) the problem of the relationship between the observer and the subject.

I shall emphasize the first two issues and make only passing remarks towards the third. I discuss Haag's "fieldwork" below. The second issue I discuss in the section on Durrell's plagiarisms.

Anthropology is closely affiliated with archaeology, and Haag told me that he once wanted to be an archaeologist. "Fieldwork" defines both cultural anthropology and archaeology. Anthropologists and archaeologists teach in colleges and universities, and they write their articles and books in the comfort of modern cities. But any archaeologist worth his or her salt has a "dig", an excavation closely identified with the archaeologist's particular field of expertise. I do not recall that Haag paid much attention to current theoretical issues related to the writing of ethnographies, that is, to what extent an anthropologist can objectively study an alien society.[7] He was interested in "fieldwork" per se, as praxis.

Haag's emphasis on proving something in the field had a direct bearing on his opposition to the Academy and its so-called ivory tower. He was especially opposed to the Academy's theoretical approaches to the study of literature. He saw himself as an outsider, as someone outside the traditional academic domain of literary criticism. I think he also relished his role as outsider (or "heretic" in his advocacy of biographical criticism, to be discussed later). It gave him the opportunity to turn on his "blowtorch" to full force.

Metaphorically speaking, Haag's main historical "dig" was Egypt, the city of Alexandria in particular. His primary literary "dig" was the study of Lawrence Durrell, and he frequently described his literary and biographical analyses as forms of "archaeology". The comparison is not farfetched; indeed, it has a noble lineage. For Haag was like Sigmund Freud, who was fond of a similar metaphor. Freud famously associated psychoanalysis with

---

[7] For an explanation of some of these issues, see Geertz, *Works and Lives*, pp. 1-24.

archaeological research.[8] His study in Vienna even featured ancient artifacts. Richard H. Armstrong has written a book on Freud's "compulsion for antiquity", and he notes that "[Freud's] desk [was] lined with ancient figurines, as immortalized in Max Pollack's [sic] 1914 etching".[9] So too Haag's home in Belsize Park had its garden mirror of Roman design. I would not be surprised if Haag also had a collection of artifacts similar to Freud's.

Anthropologists and archaeologists are both well known for their fieldwork in far-off places. That professional requirement determined how Haag approached his study of history, literature, and Lawrence Durrell. He went into the field to study places firsthand and to interview people relevant to his purpose. Archaeologists follow a rigorous methodology: they record and chart their findings. As Haag said on another occasion, "I am trying to chart [Durrell's] inner and creative life".

Haag related a story which illustrates his methodology. He did not intend the story as an illustration of his method of fieldwork. He told the story as something interesting in its own right. I find it, however, instructive and will paraphrase and excerpt his account, which is too long to quote in full.

Haag met the famous writer Patrick Leigh Fermor (1915-2011) at his home in Kardamyli in the northern Mani. The town is near a wild and rugged region of the Peloponnese. Haag called that region "one of the wildest places in Europe" and noted that "Durrell did not like the Mani and told me it was 'Methodist Greece.'" The year is unspecified, but it was probably two decades after the publication of Leigh Fermor's *Mani: Travels in the Southern Peloponnese* (1958).

So, Haag read *Mani* closely. He was intrigued by Leigh Fermor's account of a traverse across a particularly treacherous mountain gorge and the neighbouring terrain. Based on his own knowledge of the Mani, Haag did not believe the account was accurate. He found it too "vague". So in typical Haag-like fashion, he decided to retrace Leigh Fermor's journey on

---

[8] See "The Aetiology of Hysteria" (1896) in Freud, *Standard Edition*, vol. 3, p. 192. In this well-known essay, Freud uses the extended metaphor of the exploration and reconstruction of "archaeological remains" (i.e., stone ruins and material culture) as being analogous to the methodology of psychoanalysis. The long passage ends with the Latin tag, "*Saxa loquuntur* [stones speak]!"

[9] Armstrong, *Compulsion*, p. 36. Max Pollak (1886-1970) made the etching of Freud at his desk surrounded by "ancient figurines". Armstrong uses the etching for the dust-jacket illustration of his book, *A Compulsion for Antiquity: Freud and the Ancient World* (2005). Pollak's original etching, *Sigmund Freud Seated at His Desk,* is located in the Freud Museum, London.

foot. A friend accompanied him, presumably because of the dangers involved. The trek was long and arduous. It apparently lasted several, unspecified days and turned out to be, in Haag's words, "about the most stupid thing I have ever done". On the summit of Mount Taygetus, "the highest mountain in the Peloponnese", they found a "dead body", confirming the prudence of travelling with a companion. They encountered further difficulties and hardships. Then, at the end of the traverse, successfully accomplished, "we were later told by locals that nobody had ever accomplished such a daring and stupid feat before". In 2007, Haag concluded that "Paddy Leigh Fermor was a cissy. He made his traverse sound so hard, but it could not have been a patch on ours".[10]

Haag's telling of the story is dramatic, full of danger, and worthy of Durrell's descriptions of the mountainous regions of Yugoslavia in his adventure novel *White Eagles over Serbia* (1957). The Durrellian correspondences are prominent and revealing. Durrell did not like the Mani but Haag clearly does and accepts the challenge. Durrell knew Leigh Fermor, and so Haag meets him. Leigh Fermor was also very famous. His commando exploits on Crete during the Second World War were heroic and legendary, and he has been called the greatest British travel writer of his generation.[11] Durrell too was famous and a great writer of the Mediterranean landscape, although he was not an adventurer.

Among its various meanings, Greek *agón* (ἀγών) denotes a contest or some personal struggle or trial. A primary example of the *agón* was the athletic competition,[12] ultimately resulting in the Olympic Games. There, on the field of athletics, the contest between rivals determined who was the best, the ἄριστος. On the field of combat, Achilles supposes himself "the best of the Achaeans" (*Il.* 1.244) and later proves it by killing Hector, the Trojan champion, in personal combat (*Il.* 22.325-66). This struggle for supremacy exemplifies Haag's traverse across the Mani. In a metaphorical sense, Haag engages Leigh Fermor in a physical contest. He finds Leigh Fermor's work a personal challenge. He then goes out to beat the famous writer and adventurer at his own game. In the end, he wins the contest and proclaims that his "patch", his badge of distinction, has earned him — figuratively and most probably unconsciously — the laurel of victory.

Lawrence Durrell's presence hangs like a ghost behind Haag's exploit on the Mani. I wonder if Durrell was not, in some strange way, also

---

[10] See *OED* 3rd, s.v. *patch* at P1, for the British colloquial phrase, "not a patch on", which is equivalent to "in no way comparable, not nearly as good as".

[11] H. Smith, "Literary Legend", 2 March 2007.

[12] See *Intermediate Greek-English Lexicon*, s.v. ἀγών: "II. 2. *the contest for a prize at the games*".

part of the contest, and Durrell's spectre may illustrate Haag's close identification with his subject, his lack of objectivity. Thus, we have before us the third anthropological issue that questions the degree to which an observer can accurately describe what he or she observes.[13]

Whatever the case, Haag is not modest in his accomplishment. True, he is self-deprecating — he twice refers to his own stupidity — but he is not so stupid as to hike in the Mani alone. His self-criticism is a rhetorical flourish, a kind of paralipsis — the art of saying something by denying to say anything. Haag's self-deprecation serves to highlight his own boldness and audacity. Immodesty aside, the story illustrates well the extent to which Haag would go to prove a point. His method was to do "fieldwork", no matter what the costs, no matter how difficult the endeavour. His mentors Mary Douglas and Phyllis Kaberry would have been proud of him — and rightly so.

Fieldwork serves as an introduction to Haag's unfinished biography of Lawrence Durrell. Haag found his inspiration for undertaking the biography out in the field — while sitting in the White House on the island of Corfu. Durrell made the house famous in *Prospero's Cell*, where he describes it as "a white house set like a dice on a rock already venerable with the scars of wind and water" (*PC* 12). In that same paragraph, Durrell calls the "bare promontory" of "metamorphic stone" a "*mons pubis*". The description of the promontory has obvious sexual connotations. For both Durrell and Haag, the image probably connotes Kalami as a womb, as the matrix of an important beginning.[14]

Haag was never precise about his dates (just as Durrell wasn't), but I understand the occasion at Kalami to have occurred sometime in the early 1990s. (Lawrence Durrell died on 7 November 1990 in Sommières, France.) In 2006, Haag described to me his revelation on Corfu:

> At Kalami in March (good time to be there, bad winter, therefore no people, so it seemed something like 1935)[,] I spend several days wandering in and out of the White House where Durrell and Nancy lived. The family gave me the keys and I would go day and night, just sitting there sometimes, or looking out the windows, or listening to the waves, watching storms — *The Black Book* begins with a lightening [sic] storm: I could *never* have started this book in the summer, Durrell says at the start

---

[13] Geertz, *Works and Lives*, p. 9: "The clash between the expository conventions of author-saturated texts and those of author-evacuated ones that grows out of the particular nature of the ethnographic enterprise is imagined to be a clash between seeing things as one would have them and seeing them as they really are".

[14] Pine, *Mindscape*, pp. 162-63.

of *The Black Book*.[15]

Haag is describing the moment of inspiration when he decides to undertake his biography. The year 1935 is when Lawrence Durrell started writing his first major novel, *The Black Book*. Its famous opening sentences are — "The agon, then. It begins" (*BB* 21).

The *agón* can also include a literary struggle.[16] Writing *The Black Book* became Durrell's *agón* in the sense that the undertaking became the first truly important accomplishment of his early career. T. S. Eliot, Durrell's mentor at Faber and Faber, recognized the novel's importance with his famous encomium, quoted on the book's dust jacket: "Lawrence Durrell's *Black Book* is the first piece of work by a new English writer to give me any hope for the future of prose fiction".

Durrell's *agón*, then, is *The Black Book*, and its opening section sets the scene for the author's forthcoming struggle. The opening is rich in imagery associated with death and winter, the physical and psychological context of the author's trial. But it does not describe a dramatic "lightening storm". There is a storm with "thunder" but no "lightening", and Durrell's sentence actually reads, "I could not have begun this *act* in the summer" (*BB* 22; my italics). Close but not accurate. Haag's use of "never" occurs several times elsewhere and will have repercussions.

Haag is quoting from memory, and his slips reveal something about himself. His *I* seems to conflate with Durrell's *I*. Haag replicates Durrell's experience. He wanders around the empty house at Kalami seemingly lost and distraught, as though he were summoning up ghosts. My impression of this description is that Durrell's "agón" or "act" becomes Haag's future "book", the plans for his biography of Lawrence Durrell. Biographers occasionally do this kind of thing.[17] They identify closely with their subjects, and this is especially true of Michael Haag. He decides to undertake his own *agón*, as he too sits in the White House and watches a storm gather over the Ionian Sea. Only his description is more dramatic than Durrell's. The turbulent setting was memorable for both writers, but Durrell completed his *agón* — his first great literary work — and Haag *never* completed his magnum opus.

---

[15] Email 8 September 2006. My italics.

[16] Joho, "Burckhardt and Nietzsche", p. 267: "The paradigmatic manifestation of the agonal spirit was athletic contest, but it took on a great variety of different forms and was eventually disseminated throughout all spheres of life, ranging from poetry to politics and from education to social entertainment".

[17] Cf. Andrew Wilson, *Patricia Highsmith*, pp. 464-65. In his epilogue, Wilson's *I* appears, and he puts on Highsmith's dressing gown and thinks about her.

Haag's favourite novel in the *Quartet* was *Justine*. He had a provocative interpretation of Durrell's use of French *jamais* (never). In *Justine*, the word recurs in the names of a French song and perfume, *jamais de la vie* (idiomatically, "not on your life"; literally, "never of life") (*Quartet* 94, 155). Haag interpreted the reference as "a running joke with Durrell" and then commented:

> Durrell's motif of *jamais de la vie* is a variation on Nevermore: Alexandria: City of Impotence — it is not a fruitful or productive place in Durrell's terms, which is why the artists, the would be artists, Darley and Clea have to get away.[18]

Haag alludes to Edgar Allan Poe's famous (and notorious) poem, "The Raven" (1845). But Durrell's references are not a joke — impotence is no joke — and "The Raven" is a long poem which goes nowhere. Its diction is archaic and obsessive. The Raven "croak[s]" and "quoth". And the all-too-insistent refrain — "Quoth the Raven 'Nevermore'" — connotes death and loss as much as impotence, which is a common but speculative gloss on Poe's "Nevermore". Poe was another obsessive and tormented genius, much as Durrell was.

Perhaps these traits are what caught Haag's eye and caused him to make the connection between *jamais* and *nevermore*, which is just an echo of the earlier phrase in the poem — "nothing more". On another occasion, Haag wrote: "Durrell's greatest demon, I suspect, is not darkness but emptiness — that there is nothing there". Emptiness lies at the heart of Durrell's epigraph for one of his best collections of poems, *The Tree of Idleness* (1955): "The notion of emptiness engenders compassion. Mila Repa". Milarepa (1025-1135) was a Buddhist and Tibetan sage, but the Buddhist notion of emptiness (Sanskrit *śūnyatā*) as ultimate understanding is not what Haag had in mind. Despite the epigraph, Haag interpreted Durrell's notion of emptiness as pure nihilism. On Durrell's creativity, he remarked "Creation is continuous activity whose essence is flux — until you arrive at nothingness".

Haag too was a writer of "continuous activity". He wrote many books, and he never stopped moving. His long walks in the Mani and on Hampstead Heath were part of his ceaseless activity. Haag's readings of Durrell were always original and provocative, but, like the croaking of Poe's Raven of one note, they have a dark and obsessive ring. At times Haag seemed to speak through Durrell and to say something about himself.

---

[18] Email 2 September 2007.

VII. Durrell's "World"

Near the beginning of *Prospero's Cell* Durrell says "Other countries may offer you discoveries in manners or lore or landscape; Greece offers you something harder—the discovery of yourself" (*PC* 11). Durrell's claim is a big one, and he does not directly explain or justify it later in his book, although I believe the reader intuits his meaning as correct. Durrell's assertion about obtaining self-knowledge, however, is not new. Goethe says something similar near the beginning of his *Italian Journey* (1816-1817): "My purpose in making this wonderful journey is not to delude myself but to discover myself in the objects I see". Goethe supports his claim with many subsequent references to discoveries related to his own being.[19] By the time of the London publication of *Sicilian Carousel* (1977), Durrell had read Goethe's *Italian Journey* (*SC* 39).

So, what does Durrell mean by "the discovery of yourself"? I suggest — and I believe Haag would agree — that Durrell was referring to the creation of his "own world". I believe that this creation is felt or intuited by many readers who find the book captivating. This kind of reading experience is not a matter of an author explaining himself or herself in the manner of someone undergoing a journey of psychoanalytic self-discovery. It is far more subtle and mysterious. It is almost mystical, for Haag saw another aspect of Durrell's private world, his world of writing. Through his writings, Durrell could influence reality and make things happen. As Haag wrote, "There are times I think Durrell writes himself into his life, his writing makes things happen, makes things real".

This idea is really just an extension of Durrell's perennial theme that dream and reality are indistinguishable. We see this near the beginning of *Prospero's Cell* when Durrell says, "It is a sophism to imagine that there is any strict dividing line between the waking world and the world of dreams" (*PC* 11); the theme recurs during the pool scene at the shrine of Saint Arsenius (*PC* 16); and it reappears with the primacy of "the kingdom of your imagination" at the end of *Clea* (*Quartet* 877). The theme appears once again in *Sicilian Carousel*: "We have been brought up to believe that facts are not dreams—and of course they are" (*SC* 36).

In this context, also near the beginning of *Prospero's Cell*, Durrell calls his experiences on Corfu a "world": "This is become our unregretted

---

[19] Goethe, *Italian Journey*, p. 40. On p. 135, Goethe repeats this claim: "Nothing, above all, is comparable to the new life that a reflective person experiences when he observes a new country. Though I am still always myself, I believe I have been changed to the very marrow of my bones". For similar statements, see pp. 135, 143, 341, 394, 404, 482.

home. A world. Corcyra" (*PC* 12). He later describes his world poetically: "World of black cherries, sails, dust, arbutus, fishes and letters from home" (*PC* 20). Then at the end of his book, Durrell reflects on the ravages of the Second World War and speaks of his Greek friends as "recovering [...] into a small private universe: a Greek universe. Inside that world, where the islands lie buried in smoke, where the cypresses spring from the tombs, they know that there is nothing to be said" (*PC* 132). "The Greek universe" is surely Durrell's "private universe", his "world". Only now the enclosed world differs. The devastation of the war has taken its toll. Instead of lively images and homely words, Durrell's world also contains burial imagery and empty silence, which will eventually become as prophetic and portentous as Hamlet's last words, "The rest is silence".

Shakespeare's *Hamlet* was one of Durrell's favourite plays; he identified closely with the troubled prince. In 1936, when he was young and optimistic, Durrell told Miller that Hamlet's final words were "a brief but witty epitaph" (*DML* 22). The comment was lighthearted, almost jocular. But that attitude would later change, as his sad epilogue to *Prospero's Cell* shows.

That Durrell had his "own world" has long been noted, undoubtedly many times. In 1978, Carol Marshall Peirce attended a lecture given by John Wain of Brasenose College and summarized it in her article, "A Reading of Durrell's Map: John Wain's Oxford Lecture". At the time, Wain was Oxford Professor of Poetry. According to Peirce, Wain said that Durrell "has a place and a *world*".[20] On 5 July 2007, Anna Lillios, former president of the International Lawrence Durrell Society, posted an inquiry on the ILDS listserv: "Why are so many men interested in Durrell studies, i.e., most of the respondents in the discussion group are male? Is it because they are fascinated by Durrell's fantasy women and the *world* he creates around them?"[21]

As Wain, Lillios, and others have observed, Lawrence Durrell clearly had his "own world", but what exactly was it? Michael Haag had an answer which extends far beyond Wain's comments on Durrell's Mediterranean landscape and Lillios's idea of a male world of sexual fantasy.

Haag considered Durrell's "best books" to be *Prospero's Cell* (1945), *Bitter Lemons* (1957), and *The Alexandria Quartet* (1960), with an emphasis on *Justine* (1957). He also believed in 2007 that after 1960 "[Durrell] lost it. His hold on the real was never very secure, and that

---

[20] Carol Peirce, "Reading", p. 3. My italics.
[21] Lillios, 5 July 2007. My italics.

included [his fictional] characters, while his ideas were eclectic, entertaining, and also inconsistent and undeveloped". To say that Durrell reached his peak with the publication of the *Quartet* presents a big problem for his biographer. Durrell lived, wrote, and published for another thirty years. What does a biographer say about those years other than to map out a course of dismal decline? That was Haag's problem. We did not discuss it, but some problem — or perhaps something like it — prevented him from completing his biography.

Nevertheless, of the three "best books", Haag took *Prospero's Cell* to hold a position of crucial importance because it created a "world" in which Durrell found a haven, a "small private universe", and one in which he could freely exercise his imagination and could possibly influence the real world.

VIII. Durrell's Plagiarisms

One aspect of this creative process was Durrell's habit of plagiarisation. Haag took it as a given that Durrell, when writing *Prospero's Cell*, plagiarised a substantial amount of material from Sophie Atkinson's *An Artist in Corfu* (1911).[22] Haag was not the first to discover such plagiarisms,[23] but he saw no need to excuse Durrell's theft as a matter of "sources" or "borrowings", the usual literary interpretation.[24] Instead, he saw Durrell as deliberately stealing Atkinson's words and her scenes of Corfiot life. He saw these plagiarisms as essential to his biography ("the stuff of my biography of Durrell") and part of a pattern that needed to be explained ("I need to make my case about Durrell, explaining how all [h]is peculiarities added up to the writer he was").

---

[22] Sophie Atkinson, *An Artist in Corfu* (Boston: Dana Estes, [1911]. My copy is the Boston edition. The book was also published in London at Herbert & Daniel, in the same year. My edition does not contain a copyright symbol or statement of copyright, but Haag said that made no difference, for the copyright still held without formal notification.

[23] In 2000, at the conference of the International Lawrence Durrell Society on Corfu, Hilary Whitton Paipeti gave a paper listing most of the instances where Lawrence Durrell had "borrowed" from Atkinson. My thanks to Richard Pine for this reference.

[24] For a general description of this problem, see William Leigh Godshalk, "Some Sources of Durrell's Alexandria Quartet", in *Critical Essays on Lawrence Durrell*, ed. Alan Warren Friedman (Boston: G. K. Hall, 1987): pp. 158-71. In an email to the ILDS listserv on 21 May 2007, Godshalk called Durrell's plagiarisation "pilfering". *Pilfering* is not the same as *plagiarisation*. *Pilfering* diminishes the force of *plagiarisation*.

In other words, like a good anthropologist, Haag felt he had to account for the many instances of personal phenomena — separate and divergent, the "stuff" of personality — and to find the organizing principle behind them. In a cultural context, this is the approach that Bronisław Malinowski advocates: *"Only laws and generalizations are scientific facts*, and field work consists only and exclusively in the interpretation of the chaotic social reality, in subordinating it to general rules".[25] So, Haag looked for first causes, for generalizations. He looked for the One over the Many: "I follow strands and notice patterns and I link them to events, and I begin to see what made Durrell as man and writer, what made his genius what it was. Again things arise and coalesce". When "things arise and coalesce", they cohere, they form a unity, they become a first cause, a principle, a generalization. Haag's search for unity over diversity also appears in his last book, *The Durrells of Corfu* (2017). The book purports to be about the whole family of Durrells on Corfu, but its underlying subject is really Lawrence Durrell himself.[26]

Haag offered the tentative "hypothesis" that Durrell was prone to plagiarisation during periods of severe stress and "self doubt". The writing of *Prospero's Cell* in Egypt and *Caesar's Vast Ghost* in Provence coincided with such times. Egypt during the Second World War was one of those situations where Durrell suffered the loss of Greece, a broken marriage to Nancy Myers, and a separation from his daughter Penelope Berengaria. A second such situation occurred near the end of his life when his daughter Sappho Jane committed suicide in London. These two periods resulted in either depression or alcoholism.

Plagiarism, however, indicated something much more than momentary weakness brought on by acute distress. For Haag interpreted plagiarism as no small flaw in Durrell's personality; rather, it also connected to his role as an artist. So Haag further elaborated:

> All writers are magpies, but this goes a step further [Durrell plagiarising Sophie Atkinson]. It seems to me part of Durrell's general project of taking apart and reconstructing the world because he needs to do so, because for him there is something fundamentally wrong with the world from the outset — and even though he is enjoyed precisely for his celebration of life and those parts of the world where fortune brings him.[27]

---

[25] Malinowski, *Magic, Science and Religion*, p. 238. Original italics. This passage is also cited and emphasized by Geertz, *Works and Lives*, p. 81.
[26] See Chapter Five above.
[27] Email 13 July 2007.

Thus, Haag links Durrell's plagiarisation to the creation of his "world".

The theft, however, could have been disastrous. Had Durrell's publisher Faber and Faber discovered his plagiarism, Haag believed that Durrell's career at Faber would have dramatically ended. He based this opinion on a meeting with a friend who was a retired editor at Faber. They had dinner one evening at Haag's flat in Belsize Park, and he reported his friend as saying, "The entire edition of *Prospero's Cell* would have been pulped and Durrell would never have signed a contract again [with Faber]. His writing career would have been over". Whatever the case for Faber's hypothetical discovery, Haag was interested in two issues about Durrell's risky behaviour: what it said about his "world" and how to account for it in terms of his personality.

The latter is the easier to discuss. Plagiarisation follows from Haag's basic premise about Durrell's behaviour as he expressed it in 2007: "My Basic Theory About Durrell [sic] is that he invented everything". Examples of plagiarism recur in Durrell's oeuvre. They have a pathological consistency. Another example occurs in *Balthazar* when he lifts a passage from R. Talbot Kelly's *Egypt: Painted and Described* (1902). And another occurs in his last work, *Caesar's Vast Ghost* (1990), when Durrell lifts a passage from Haag's own note to his edition of E. M. Forster's original *Alexandria: A History and a Guide* (1922).[28]

A possible corollary to the "Basic Theory" is Haag's previously quoted contention that Durrell had a tenuous "hold on the real". Haag may have later developed a more sophisticated explanation for Durrell's plagiarisms, but his "Basic Theory" of 2007 has one troubling implication: Durrell plagiarised because he had difficulty distinguishing his private world from reality. But did he?

Haag was a meticulous critic and researcher. He also believed that Durrell attempted to conceal his indebtedness to Sophie Atkinson. In his "Brief Bibliography" to *Prospero's Cell*, Durrell listed Atkinson's name as "S. Atkinson" (*PC* 140). He gives the full names of two other sources — but not Atkinson's, whose full name appears on the title page of her book.[29] So, Haag argued that the "S." for *Sophie* is a "clear" and deliberate

---

[28] For *Balthazar*, see Chapter One above. For *Caesar's Vast Ghost*, compare Lawrence Durrell's description of the Battle of Actium on pp. 130-31 of *CVG* with Michael Haag's long note in his 1986 edition Forster's *Alexandria* (pp. 247-248, n. 29).

[29] NB two other names in the bibliography. "D. T. Ansted" is the author's name on the title page of *The Ionian Islands,* and "Viscount Kirkwall" is the way his name is indicated in all the sources I've been able to check. Incidentally, Durrell misspells Ansted's name as "Anstead". See *PC* 89, 90, and 140.

"omission". If this is the case, then Durrell knew what he was doing — committing plagiarism and trying to hide the fact — and the matter then becomes one of ethics. That leaves unanswered one big question about Durrell — was he unethical? I do not know how Haag answered that question. My response is that Durrell was occasionally unethical and probably more often than he should have been.

Haag also saw Durrell's plagiarism as providing one major benefit in assessing his abilities. It demonstrated the great superiority of Durrell's artistic abilities over Atkinson's. Plagiarism, then, became Haag's key into Durrell's "world". It enabled him to compare a great writer to one of lesser abilities. So he comments on the quality of Durrell's and Atkinson's writings:

> An important quality of Durrell's writing, to my mind, is the way he draws the reader into his world. It is a world he creates by *dismantling* this world and building another in which he feels better — feels unburdened, playful, free or whatever. As I have said before, I think Durrell finds it necessary for his own well being to create such a world and to have it validated by readers. *Prospero's Cell* achieves that beautifully; and he used Sophie's text in a way that gives it that dreamworld quality it did not have in her hands. She writes about the world; he writes about his world, and in making the world his he appropriates of it what he likes, including what she has written.[30]

Here, Haag's use of "dismantling" and creating another world is crucial. I do not think he would equate this process to Durrell's idea of the "Heraldic Universe", which, I believe, is some realm analogous to Platonic Forms. That is to say, the "Heraldic Universe" is a dimension beyond the mundane world we live in. Moreover, "dismantling" as a form of creation is a part of Haag's "Basic Theory" that Durrell "invented everything". He argued that Durrell's use of the initial "S." (for Sophie Atkinson) corresponds to the initial "N." (for Nancy Myers) in *Prospero's Cell* (*PC* 11) and the initial "E" (for Eve Cohen) in *Reflections on a Marine Venus* (*RMV* 16). All these shorthand references to real women, in Haag's analysis, are examples of Durrell's deliberate truncation of personal names — in the sense of altering reality itself — in order to create a world of his own.

Not all of these references are to women; if they had been, then Durrell would have been open to the charge of misogyny. One important male appears. Following Haag's line of reasoning, the ultimate truncation would be "Count D." in *Prospero's Cell*, who is first mentioned in the

[30] Email 7 August 2007. My italics.

book's dedication and later developed in full. Ignoring his advanced age, the Count resembles Durrell in physical appearance: "The old Count, a man of about sixty, was stocky and heavily built; he possessed a pair of remarkable eyes set in a head which was a little too big for his body" (*PC* 75). He also sounds like Durrell delivering one of his maxims: "Philosophy […] is a doubt which lives in one like hookworm, causing pallor and lack of appetite" (*PC* 77). Haag saw the Count as being Lawrence Durrell in disguise, recreated as an aristocrat living on Corfu.[31] Count D., then, may serve as the final proof of Haag's argument — QED.

What Haag hints at in this passage, but does not fully explain, is the nature of Durrell's private world. Haag calls it a "dreamworld", but I would further specify that it is a world of loss and memory ensconced within a dream. It has a very Proustian quality. All of Durrell's "best books" — to which I largely concur with Haag — along with his best poetry — have that characteristic.

Although Haag considered Lawrence Durrell the superior artist by far, that did not mean he disparaged Atkinson's work. He was just and fair. And he made that clear when he said, in the context of discussing Atkinson, "I do think that people should be remembered for what they have contributed". He wanted to give Sophie Atkinson her proper due. He even went so far as to create a biographical entry for her on Wikipedia. I suspect that Haag believed that Durrell had wronged Atkinson by not giving her full credit for her work. He may have also wanted to make amends on Durrell's behalf. This suspicion, however, harbours one troubling possibility. If true, not only does Michael Haag seem to be speaking *for* Lawrence Durrell, he seems *to be* Lawrence Durrell.

IX. Enigma Machines

When discussing Durrell's poetry, codebreaking was one of Haag's favourite tropes. One of our exchanges on the German "Enigma Machine" brought up the topic. During the Second World War, the Germans used that intricate device for encoding messages transmitted within the upper echelons

---

[31] See also, MacNiven, *Lawrence Durrell*, p. 293. In his biography of Durrell, MacNiven sees Count D. as "a composite character grounded on several of Larry's Corfiot friends". Others who agree with MacNiven include Hilary Paipeti, Theodore Stephanides, and Richard Pine. I disagree with these views, which see the aristocrat as a conglomerate of traits gathered from other people. Those views, in my opinion, ignore the count's basic character as Durrell presents it. I agree with Haag — Count D. is Lawrence Durrell himself and should probably be seen as how he wants to see himself, however jokingly.

of military units. The encrypted traffic was almost unbreakable, were it not for the work of British cryptologists, Alan M. Turing in particular. The breaking of the Enigma code is one of the great stories of British Intelligence.

As Haag pointed out, however, the Enigma Machine was not part of the spy story related to British Intelligence in Egypt, rather it was the discovery of the use of Daphne du Maurier's famous novel, *Rebecca* (1938). The British captured a German Morse code operator in the western desert and found in his possession a copy of the novel. The radio operator didn't understand English; he was using *Rebecca* as an encryption pad for passing radio traffic. The low-level code, a form of simple substitution, was based on du Maurier's text.

As Haag briefly mentions in his *Alexandria: City of Memory*, Daphne du Maurier (1907-1989) wrote *Rebecca* in Alexandria out of sheer boredom. She was "bored […] stiff" because of her social obligations as the wife of a British lieutenant colonel stationed in the city.[32] Her husband later became Lieutenant General Frederick Browning, who was famous for his comment about the failed assault on a bridge in Arnhem, Holland ("a bridge too far"). In Alexandria, the couple lived in a rented bungalow near Ramleh and the Corniche. Their living conditions were undoubtedly posh and exclusive, not unlike Durrell's living arrangements in Cairo and Alexandria.

In her biography of the English author, Margaret Forster mentions that du Maurier saw herself as a sexual "half-breed".[33] She was bisexual but reluctant to admit her sexuality. Her marriage was complicated. Browning had mistresses. Du Maurier had an alleged affair with the actress Gertrude Lawrence. These facts Haag did not mention, but he was probably aware of them. The unusual couple could have easily joined the ranks of Durrell's exotic Alexandrians, those "inquisitors of pleasure and pain" (*Quartet* 350). But that didn't happen. Whatever her experiences in Egypt, a bored du Maurier, living in a historic city with all its oriental allure, took refuge in writing a mystery set faraway on her native Cornish coast and whose plot resembles Charlotte Brontë's *Jane Eyre* (1847). She completely rejected the city made famous by Cavafy and Forster and later memorialized by Durrell and Haag himself. Coincidentally, Durrell was also bored. He had initially rejected Egypt, as he revealed in a letter of early July (?) 1958 to Henry Miller: "I loathed Egypt" (*DML* 320). Durrell and du Maurier never met, but they shared intriguing similarities.

[32] Haag, *City of Memory*, pp. 167-68.
[33] M. Forster, *Daphne du Maurier*, p. 418.

Haag found the complementary stories of Daphne du Maurier in Alexandria and German espionage in Egypt as just too weird and compelling to ignore — or too much, in Desdemona's reported words, "passing strange" (*Oth.* 1.3.160). The stories seemed to bewitch Haag just as Othello's storytelling had bewitched Desdemona. Haag's fascination with du Maurier is an insight into his fascination with Durrell's personality.

Taken as a pair, du Maurier and Durrell, their personalities and works were ironic, fantastic, and prophetic. *Rebecca* as decryption key became Haag's metaphor for understanding Lawrence Durrell. Du Maurier's life and fiction had coincidences as they pertained to Durrell's own life and fiction. The city of Alexandria is an obvious connection; another is sexual promiscuity. I would also suggest that du Maurier's bisexuality was reflective of Durrell's idea of Alexandria as "the great winepress of love" (*Quartet* 18), where bisexuality or the "bisexual psyche" is a major theme.[34] As Haag said, "Durrell's *Rebecca* is his life story". That is to say, Durrell's biography is the basis for breaking the "code" of his poetry. As Haag further explained, "It is not *Rebecca* that is Durrell's life story. But the role played by *Rebecca* in the war is the role played by Durrell's life story in decoding his poems".

Poetry as encryption, then, served as a way for Durrell to deal with his deepest problems and — paradoxically — as a way to conceal them. Haag was not referring to all of Durrell's poetry, of course, but to many of his important poems. So he argued:[35]

> LD's more painful memories being idiosyncratically buried in poetry where they serve a dual function. Firstly, as a compressed trigger to release the emotive memories associated with the poem[']s theme and secondly as a means to efficiently encrypt his most intimate experiences ... this is selfish art at its best and double the fun for LD as his innermost is exposed, and thereby ventilated, without being readily available to prying eyes which have not the benefit of his decoding subjectivity.

The immediate objective of this exercise appears as an italicized refrain in "At the Long Bar" (1955): "*The sickness of the oyster is the pearl*". The ultimate objective is to render this exercise unnecessary, as expressed in italicized lines from "Conon in Alexandria" (1945), where a man is "*engaged in bitterly waiting / For the day when art should become unnecessary*".

---

[34] Pine, *Mindscape*, p. 90.
[35] Email 22 July 2007.

But Haag's emphasis on biographical interpretation created problems, for this critical approach was anathema to American Formalism or "New Criticism" of the 1940s and 1950s, which treats poetry as a "verbal icon". It considers the text alone as sufficient for interpretation. New Criticism eschews biography,[36] and to indulge in it is to commit the "*biographical heresy*".[37] As Harry Levin explained as late as 1984, "It is no longer acceptable to identify the author's personality with his vicarious *persona*".[38] Haag broke decisively with this tradition; he became a "heretic". He saw Lawrence Durrell himself as the ultimate "Enigma Machine" and his life story as essential for understanding some of his most important and intimate poetry. Haag's approach has major consequences, for his emphasis on biography contrasts sharply with the Formalist rejection of biography. This opposition can lead to radically different interpretations of Durrell's poetry.

The "biographical heresy", however, has lost some of its pejorative force in contemporary criticism. Marina MacKay, for example, is a professor of English at St Peter's College, University of Oxford. In her recent book, *Ian Watt: The Novel and the Wartime Critic* (2018), she argues for what is essentially a biographical approach to literary interpretation, as evidence in the work of the great literary critic, Ian Watt (1917-1999). Watt was a British officer during the Second World War and a prisoner of war of the Japanese for three-and-a-half years. He spent much of that time in Thailand in Japanese prison camps, which provided forced labour for the construction of the Burma-Thailand Railway and possibly the notorious "Bridge on the River Kwai". Years later after the war, as a scholar, Watt wrote what is probably the best critical study of the early English novel, *The Rise of the Novel: Studies in Defoe, Richardson and Fielding* (1957). MacKay shows how Watt's wartime experience influenced his writings in a reticent, "stiff-upper-lip" manner.[39] She also quotes from the Preface to William Empson's *Seven Types of Ambiguity* (1947). The quote provides a neat comment on one kind of literary interpretation: "There is always an

---

[36] Wimsatt, *Verbal Icon*, p. 10: "Yet there is danger of confusing personal and poetic studies; and there is the fault of writing the personal as if it were poetic".

[37] *Critical Tradition*, p. 728.

[38] Levin, "Implication of Explication", p. 101. Original italics.

[39] MacKay, *Ian Watt*, p. 42: "Perhaps it is not surprising that Watt's war experience is largely unspoken in his published work: he was a critic rather than a creative writer, after all. But this special kind of reticence seems to me attributable in part to his membership of a generation of mid-century British literary critics who were never attracted to contemporary dogmas about the irrelevance of the writer's intentions and the critic's ability to interpret them, but, on the contrary, expected from serious readers a high level of what we now call emotional intelligence".

appeal to a background of human experience which is all the more present
when it cannot be named".[40] That statement exemplifies the work of Ian
Watt. It also applies to Michael Haag's biographical interpretation of the
work of Lawrence Durrell.

X. Biographical Poetry: "The Tree of Idleness"

"Biographical poetry" is my term. It is awkward, and Haag did not use it.
Beyond his emphasis on biography, he never used a specific term for his
idea. I don't know if he ever formulated one. True, some may object —
Durrell writes highly personal poetry — so what? Biological poetry may be
simply an alternative term for lyric poetry — and a clumsy one at that. Many
of Durrell's poems are indeed lyrics: a short poem where a solitary speaker
expresses some particular feeling, such as the aubade, "This Unimportant
Morning" (1944). Also, the Greek poet Sappho wrote lyric poetry, and
Durrell greatly admired the "Tenth Muse". He named his second daughter
after her. But lyric poetry was clearly not what Haag had in mind. As
previously mentioned, he saw biographical poetry as the "release" and
encryption of some deep anxiety, resulting in the poetic artifact, as Durrell
himself expresses in "Cities, Plains and People I" (1943), "Until your pain
become a literature". Perhaps "psychic poetry" is less cumbersome and
more appropriate, if not entirely satisfactory.

Durrell's great poem "The Tree of Idleness" is not easy to
understand. Durrell wrote the poem during his years on Cyprus (1953-
1956), and it became the title of an important book: *The Tree of Idleness
and other poems* (1955). I choose this poem because Haag saw Durrell's
three years on Cyprus as crucial to his development as poet and person. In
those years, Durrell was very productive as a creative artist. At the same
time, his private life was in turmoil and underwent substantial changes. This
poem reflects outward and inward circumstances.

I will not give an extended analysis to this poem. Isabelle Keller-
Privat has already provided a thorough literary analysis in her recent book
on Durrell's poetry. She has many good things to say about Durrell and his
poetry; this is especially true in the way she brings in the French poet Paul
Valéry (1871-1945) to illuminate her points on the "dream process".[41] She
also cites to good effect French Symbolists such as Charles Baudelaire
(1821-1867), Arthur Rimbaud (1854-1891), and Stéphane Mallarmé (1842-
1898). But her close analysis of "The Tree of Idleness" is essentially in the

---

[40] Empson, *Seven Types of Ambiguity*, p. 16.
[41] Keller-Privat, *Lawrence Durrell's Poetry*, pp. 130-36; p. 133 on Valéry.

mode of Formalism or New Criticism. She sticks primarily to the text itself and has little to say about its interaction with Durrell's personal life and struggles beyond noting, "the outer and the inner rift, the historical and the personal".[42] In the end, her interpretation of the poem is sanguine ("Anxiety is eventually annihilated in the second half of the poem"),[43] whereas Haag most probably did not see any indication of the cessation of anxiety. Just the opposite. He saw Durrell's vision and disposition as fundamentally bleak. As previously noted, Haag rejected the Formalist approach in favour of a biographical interpretation. So, I will concentrate on a few of Durrell's puzzling images and attempt to show how Haag treated them — or might have treated them.

I quote "The Tree of Idleness" in full. It is a fairly short poem of seven quatrains and one final line, twenty-nine lines in all. Six of the quatrains have rhymes at the end of the first and last lines, thus locking the lines of each quatrain together. This pattern seems to be broken with the last quatrain and the final line. I will argue that the last quatrain (ll. 25-28) is a deliberate deception in the sense that its arrangement on the page is misleading. The actual quatrain contains lines 26-29.

The Tree of Idleness

I shall die one day I suppose
In this old Turkish house I inhabit:
A ragged banana-leaf outside and here
On the sill in a jam-jar a rock-rose.   4

Perhaps a single pining mandolin
Throbs where cicadas have quarried
To the heart of all misgiving and there
Scratches on silence like a pet locked in.   8

Will I be more or less dead
Than the village in memory's dispersing
Springs, or in some cloud of witness see,
Looking back, the selfsame road ahead?   12

By the moist clay of a woman's wanting,
After the heart has stopped its fearful
Gnawing, will I descry between
This life and that another sort of haunting?   16

[42] Keller-Privat, *Lawrence Durrell's Poetry*, p. 134.
[43] Keller-Privat, *Lawrence Durrell's Poetry*, p. 133.

No: the card-players in tabs of shade
Will play on: the aerial springs
Hiss: in bed lying quiet under kisses
Without signature, with all my debts unpaid   20

I shall recall nights of squinting rain,
Like pig-iron on the hills: bruised
Landscapes of drumming cloud and everywhere
The lack of someone spreading like a stain.   24

Or where brown fingers in the darkness move,
Before the early shepherds have awoken,   26
Tap out on sleeping lips with these same
Worn typewriter keys a poem imploring

Silence of lips and minds which have not spoken.   29

The physical location of "The Tree of Idleness" is clear. Durrell's
note states: "The title of this book is taken from the name of the tree which
stands outside Bellapaix Abbey in Cyprus, and which confers the gift of
pure idleness on all who sit under it".[44] The "old Turkish house" refers to
the house Durrell purchased and refurbished in Bellapaix, a village located
in the hills above Kyrenia. In his memoir *Bitter Lemons* (1957), Durrell's
description of both house and Bellapaix provides some of the imagery used
in the poem: "banana-leaves", "the mournful whining of a mandolin", and
an early morning departure "at about half past four", when "I rose […] with
the shepherds and scrambled down to the Abbey".[45]

What is not clear, indeed puzzling, is Durrell's psychic landscape
as expressed in the imagery of lines such as "On the sill in a jam-jar a rock
rose" (l. 4) and "Or where brown fingers in the darkness move" (l. 25). Haag
gave these images a biographical reading — both "jam-jar" and "rock rose"
as being cryptic references to Durrell's young daughter Sappho Jane (1951-
1985), who is unnamed and who was then about three or four. In 1955, the
approximate time of the poem's composition, Durrell was under considerable
stress. He and his wife Eve had a stormy marriage. In mid-August 1955,
Eve leaves Durrell for London and takes her daughter with her.[46] The poem
suppresses or condenses a tumultuous situation into a few images.

---

[44] L. Durrell, *Tree of Idleness*, p. 7.
[45] *BL* 56 and 126. As Keller-Privat points out, this early awakening is also mentioned
in Durrell's letter of about November 1953 to Henry Miller. See Keller-Privat,
Lawrence Durrell's Poetry, p. 135. See also *DML* 275.
[46] Chamberlin, *Durrell Log*, p. 103.

Haag interpreted the "jam-jar" containing a "rock-rose" as the invention of a child, one who sleeps with her father and whose "brown fingers" come from playing in the sun. To prove his point, he could have further examined the poem's structure. Line 25, which contains those "brown fingers", is dislocated. It is not part of the poem's overall structure of seven quatrains, for the rhymes "awoken" and "spoken" define the final quatrain, lines 26 through 29. You might call line 25 an "orphan" — it is separated from the matrix of the poem, from its family of quatrains, if you will — and it suggests two meanings: Durrell as orphan and Sappho Jane as one.

The orphan as literary trope occurs frequently in *The Alexandria Quartet*. The trope ranges from an association with several characters to the final comparison of turning the entire city of Alexandria into an "orphanage".[47] Becoming an orphan had traumatic consequences in Durrell's personal history. During times of stress, as during the start of the journey in Sicily in 1975, he compared himself to becoming an orphan: "All my journeys start with a kind of pang of anxious doubt—you feel yourself suddenly an orphan" (*SC* 21). He surely felt himself an orphan when he was forced to take the journey of leaving India at age eleven, and now his daughter will become half an orphan after she is separated from her father. Given the prevalence of this trope in Durrell's oeuvre, Haag would have looked for a generalization, an overriding principle, which lay behind this odd imagery and structure in "The Tree of Idleness". He would try to explain the origin of Durrell's impulse that "you feel yourself suddenly an orphan".

So, as he may have argued, the childish imagery in "The Tree of Idleness" conceals a "pining" (l. 5) for the innocence of childhood. This accounts for the references to "banana-leaves" and a "pining mandolin", both of which evoke Durrell's childhood in India. At his first visit to the house in Bellapaix, Durrell describes a storm which suggests the stirring of early memories of India. Then he was "stirred by a vague interior premonition which I could not put exactly into words" (*BL* 56).

The "idleness" of the title also evokes childhood innocence. Durrell's poem "Cities, Plains and People I" begins with the line, "Once in idleness was my beginning". Idleness is also a familiar Romantic and Victorian trope of childhood, along with, incidentally, the pleasure of eating jam. So, in "To My Sister" (1798), a grown-up Wordsworth tells Dorothy, "We'll give to idleness", and then they will enjoy the day like children free

---

[47] See the following pages in the *Quartet*: Nessim (30), Scobie (129, 719), Narouz (577), Mountolive (584), Darley and Clea (669), and Alexandria itself (732).

of "toiling reason" and constraints. And so George Eliot describes a young Maggie Tulliver in *The Mill on the Floss*: "Maggie didn't know Tom was looking at her: she was seesawing on the elder bough, lost to almost everything but a vague sense of jam and idleness."[48]

Identifying Sappho Jane also opens the poem to an obvious comparison with the poetry of Sappho of Lesbos (c. 630-c. 570 BC). Greek Sappho was a major influence on Durrell. His second daughter bears her name, and he wrote a play about the poet, *Sappho: A Play in Verse* (1950).[49] Haag did not discuss this comparison, however. Nevertheless, "The Tree of Idleness" has similar Sapphic themes: death, love, loss, separation, remembrance. Durrell's likely source for Sappho's poetry was *The Oxford Book of Greek Verse in Translation* (1938).[50] From that collection, I emphasize "Parting" (pp. 208-09) and "Night" (p. 211). The editors and translators provide the titles of these poems. C. M. Bowra translates "Parting", and J. M. Edmonds translates "Night".

"The Tree of Idleness" moves towards solitude and loneliness, as also seen in Sappho's "Night" (fr. 168B) and its final line, "Alone I lie". Durrell's poem begins and ends in futurity (future tenses), with poetry or remembrance as the vehicle for immortality. In the second stanza of "Parting" (fr. 94), Sappho uses remembrance to similar effect: "To her I made reply: / 'Go with good heart, but try / Not to forget our love in days gone by.'" I see Durrell's final setting as a bed, which is also the case with Sappho's "Night", a poem which Durrell could have written or imitated:

> The Moon is gone
> And the Pleiads set,
> Midnight is nigh;
> Time passes on,
> And passes, yet
>   Alone I lie.

---

[48] Eliot, *The Mill on the Floss*, vol. 1, p. 79 (bk. 1, ch. 6).

[49] The play was originally titled *Sappho: The Tenth Muse*. See Vol. 2, p. 55 of *Lawrence Durrell's Endpapers and Inklings 1933-1988*.

[50] I thank Chancellor's Professor Andrew Stewart, Departments of History of Art and Classics, University of California, Berkeley, for suggesting Durrell's probable source: *The Oxford Book of Greek Verse in Translation* (1938). See also, *Greek Lyric I: Sappho and Alcaeus* (1982). "Parting" of the Oxford anthology is fr. 94 of the Harvard edition, and "Night" is fr. 168B. Although the one-line fr. 147 is not included in the Oxford anthology, it continues the theme of remembrance as immortality and appears in *Greek Lyric I*: "Someone, I say, will remember us in the future".

"Night" resembles Durrell's "Lesbos" (1953), the first poem in the collection *The Tree of Idleness*. Lesbos was of course the home of Sappho, and Durrell's "Lesbos" begins with "The Pleiades are sinking calm as paint" and ends with a speaker, presumably alone in bed and accompanied by "the dispiriting autumn moon". Sappho Jane and Sappho of Lesbos seem to share a similar identity, in Durrell's mind at least.

The Sapphic background of Durrell's "Lesbos" requires further explanation and, if I may, a short excursus into paleography. Sappho's "Night" surely appealed to Durrell because the tone is highly personal. Many scholars, however, have rejected fr. 168B as part of Sappho's corpus.[51] Ulrich von Wilamowitz-Moellendorf, Edgar Lobel, and Denys Page found the tone's intimacy, among other linguistic and historical considerations, alien to the genre of Greek lyric poets.[52] That rejection was in turn questioned with the discovery in 2004 of a second poem within fr. 58. Another papyrus fragment, found in the cartonnage of a Ptolemaic mummy from the Fayum Oasis southwest of Cairo, revealed the second poem, which is sometimes called "the Tithonus poem" because of the reference to the myth near its end.[53] In that poem, Sappho anguishes over the hardships of old age and speaks in a manner previously thought unlikely.[54] Durrell was probably unaware of the controversy over the authenticity of fr. 168B. But, since the Oxford anthology included the poem, I assume he considered it authentic and so chose to write his "Lesbos" as a

---

[51] *Greek Lyric I,* p. 173, n. 2: "ascription rejected by Wilamowitz, Lobel, Page".

[52] The arguments for and against fr. 168B are too detailed for my discussion. For a sample of the disagreements, see the exchange between Gomme, "Interpretations", pp. 255-66, and Page, "ΔΕΔΥΚΕ ΜΕΝ Ἁ ΣΕΛΑΝΑ", pp. 84-85. Gomme questions how fr. 168B, "which can charm most men's ears", could be "banished" from Sappho's corpus (p. 265). Page does not consider the fragment authentic but acknowledges the poem's "charm". His answer is technical and leaves unexplained why some scholars (Gomme, Higham, Bowra, and Anne Carson, poet and classicist) choose to ignore his argument that no linguistic "evidence" warrants the poem's inclusion in the Lesbian corpus (p. 84). In her *If Not, Winter: Fragments of Sappho* (2002), Anne Carson includes fr. 168B in Sappho's corpus, although she notes, "not included among Sappho's fragments by most modern editors" (p. 382). In my opinion, the irresistible "charm" of fr. 168B says something about Sappho herself, real or imagined, and deserves serious consideration.

[53] See M. West, "New Sappho Poem", p. 8. West provides a translation and commentary on Sappho's Lesbian-Aeolic Greek. He emphasizes, "In the new poem, however, the focus is on Sappho herself". See also, Carson, "Beat Goes On", 20 October 2005. Carson also provides commentary and translation. For an extensive analysis of the Tithonus poem, see *New Sappho on Old Age* (2009).

[54] I thank Professor Stewart for these comments.

Chapter Six

contribution to the Sapphic tradition in an equally personal mode, as he may have understood her poetry.

Aside from what Haag might have said, what he did say was that the message of "The Tree of Idleness" was encoded in its last line, namely, the poem is essentially a secret which Durrell wishes or "implore[es]" to be kept secret: "[I]t is a poem, one which is asking lips and minds to be silent — to give nothing away". In a privately printed monograph, *A Writer in Corfu*, Richard Pine asks the question, "What is a secret?" He answers, "A secret is a dark place that punctuates the process of transition from private ritual to public drama".[55] Durrell's use of the secret as a form of personal therapy follows this pattern but with one major qualification: his "public drama" — to wit, his published poetry — occasionally remains "dark" and obscure. Deliberately so. Haag recognized this paradox. In discussing Durrell's *Private Drafts* (1955), a collection of poems privately printed on Cyprus, Haag restated his analysis of Durrell's intent: "It is as though it is yet another way of saying yet not saying." "Saying yet not saying" is just another way to encrypt feelings.

Haag's idea of Durrell's silence at the end of this poem is radically different from Keller-Privat's. Haag sees silence as a way for Durrell to impose some kind of equanimity; Keller-Privat sees Durrell's use of silence as an act of liberation. Haag sees Durrell exercising tight control over his feelings; Keller-Privat sees Durrell achieving peace, the "tender complicity of brotherly souls that give birth to the poem".[56] These are very different interpretations stemming from very different critical approaches.

Poetry as encryption brings up again the story of Daphne du Maurier's *Rebecca*. The Germans used her novel as an encryption pad for passing messages through radio traffic. Haag was fascinated by this process; he studied the literature describing the incident (e.g., Ken Follett's novel, *The Key to Rebecca* [1980]). And, when he analyzed "Tree of Idleness", he duplicated (unintentionally) the sound of a radio operator tapping out Morse code:

> Referring to the stanza beginning with 'No', Durrell (or the persona if you like) says what 'I shall' do. I shall lie in bed etc. I shall recall nights, etc. I shall *tap* out, etc. He places the word 'or' between the second and the third, so that it could read I shall lie in bed, I shall recall nights, or I shall *tap* out, so that as an alternative to lying in bed, recalling nights, instead I shall *tap* out. And what he *taps* out is a poem.[57]

---

[55] Pine, *Writer in Corfu*, p. 23.
[56] Keller-Privat, *Lawrence Durrell's Poetry*, p. 136.
[57] Email 22 July 2007. My italics.

Haag refers to the tapping of "typewriter keys" mentioned in lines 27 and 28. The tapping, however, could equally apply to a telegraph key tapping out code.

It remains largely moot, however, whether or not Durrell himself was aware of this possibility. He was in Egypt at the time of the German espionage plot, but I cannot find him making any references to du Maurier's *Rebecca*. On the other hand, Durrell clearly knew about cryptography and codes based on literary texts; for, in *White Eagles over Serbia* (1957), also written on Cyprus around the troubled times of "The Tree of Idleness", he describes his protagonist Methuen using Thoreau's *Walden* as a "private code".[58] Once again, Durrell's "private code" could also apply to his own poetics.

Methuen is a secret agent and a man of derring-do. He is a fascinating character, and *White Eagles* is another of Durrell's "potboilers" written during a stressful period. It follows in the footsteps of *The Dark Labyrinth* (1947) and anticipates *Sicilian Carousel* (1977). Writing these "minor mythologies", as Richard Pine classifies these works,[59] might have enabled Durrell to indulge in a bit of escapism when he needed it most.

The spy and adventurer Methuen could have been modelled on Patrick Leigh Fermor, who, like Methuen, belonged to a Special Operations unit. Durrell and Leigh Fermor met in Egypt during the Second World War and became lifelong friends. Methuen could also be a projection of the type of bold figure Durrell wished himself to be. But this is just speculation. Whatever his motivation, Durrell knew about cryptography, he knew how it worked, and he left a small clue in a minor piece of fiction to show that he knew. As Haag commented in a different context, this is a subtle way of "saying yet not saying".

Finally, the metaphor of "a laborious private code", based on Durrell's very own words, is also a handy way to characterize Michael Haag's literary and biographical interpretation of the life of Lawrence Durrell. That "private code" Haag struggled to break, and it may have ultimately broken him. If you wrestle with the angel, you become like the angel — and you suffer the consequences.

Furthermore, as previously noted, I believe that Haag saw his traverse across the Mani as a kind of *agón*. He also viewed the writing of his planned biography of Lawrence Durrell as another *agón*, one which compares to Durrell's writing of his breakthrough novel, *The Black Book*.

---

[58] *WES* 28: "The book was *Walden* [...] out of which he [Methuen] had evolved a laborious *private code* for keeping in touch with Dombey". My italics. For date of composition, see Chamberlin, *Durrell Log*, p. 98.
[59] Pine, *Minor Mythologies*, pp. 411-16.

The Greek *agón,* however, was not an entirely glorious experience. Long ago Jacob Burckhardt (1818-1897) and recently Tobias Joho have noted that *agón* is directly related to *agony.* Joho comments on Burckhardt's idea of the "dark side" of the *agón* and writes, "While bright luster and nearly superhuman glory attached themselves to victors at the great athletic contests, they also suffered from psychic deformation induced by pent up suspense and enervating tension."[60] Joho subtitles his essay, "the dark luster of ancient Greece". "Dark luster" also resonates in the oeuvre of Lawrence Durrell, for the image — "dark crystal" — appears twice in *Prospero's Cell* (pp. 11 and 133) and once in the poem "Letter to Seferis the Greek" (1941). The effect is similar, a sense of revelation mixed with foreboding. And perhaps — just perhaps — Michael Haag experienced something similar to this dark description.

XI. Unfinished But Not Unimportant

I have not presented a full and complete account of Michael Haag's ideas about Lawrence Durrell. I am merely presenting some of his ideas as we discussed them in various contexts and situations. I was not always in accord with his views, for Haag and I had disagreements, some quite profound. (Haag was cautious and unwilling to push his arguments as far as I would on occasion.) But I am trying to be faithful to his various interpretations as I understand them and to his general line of argument as I see it. No doubt Haag would have disagreed with some of my points. That was the nature of our back-and-forth exchanges. Nevertheless, I also intend this memoir as a tribute to Haag's accomplishments. He radically changed my reading of Lawrence Durrell's works — he opened up new vistas — and I thank him for that opportunity, however belatedly.

If I may indulge in a metaphor which Haag may have approved of, this memoir is like the fate of the Great Library at Alexandria. After the loss of the library's contents, archivists and scholiasts gathered together the fragmented papyri and other surviving documents to form a corpus which barely hinted at the extent of its vast and vanished holdings. In a very small way, this is what I am doing.

Haag's biography of Lawrence Durrell was unfinished, but his research and developing interpretations should be made available to stimulate further discussion of these two writers — one great, the other important — Lawrence Durrell the poet and Michael Haag the historian.

---

[60] Joho, "Burckhardt and Nietzsche", p. 275.

In conclusion, I would like to repeat what Haag himself said of the painter and writer Sophie Atkinson, whom he championed: "I do think that people should be remembered for what they have contributed". And so should Michael Haag also be remembered.

Plate 1 Alexandria, the White City (licenced by Alamy on 16 October 2021)

Plate 2 Ambron Tower (© Michael Haag, 2004)

Plate 3 David Green (left) and Michael Haag (right) (© Denise Tart, 2015)

Plate 4 Haag's Garden Mirror (© Denise Tart, 2015)

Plate 5 *Fowling in the Marshes* (British Museum EA 37977; reproduced by courtesy of the British Museum)

Plate 6 *Cleopatra on the Terraces of Philae* (1896) (Frederick Arthur Bridgman. Wikimedia Commons)

Plate 7 Tomb of the Diver, ca. 470 BC (National Archaeological Museum of Paestum. © Michael Johanning, 2001. Wikimedia Commons)

PART THREE:

DURRELL'S ART

Introduction to Part Three

In his conversation with Eckermann on 2 April 1829, Goethe famously said, "I call the classic *healthy*, the romantic *sickly*".[1] Thomas Mann further developed this idea and applied it to German Romanticism. He believed that the Romantic artist was essentially diseased, that he suffered from an abnormal condition separating him from the lot of most men. Mann's art — works such as *Death in Venice* (1912), *The Magic Mountain* (1924), and *Doctor Faustus* (1947) — explore this theme in various ways. Mann's particular diagnosis of creativity is especially true of Lawrence Durrell. For his great achievement as an artist is directly connected to what might be called a study of his special abnormality. Durrell may have considered himself a postmodern writer, but his roots were strongly indebted to English and American Romanticism in their flirtation with romantic irony (or authorial fabulation) and Romantic notions of incest, sexuality, death, and the Gothic. We have already seen some of these motifs at work in Durrell's literary treatment of George Gordon Byron, Emily Brontë, and Edgar Allan Poe. The following essays will look at Lawrence Durrell's art in terms of the fabulation of his own identity and his ability to rework Virgilian pastoral and ancient Egyptian art to suit his own needs.

---

[1] Goethe, *Conversations*, p. 305. Original italics.

CHAPTER SEVEN

FABULATION[1]

Lawrence Durrell's *Sicilian Carousel* (1977) is generally held in low esteem. Durrell himself calls it "fabricated and pot boiled", and Ian MacNiven concurs in his definitive biography.[2] Moreover, Richard Pine in his *Mindscape* calls it "the weakest of his 'island portraits'".[3] I disagree with these opinions, so I'll provide some remarks defending the book's merits. I base this defence on a rejection of what Durrell dismisses as "fabricated". If fabrication is to be taken seriously as criticism, then much of his nonfiction should also be rejected. Durrell was a fabulator. He was a compulsive storyteller in both senses of the word, both raconteur and liar, intentional or not. Yvette Cohen, his second wife, found his stories "endlessly fascinating and amusing", according to Michael Haag, but she also said that although "'he would make things up on the spur of the moment to suit the occasion, he believed what he said'".[4] Or did he? How could she know what he thought? What is certain is that Durrell was a master of adapting to various situations — fabrication served his personal needs.

I would like to look at *Sicilian Carousel* as a *summa*, that is, as a summation of Durrell's personal anxieties as they become infused in a Mediterranean landscape. This is a different "spirit of place", a true "island of the mind". I am not treating the book as travel literature, as a journey full of interesting places, peoples, and experiences. Examples of *summa* in English literature include the Old English *Beowulf*, Chaucer's *Canterbury Tales*, and Joyce's *Ulysses*. They encapsulate an age. Yes, this is heady company and a lot to claim for Durrell's small book. But bear with me. I limit my claim to Durrell himself, who encompasses a world, if not an age.

Summa means the summation of a tradition. Durrell has Martine use the word to summarize her experiences on Sicily. More on Martine later.

---

[1] Originally published as "Remarks on *Sicilian Carousel* and Its Fabulator" in *Islands of the Mind: Psychology, Literature and Biodiversity*, edited by Richard Pine and Vera Konidari (Newcastle-upon-Tyne: Cambridge Scholars Publishing, 2020).
[2] MacNiven, *Lawrence Durrell*, p. 617.
[3] Pine, *Mindscape*, p. 54.
[4] Haag, *City of Memory*, p. 250.

She serves in this book as a kind of feminine *alter ego*. She's already dead when Durrell arrives on the island, but she remains alive through her letters. (These letters, by the way, Durrell "invented", as he confesses in Paul Hogarth's *The Mediterranean Shore* [1988].)[5] In one of the letters, Martine comments on the city of Taormina: "Taormina, the old Bull Mountain—I'm so glad I followed my instinct and saved it for the last. It was like a kind of *summation* of all that went before, all the journeys and flavours this extraordinary island had to offer" (*SC* 207; my italics).

How is *Sicilian Carousel* a *summa*? Let's begin with the title. Durrell is a poet who cherishes images and metaphors; for good reason he invents his own Heraldic Universe. A carousel is an amusement ride full of unusual creatures — gaily decorated horses, unicorns, dragons, and so on. So too Durrell's fellow travellers, all invented, are equally unusual, characters such as the British army veteran, the British Bishop, the English schoolmaster, the French couple, and the German blonde who walks naked in the moonlight. With the possible exception of Deeds, the army veteran, these are colourful types but not unique individuals. They are stock characters. Similar to Chaucer's array of type characters, Durrell offers a cross section of his European society. For example, near the top of the medieval social scale, we find Chaucer's Knight: "A KNYGHT ther was, and that a worthy man".[6] Befitting his high station, the knight appears first among the pilgrims in the General Prologue to *The Canterbury Tales*. In a similar fashion, Durrell's Colonel Deeds makes the first appearance of the author's travelling companions. Deeds is a worthy veteran of El Alamein, just as Chaucer's Knight is a worthy veteran of wars against the Muslims.[7] More on Deeds later.

Durrell conceives of a summation as a circle. His last book, *Caesar's Vast Ghost* (1990), concludes with the cryptic poem, "Le cercle refermé", which describes his own life as a closed circle. At the end of the poem, Durrell says his "last goodbye". These are in effect his dying words. Durrell's circle ends in death, and death, or anxieties about dying, permeates his work. The very title *Sicilian Carousel* suggests a circle, both as a carousel spinning on its axis and as a journey around the island. Durrell

---

[5] Hogarth, *Mediterranean Shore*, p. 100.

[6] Chaucer, *Riverside Chaucer*, p. 24 (I[A] 43).

[7] See Lawrence Durrell, *Constance* (1982), third novel of *The Avignon Quintet*. In a sense, Colonel Deeds also fought the infidel. In the vernacular of the Second World War, he fought "the Hun". Although Deeds does not use the term, a character in *Constance* says of the war against the Germans, "Our war against the Hun is just, and we must win it" (*Quintet* 642). *Hun* was surely part of Deeds's "lingo of El Alamein" (*SC* 24).

tours Sicily in a little red bus called the "Sicilian Carousel", and the path of the journey forms a circle rotating in a clockwise direction, beginning in Catania and ending in Taormina. The journey is the analogue of a clock beginning in the darkness of evening and ending in the twilight of dawn.

Carousel is an unusual word in Durrell's vocabulary. I cannot find it elsewhere in his prose or poetry. Its rarity suggests some special significance. According to MacNiven, Durrell did indeed travel around Sicily on an unnamed bus,[8] but I doubt the tour was called "Sicilian Carousel". The name is probably a disguise or screen. Perhaps it has childhood significance. I associate a carousel with childish play and pleasure, and childishness in its various forms permeates *Sicilian Carousel*.

J. D. Salinger's most famous book is *The Catcher in the Rye* (1951). As Brewster Chamberlin notes in his chronology of Durrell's life, Salinger's novel was one of the important books of 1951.[9] Salinger's title alludes to an anxiety about avoiding death — catching someone before he or she falls off a cliff. Near the end of the novel, the hero finds solace in riding a carousel in Central Park, New York City.[10] The trope of the carousel became Michael Mitchell's classic illustration for the first edition of the novel's dust jacket: a sketch outlines the fanciful figure of "a big, brown, beat-up looking old horse".[11] The image of the carousel "going round and round" dominates the ending,[12] and the story reconciles itself in the innocence of childhood. Perhaps Durrell's symbolic carousel has a similar function. Perhaps it has Freudian significance and deflects the morbid associations of a circle with childish merriment. So Durrell's title sets the tone for the book — one of lightheartedness mixed with sadness.

Durrell's tone is anxious but also relaxed, unpretentious, and self-deprecating. The first sentence of *Sicilian Carousel* begins offhandedly,

> As I explained to Deeds more than once during the course of our breakneck journey round Sicily in the little red coach, nobody has ever had better reasons than I for not visiting the island. (*SC* 17)

He then explains his hesitation by referring to Martine's death on Sicily. Deeds listens politely and then answers, "But you seem to be enjoying [the journey] very much". Poetry is largely about compression, and the opening paragraph compresses a great deal — avoidance as negation (not doing

---

[8] MacNiven, *Lawrence Durrell*, p. 617.

[9] Chamberlin, *Durrell Log*, p. 89.

[10] Salinger, *Catcher in the Rye*, pp. 224, 272.

[11] Salinger, *Catcher in the Rye*, p. 273.

[12] Salinger, *Catcher in the Rye*, p. 275.

something unwanted) — journey as "breakneck" speed (a suggestion of death) — journey as humorous "little red coach" (a comic deflection) — death as woman with a beautiful name (a euphemism for ugliness) — and finally Deeds's counter argument which deflates the narrator's seriousness. Thus, the opening tone suggests some vague anxiousness, but the author is still able to poke fun at himself. This is Durrell at his best. He's in full control of his anxiety.

This kind of self-control also concludes his book on Cyprus, *Bitter Lemons* (1957). The beautiful poem of the same name, "Bitter Lemons", summarizes three years of tumultuous events and experiences in only thirteen lines. Durrell's stay on Cyprus coincided with the violence of the Greek struggle to unite the island with the mainland and with the dissolution of his second marriage to Yvette (Eve) Cohen. The poem, however, is quiet. No sound of gunfire in the background and no suggestion of marital discord. The speaker — Durrell himself — stands on a headland overlooking the "Greek sea", a misnomer for the eastern Mediterranean, remembers the past without mentioning the past, and listens to the repetition of waves as they mimic the lines, "Keep its calms like tears unshed / Keep its calms like tears unshed" (*BL* 252).

Equanimity is also characteristic of pastoral poetry, Virgil's *Eclogues* in particular. Pastoral poetry creates an ideal environment (replete with shepherds, springs, and shady trees) in order to alleviate the troubles of the world. Death is among them. The traditional founder of this genre is Theocritus, who wrote his *Idylls* in Hellenistic Alexandria but set them in his native Sicily. Durrell knows this. He mentions Theocritus (*SC* 185) and makes a point of visiting the famous spring of Arethusa. Milton mentions this fountain in "Lycidas" (l. 85), a pastoral poem commemorating the death of a friend. Durrell's Arethusa, however, is cluttered with "a Coke bottle and a newspaper" (*SC* 85). Such is modern pastoral. He updates the convention, but the motif of death lingers. Death lurks in the pastoral landscape. The *topos* is called "*Et in Arcadia Ego*" ("Even in Arcadia there am I", where *I* refers to the personification of Death),[13] and it resounds throughout Durrell's world.

In *Sicilian Carousel*, Durrell follows many of the conventions of pastoral poetry, both in terms of atmosphere and personages. Pastoral abounds with spots of rural refuge. The technical term is *pleasance*. In Virgil's *Eclogues*, the bucolic scene typically begins during the heat of noon. Here is one of Durrell's descriptions:

---

[13] Panofsky, *Meaning in the Visual Arts*, p. 307.

> I walked a little way and entered a vineyard where I found a patch of grass, almost burned brown by the summer heat. Here I lay down in its warm crackling cradle, dislodging swarms of crickets which hardly ceased their whirring as they retreated. The earth smelt delicious, baked to a cinder. Ants crawled over my face. In my heat-hazed mind dim thoughts and dreams and half-remembered conversations jumbled themselves together as a background to this throbbing summer afternoon with the cicadas fiddling away like mad in the trees. (*SC* 122)

The scene is Virgilian, but Durrell also alludes to Aesop's fable of the ant and the cicada (no. 140). Aesop sides with the industrious ant, who toils during the summer while the cicada fiddles away, whereas Durrell finds himself pestered by ants as he dreams to the background music of cicadas. Of the two insects and their symbolic roles, Durrell was definitely a cicada or a cricket, an image occurring throughout his poetry and prose. The opening to *Justine* includes the poetic line: "A sky of hot nude pearl until midday, crickets in sheltered places" (*Quartet* 17).

Another device used by Theocritus and Virgil is the dialogue between two shepherds. They engage in verbal contests. Durrell doesn't employ duelling shepherds, but he does carry on a friendly competition with his travelling companion Colonel Deeds, a veteran of Montgomery's Eighth Army, who "speaks the lingo of El Alamein" (*SC* 24). Deeds is one of Durrell's many *alter ego*s. Deeds, as his name indicates, is practical. He is like Aesop's industrious ant. He is a down-to-earth, no-nonsense guy. Moreover, he is literally down-to-earth because he works for the Allied Graves Commission, which tracks down war dead from the Second World War (*SC* 24). *Et in Arcadia Ego.*

The pastoral world is small and confined to a narrow space and a few characters. The main players gather together from elsewhere, but they are not real strangers. They share common experiences. Durrell's minibus travelling around the home of pastoral poetry conforms to this literary convention. The convention is an old one — Chaucer's pilgrims on the way to Canterbury come to mind — and it may seem contrived or "fabricated", but I will suspend my disbelief and grant the author this implausible plot. This convention is especially true of the characterizations of Durrell himself and Deeds. So, Deeds and Durrell were in Cairo together during the war, and they were both on Cyprus during the struggle for *enosis*, unification with the Greek mainland. Although they never met, they knew the same people and places. And what they especially have in common is Martine, Durrell's close friend from Cyprus, whom Deeds calls "a good-looking blonde", who is also "rich" and "spoiled" (*SC* 25). Leave it to Deeds the blunt veteran to say what Durrell the discreet writer will not.

Martine is a crucial element in this version of Durrell's pastoral world. Her characterization is based on Marie Millington-Drake, whom Durrell met on Cyprus in 1953 and who serves as a kind of muse for his fictional memoir. She was indeed "blonde", and blondeness is a distinctive feature among Durrell's women, real and fictional. Two real-life examples include Nancy Myers, his first wife, and Claude-Marie Vincendon, his third wife. And then there are those two women whose names become the titles of novels: Clea of *The Alexandria Quartet* and Constance of *The Avignon Quintet*. Durrell was drawn to Millington-Drake, but, according to MacNiven, he called her — to her face no less — "crazy and shallow".[14] He knew a serious relationship with her would never work. Nevertheless, she gets mentioned many times in *Bitter Lemons*. She flits in and out of the story like a gorgeous nymph. Notwithstanding Deeds's criticism of Martine, this mercurial aspect of Millington-Drake is not exactly what gets portrayed in *Sicilian Carousel*.

In Sicily, Martine is beautiful and elusive, but Durrell's sense of her death seems disproportionate to the person he knew on Cyprus. I would argue that Martine is a highly idealized version of Marie Millington-Drake, on whom Durrell could project his feelings of death and loss. I loosely use "project" as the psychoanalytic concept of transferring one's personal feelings onto another person or thing.

Why the projection? In one of his poems, "Cities, Plains and People" (1946), Durrell uses the phrase "Until your pain become a literature" (*CP* 159). It is fairly easy to identify pain in Durrell's life. Aside from being torn from the India of his childhood, he suffered numerous personal losses beginning with the death of his father in India, a broken first marriage to Nancy Myers, another broken marriage to Yvette Cohen, and the untimely death of his beloved Claude-Marie Vincendon. How these events "become a literature" is more complicated.

I propose this hypothesis. Durrell is at heart a mythmaker. He is like William Blake, one of his favourite poets, but unlike Blake he creates his own mythology in an attempt to deal with personal anxieties. I see this as connected in some strange way to his notion of the Heraldic Universe. As I said before, he thinks in images and metaphors, but I'm uncertain as to how much control he has over this process. His use of myth and pastoral illustrates this problem. In *Sicilian Carousel*, Durrell addresses the deceased Martine and speculates on the nature of the Greek garden in Homer's *Odyssey* (*Od.* 7, 114-16). Gardens are an aspect of pleasance. Durrell comments, "In the culture which followed [the garden landscape], each

---

[14] MacNiven, *Lawrence Durrell*, p. 405.

plant and flower had its story, its link with the mythopœic inner nature of man—which he can only realise when he has a chance to dream" (*SC* 70). Durrell may think his dreams are idyllic, but underneath they are nightmares.

Consider how he uses Martine in his narrative. Like Edgar Allan Poe, Durrell indulges himself in the myth of the death of a beautiful woman. Poe linked death and beauty: "The death [...] of a beautiful woman is, unquestionably, the most poetical topic in the world".[15] The linkage develops the Neo-Classical or Romantic notion of "the sublime" as both exalting and terrifying.[16] In the Romantic reworking of this myth, Dante's Beatrice fits the profile, so too Shakespeare's Cleopatra. Martine, however, is closer to Shakespeare's heroine in maturity and "infinite variety" (*Ant.* 2.2.248).

Ralph Waldo Emerson called Poe "The Jingle Man", a term which derisively referred to Poe's penchant for rhymes of the nursery variety and, possibly, for nursery tales.[17] His love poem "Annabel Lee", his last poem, begins like a fairy tale and immediately enters a fairy landscape:

> It was many and many a year ago,
>   In a kingdom by the sea,
> That a maiden there lived whom you may know
>   By the name of Annabel Lee;—
> And this maiden she lived with no other thought
>   Than to love and be loved by me.[18]

Poe concludes "Annabel Lee" with the image of the poet and his childlike bride lying together:

> And so, all the night-tide, I lie down by the side
> Of my darling—my darling—my life and my bride,
>   In the sepulchre there by the sea—
>   In her tomb by the sounding sea.[19]

---

[15] Poe, *Essays and Reviews*, p. 19.

[16] Edmund Burke (1729-1797) provides a classic description on the relationship between the sublime and terror. See Burke, *Philosophical Enquiry*, 58 (Pt. II, Sec. IV).

[17] See McGann, *Edgar Allan Poe*, pp. 1 and 183-98. McGann mentions Emerson's famous dig and discusses "the Dantean myth of Beatrice" in the context of Poe's "Annabel Lee".

[18] Poe, *Poetry and Tales*, p. 102.

[19] These final four lines appear in an earlier version of the poem, as published in *Selected Writings of Edgar Allan Poe* [1956], p. 47. I assume Durrell kept this version in mind when he developed the image of "the sighing of the sea" below.

The scene is Gothic. Annabel is quite possibly a model for Martine. Both have the qualities of innocent children inhabiting a dreamscape. After her death, Martine rests in a similar state of repose, as Durrell recalls:

> Somewhere she said that she had given instructions to her lawyers to let her lie in state one whole night on the beach at Naxos, close to the sea, so that like a seashell she could absorb the sighing of the sea and take it with her wherever she was going. (*SC* 212)

Durrell's scene is similar to Poe's conclusion to "Annabel Lee". The similarities are no coincidence, for Durrell's second daughter, Sappho Jane (1951-1985), notes in her diary that her father could on occasion "improvise a Poe-like story".[20] Sappho's specific occasion, undated, was when the pair visited the grave of Durrell's third wife, his beloved Claude-Marie Vincendon.

Martine's characterization is both mythic and ambivalent. On one level she is a romanticized version of Marie Millington-Drake, but on another she resembles Ariadne of the Theseus myth. Both women are blondes, so Deeds describes Martine as one and so Hesiod describes Ariadne as another in the *Theogony*.[21] As Durrell knows, blondeness is a prominent attribute of women in folktales (Cinderella and Goldilocks) and popular culture. Hence the proverb, "Gentlemen prefer blonds [sic]".[22]

These physical attributes, however, are both cultural and historical. Durrell was a poet whose linguistic sensibilities exceeded his historical sense. Not surprisingly, he distorts prehistory when he speculates on the origin of the ancient Greek fondness for gold and golden hair:

> Why, the notion of gold being valuable may well have come from the first golden Aryan head which the Greeks saw, with its marvelous buttercup sheen. The men went mad over this hypothetical girl—Circassian or Scythian or British perhaps? Gentlemen preferred blondes even then. […] The story of Goldilocks. (*SC* 137)

Although "buttercup sheen" is a vivid image, there are several problems with this account. Namely, it is wrong, outdated, and ahistorical. Durrell's "Aryan" is a superseded term of the 19th and early 20th centuries, which took on pejorative connotations when the Nazis used it to define a racial type in the 1930s. The current term is *Indo-European*, and it applies either to a large

---

[20] S. Durrell, *Journals and Letters*, p. 58.
[21] Hesiod, *Theogony*, p. 79 (sec. 947). Durrell read Hesiod. He cites the *Theogony* in *The Greek Islands* (*GI* 32 and 66).
[22] Whiting, *Modern Proverbs*, p. 250 (G28).

language family or to an ethnic group probably originating in the Pontic-Volga steppes of Russia.[23]

Durrell's usage refers to the Indo-European intrusion of "charioteering invaders", which occurred around 1600 BC.[24] The Indo-Europeans were in fact the "Greeks" who replaced an indigenous society which Marija Gimbutas (1921-1994) calls "Old Europe".[25] Moreover, Gustaf Kossinna (1858-1931), a German linguist and prehistorian, helped to give *Aryan* racist connotations. He notoriously characterized the Aryans ("his *Germani*") as a "blonde race" epitomizing the "Nordic ideal".[26] In the early nineteenth century, a "popular choice" for the Aryan homeland was in the region of the Himalayan Mountains.[27]

Durrell's brief account of "the first golden Aryan head" reflects antiquated notions of the Aryans and also reveals his own predilections but without, I strongly emphasize, racist overtones. For two of his wives were Jewish, and he correctly refers to "the new Aryan order" as Nazi propaganda in *Constance* (*Quintet* 612). I assume his usage in *Sicilian Carousel* is innocent, although predisposed to the exotic, which is a hallmark of his style and vocabulary. The account is also self-reflexive. Durrell himself had sandy hair, was born in India, and had a lifelong attachment to the "stupendous peaks of the Himalayas".[28] So did he see himself as a blond Aryan intruder? His geographic chain of associations begins in northern India (putative home of the "Aryan") and ends in Britain ("British perhaps"). In *The Alexandria Quartet*, Ludwig Pursewarden, writer and diplomat like his creator, is another of Durrell's *alter ego*s. Pursewarden is blond, bearer of a good Germanic first name, and his mysterious epitaph reads, "Here lies an intruder from the East" (*Quartet* 383.)

Theseus is another kind of intruder. With Ariadne's help, he slays the Minotaur in the Cretan labyrinth and ends a Minoan myth. Theseus and Ariadne flee Crete, and he later abandons her on Naxos, the main island of the Cyclades. In classical sources, the myth is ambiguous. Theseus either abandons Ariadne deliberately or at the command of the gods.[29]

Now, allow me to speculate. Martine dies in Sicilian Naxos, and the poem "Autumn Lady" — subtitled "Naxos" — comes near the end of *Sicilian Carousel*. Sicilian Naxos is next to Taormina, which Martine calls

---

[23] Gimbutas, "Proto-Indo-European Culture", p. 190.

[24] Drews, *Coming of the Greeks*, p. 159.

[25] Gimbutas, *Goddesses and Gods*, p. 17.

[26] Veit, "Ethnic Concepts", p. 38.

[27] Anthony, *Horse, Wheel, and Language*, pp. 9, 48.

[28] MacNiven, *Lawrence Durrell*, p. 1.

[29] *Oxford Classical Dictionary*, p. 150, s.v. *Ariadne*.

"Bull Mountain". That designation is a fair etymology of the place name.[30] The toponym *Taormina*, however, also suggests a folk etymology, an inversion of *Minotaur*, resulting in "bull of Minos" or "Minoan bull". *Taormina* as an inversion of *Minotaur* sounds like an uncanny reference to the Minoan Labyrinth. Sicilian Naxos and Greek Naxos are not close; they are about five hundred miles apart. But Durrell emphasizes the Minoan connection the moment he sees Sicily from the air:

> From so high one could see the lateral tug of the maindeep [sic] furling and unfurling its waters along those indomitable flanks of the island. And all below lay bathed in a calm green afterglow of dusk. It looked huge and sad and slightly frustrated, like a Minoan bull—and at once the thought clicked home. Crete! Cyprus! (*SC* 18)

This is a fine example of free association. Durrell's thought processes are highly associative and owe a lot to Freud's description of "the laws of association" in *The Interpretation of Dreams*.[31] Recall the phrase "the iron chains of memory" at the beginning of *Justine* (*Quartet* 17). So, Durrell mixes, deliberately or not, his geography of Sicily and Greece. Then follows a question: If Martine is some version of Ariadne, is Durrell some version of Theseus?

I am again speculating, but it's a fact that Durrell was interested in the idea of the "confluence" of cultures and traditions. As he states in an interview with the *Paris Review* in 1960, "Eastern and Western metaphysics are coming to a point of confluence in the most interesting way".[32] Allow me to generalize on Durrell's use of "confluence". In the Theseus myth, Ariadne is the daughter of King Minos of Crete. Minoan Crete was a non-Indo-European civilization with a separate culture, which was considered, largely under the influence of Sir Arthur Evans (1851-1941), the excavator of Knossos, as sophisticated and peaceful. In *Knossos & the Prophets of Modernism* (2009), Cathy Gere argues that Minoan civilization (c. 3500-c. 1100 BC) represented a "beatnik Eden" in the 1950s. She dismisses Evans's representation of the Minoan Age as a *"Pax Minoica"*.[33]

This view of Minoan peace and florescence, however, was subsequently challenged in 1979 and afterwards. Archaeologists then began

---

[30] See *Antonio Sciaretta's Toponymy*. Taor < Siculian 'bull' (Lat. *tauros*); mina < Siculian 'mount' (Lat. *mons*). http://www.asciatopo.altervista.org/sicilia.html.

[31] Freud, *Standard Edition*, vol. 4, pp. 58-59.

[32] L. Durrell, "Art of Fiction", p. 57.

[33] Gere, *Knossos*, pp. 209 and 223. "In the 1950s ancient Crete was reinvented as a beatnik Eden of creative spontaneity and existential joy" (p. 209).

to view Minoan civilization as warlike or "militaristic".[34] But that is not how Durrell must have thought of Crete when writing *Sicilian Carousel* in 1975. His idea of Minoan Crete was probably based upon Evans's view — a culture of refined art and peaceful coexistence[35] — but one which also had a bull ritual. Durrell does not mention Evans directly, but he does allude to the "Villa Ariadne", Evans's famous headquarters located near the ruins at Knossos. Durrell attaches the name to a Sicilian villa belonging to "Loftus Adam" (*SC* 137). That personal name is another fabrication, an imperfect anagram for "Norman Douglas". (Imperfection is an aspect of Durrell's poetics — note the desultory rhymes of "Bitter Lemons".) Loftus, as he is usually called, is a character clearly based on Norman Douglas (1868-1952), the author of *South Wind* (1917).

Douglas and Loftus are a pair of Durrell's "islomanes". As Durrell first presents this idea in *Reflections on a Marine Venus* (1953), islomanes suffer from "islomania" and "find islands somehow irresistible" (*RMV* 15). Durrell reprises *islomanes* and *islomania* in *Sicilian Carousel* (*SC* 19 and 209), but he does not explain their emotional basis, namely, that they pertain to places of refuge. Loftus embodies this theme. Douglas lived on Capri in the Gulf of Naples and devoted his life to art and refined sensibilities. Similarly, Loftus was also a "relic of the Capri epoch" (*SC* 210). That epoch was peaceful — although "a trifle precious" (*SC* 209) — a brief interlude between two world wars. In 1950, during his unhappy days working in the British embassy in Belgrade, Durrell enjoyed a similar interlude of peace and creativity when he visited the island of Ischia, also in the Gulf of Naples. There he met Norman Douglas, and there he wrote "Deus Loci", a long poem celebrating the "Spirit of Place".[36]

Loftus retires to Taormina, tends his garden, and translates "the classics". He lives in his "Villa Ariadne", which is a "delightful old house built on a little headland over the sea, and buried in roses" (*SC* 210). In her memoir *The Villa Ariadne*, Dilys Powell uses Evans's villa as a complex emblem of violence and peacefulness: "The Villa Ariadne has translated the refined savagery of Minos into the stuff of scholarly domestic repose. The Villa means quiet, the Villa means a retreat".[37] So, Durrell's Villa Ariadne

---

[34] Gere, *Knossos*, pp. 222-23.

[35] See *GI* 65. In *The Greek Islands*, Durrell wanders around the ruins of Knossos and reflects: "In these quiet precincts, which in fact may be simply administrative buildings, but which exhale the kind of equanimity and poise of an architecture at once beautifully proportioned and not too sweet, one feels the presence of a race that took life gaily and thoughtfully".

[36] MacNiven, *Lawrence Durrell*, pp. 368-69.

[37] Powell, *Villa Ariadne*, pp. 185, 189.

draws a connection between Sicily and Crete, between the myth of Theseus and Ariadne, between conflict and refuge.

Nothing in Lawrence Durrell is simple. He delights in paradox and antinomies or, as Justine quotes Darley, "the antinomian nature of irony" (*Quartet* 32). A paradox contains a contradiction; it is a kind of sustained conflict. And the resolution of conflict is also a part of Durrell's idea of confluence. If Ariadne represents peace, then Theseus represents aggression. He slays the Minotaur and terminates a myth. The Theseus myth is roughly contemporary with the late warrior culture of the Mycenaean Greeks (c. 1575-c. 1200 BC), who were the invading Indo-Europeans or Durrell's "golden Aryan[s]". Homer calls them "Achaeans", "Argives", or "Danai".[38] They are the Greeks who conquered Troy and Minoan Crete. From his early days on Corfu, Durrell saw himself as one of the "Hellenes", the traditional term for *Greeks* (*PC* 23). Thus, Martine as Ariadne and Durrell as Theseus may have represented, in Durrell's mind at least, the "confluence" of two cultures.

It's not hard to imagine Lawrence Durrell as a latter-day "Odysseus" or "Ulysses".[39] His lifelong travels in the Mediterranean are a kind of odyssey. In terms of personality, Odysseus and Durrell are also similar: wily, multifaceted, and polymorphous. In the introduction to her recent translation of the *Odyssey*, Emily Wilson says that an "essential aspect of Odysseus' [sic] multiplicity is his rhetorical ability and capacity for deceit". Wilson further notes that Odysseus "usually claim[ed] to have come from Crete—the traditional home of liars".[40] Odysseus's "capacity for deceit" is just another way to discuss Durrell's capacity for fabrication.

Crete had an enduring fascination for Durrell. His novel *The Dark Labyrinth* (1947) takes place on the island, and he devotes his longest chapter in *The Greek Islands* (1978) to Crete. Crete is the home of the

---

[38] *Oxford Classical Dictionary*, p. 656, s.v. *Hellenes*.

[39] Durrell uses Greek *Odysseus* (Ὀδυσσεύς) in *The Greek Islands* and Latin *Ulysses* (*Ulixes*) in *Sicilian Carousel*. In literature, both names refer to the same legendary figure, although some argue that historically the persons were different. (For the Latin variant, see *Oxford Latin Dictionary*, s.v. *Vlixes*.) This alteration in names may indicate Durrell's sensitivity to Greek and Latin areas of influence, or it may indicate that he was fully aware of the onomastics of the name, *Odysseus*. For a good discussion of the history and linguistics of *Odysseus*, see Stanford, *Ulysses Theme*, pp. 8 and 247 nn. 3 and 4.

[40] See Emily Wilson's introduction to her recent translation of Homer's *Odyssey* (Homer, *Odyssey*, p. 62). Wilson's comment on Odysseus's mendaciousness is correct but hardly new. For a short discussion of Odysseus as liar, see Plato's *Lesser Hippias* (Plato, *Complete Works*, pp. 924-25 [365b-c]). Hippias says, "Odysseus is wily and a liar".

Minotaur and its labyrinth. It is also the home of the prophet Epimenides (c. late 7th cent. BC), who is famous for his "Liar Paradox", often stated as "Cretans always lie". Since Epimenides was himself a Cretan, his statement is a paradox, that is, false if true and true if false. This paradox is complicated and has led to much philosophical discussion far beyond the scope of this essay.[41] It is likely, however, that Lawrence Durrell would have enjoyed such speculation, for he knew about the tradition of lying Cretans, as St. Paul recounts in his Epistle to Titus (1.12) (*GI* 60). Should we look at Durrell in this context when he claims that *Sicilian Carousel* is "fabricated"? Ian MacNiven has already cast suspicion on Durrell's numerous "claims" and the extent of his truthfulness.[42]

Versions of the Minoan bull recur in Durrell's writings. It is either dangerous, sacrificial, or playful. Bull sacrifice was also the dominant symbol of Mithraism, a Roman mystery religion. Martine's letters connect her to Mithraism and the Minotaur. In one, she compares the sun to "the mithraic animal plunge hissing into the sea". In another, she describes a situation "as if a human being were wrestling with the Minotaur and having all his bones crushed with the embrace" (*SC* 156). In *Caesar's Vast Ghost* (1990), Durrell's final book, he devotes Chapter IV to "Bull-worship" and admires the playfulness of Provençal bull fighting (*CVG* 50). In Provence, the bull is not killed, as in Spain, rather it participates in a game, which is not unlike Nikos Kazantzakis's idea of bull leaping in Minoan Crete. Kazantzakis calls it "the Cretan glance".[43]

The poem "Autumn Lady" comes near the end of *Sicilian Carousel*. Titles are important in Durrell. Autumn marks the downward turn of the seasons and defines the downward turn of this poem. As Durrell comments in *The Mediterranean Shore*, the Autumn Lady is Martine.[44] "Autumn Lady" is a beautiful poem, similar to "Bitter Lemons" in tone and method. The tone sad, the method elliptical. Personal details are not given; they must be inferred.

The poem describes a woman personified as a sunken ship "with two wide / Aegean eyes". Much of Durrell's imagery sinks deep into time: in particular, Greek and Latin history and ancient Egyptian history. The personification here evokes ancient ships of the classical age.[45] The image also recalls the mysterious description of Justine as "someone beautiful,

---

[41] For a brief history of the paradox, see Sorensen, *Paradox*, pp. 93-95.

[42] MacNiven, *Lawrence Durrell*, pp. 13, 14, 40.

[43] Kazantzakis, *Report to Greco*, p. 486. In the "Notes and sources" to *Caesar's Vast Ghost*, Durrell cites Kazantzakis's *Report to Greco*.

[44] Hogarth, *Mediterranean Shore*, p. 100.

[45] Carlson, "Seeing the Sea", pp. 347-65.

dark and painted with great eyes like the prow of some Aegean ship" (*Quartet* 286). Not only Greek ships have such eyes, mysterious women in Minoan frescoes also have "great eyes".[46] Was Durrell familiar with Cretan frescoes of the Bronze Age? Yes. He comments on Martine's love of roses, and of the rose itself, he notes, "Its history is as beautiful as its flower for it goes right back into the Age of Bronze as far as fresco paintings in Crete are concerned" (*SC* 71).

A crucial line in "Autumn Lady", however, is deeply personal: "She'll sink at moorings like my life did once".[47] The years prior to 1976 were desperate ones for Durrell. Chamberlin chronicles alcoholism, affairs, wife-beatings, and Claude-Marie's unburied ashes.[48] So, it's not surprising that Durrell can say his life had slipped its "moorings".

The final stanza is most poignant. The underwater scene of the sunken boat reminds me of the famous pool scene at the shrine of Saint Arsenius in *Prospero's Cell* (*PC* 16). And what happened there materializes here as an eerie, underwater seascape. It has the feeling of a bad dream. I sense that Durrell knows this. He knows he can't do again what he once did in *Prospero's Cell*, nor what Shakespeare was able to do in *The Tempest*. Durrell can't be the magician who transforms death, as in Ariel's song, "Full fathom five thy father lies; / Of his bones are coral made; / Those are pearls that were his eyes" (*Tp*. 1.2.395-97). The most that Durrell can do is exercise poetic control — as in the penultimate line — "Let the tides drum on those unawakened flanks" — a line which remind me of the repetitive ending to "Bitter Lemons" — "Keep its calms like tears unshed". I find that many of Durrell's best lyrics are laments.

The ship *Autumn Lady* personifies Martine, and she serves as Durrell's feminine *alter ego* throughout *Sicilian Carousel*. Her voice is actually Durrell's at its most poignant and suggestive. And her sensitivities are almost Shakespearean. In *Venus and Adonis* (1593), Shakespeare can even feel the pain of an animal as small as a snail: "Or as the snail, whose tender horns being hit, / Shrinks backward in his shelly cave with pain" (*Ven*. 1033-34). Martine has similar sympathies. When she hears the noise of someone or something in distress, she first imagines a person "wrestling with the Minotaur". Then she discovers a fox, a small animal, caught in an iron trap and describes it as "half mad with pain and fright and its bloodshot

---

[46] Higgins, *Minoan and Mycenaean Art*, ill. 103 and p. 203. Among the numerous depictions of women in this book, see the illustration of the "*Parisienne*", the profile of a Cretan woman with an enhanced eye, "1550-1450 [BC], from Knossos" (p. 203).

[47] I thank Michael Haag for pointing out the importance of this line.

[48] Chamberlin, *Durrell Log*, pp. 167-71.

eyes were almost bursting from their sockets" (*SC* 156). Durrell then resorts to a mixed metaphor — the fox's "groans" weigh "a ton". The pain of the "poor red fox" thus becomes both reified and mythologized. The rhetorical strategy is not incidental to her personality. For Durrell goes out of his way to emphasize the description. The incident consumes almost a full page of exposition.

The wrestling metaphor is apt and has other uses. Wrestling with angels or demons is not an unusual activity for many artists and writers. Van Gogh and Hemingway had their personal problems and many other artists as well. In Lawrence Durrell's case, the sport took the form of an elaborate ruse, of a way to conceal and to reveal — or of "saying yet not saying", as Michael Haag argued in Chapter Six above. In spite of the book's unlikely account of an organized tour around Sicily, *Sicilian Carousel* succeeds because of its faults, because of its gross fabrications. Even Durrell's mistakes have meaning and reveal his lifelong concerns. His misidentification of the Greeks and the Aryans says more about his own preferences than about the standard histories of these peoples. Durrell's journey is a kind of spiritual journey, somewhat like Chaucer's *Canterbury Tales.* It is a summation of inventions, fabrications, and attempts to circumvent deep anxieties. Durrell invents characters such as Deeds and Martine as substitutes for aspects of his own personality. These inventions act like buffers; they shield and hide the author's secrets. And when the buffer becomes too personal, too painful, too close to the truth, such as happens to Martine herself, then it becomes further removed and turned into the poem of the ship the *Autumn Lady*, which is just a personification of an invention, an abstraction of an abstraction. At the end, when Lawrence Durrell the fabricator "wrestles with the Minotaur", we may well ask, "And just what does the Minotaur represent, what does it really mean?" The secret, however, must remain a secret. So, Durrell's cryptic answer to that important question comes at the end of "Autumn Lady":

> Let the tides drum on those unawakened flanks
> Whom all the soft analysis of sleep will find.

CHAPTER EIGHT

PASTORAL[1]

I. Cartography

surgamus: solet esse gravis cantantibus umbra,
iuniperi gravis umbra; nocent et frugibus umbrae.

Let us rise. The shade is oft perilous to the singer—perilous the juniper's
shade, hurtful the shade even to the crops.[2]
— Virgil, *Eclogue* 10.75-76

Tread softly, for here you stand
On miracle ground, boy.
A breath would cloud this water of glass,
Honey, bush, berry and swallow.
This rock, then, is more pastoral, than
Arcadia is, Illyria was.
— Durrell, "On Ithaca Standing" (1937)

Arcady, not Arcadia. *Arcadia* originates from Ancient Greek, *Arcady* from
Elizabethan English.[3] Although interchangeable, the variants are not
equivalent. When discussing Virgil's pastoral landscape, Robert Coleman
distinguishes between the Arcadia of the Peloponnese and the Arcady of
myth. He calls the latter a "state of mind", and, as Bruno Snell argues,
"Arcadia is not an area on the map".[4] Virgil first mentions *Arcadia* in
Eclogue 7.4, but it's unlikely he ever saw the remote area. Aelius Donatus

---

[1] Originally published as "Virgil and Durrell in Arcady: *Umbra*, Penumbra, and
Dark Pastoral" in *C.20: an International Journal*, issue 2, December 2019.
https://durrelllibrarycorfu.wordpress.com.
[2] Virgil, *Eclogues, Georgics, Aeneid I-VI,* p. 95. Unless otherwise noted, all
quotations and translations of the Latin are, with minor adaptations, from the Loeb
edition of Virgil's works.
[3] *OED* 3rd, s.vv. *Arcadian* and *Arcady*.
[4] Virgil, *Eclogues*, pp. 207-09, 296; Snell, *Discovery*, p. 283.

in *Vita Vergilii* says that Virgil travelled to Athens and nearby Megara; he does not record a journey to Arcadia.[5] Lawrence Durrell, on the other hand, knew Greece intimately. He stood on Ithaca in 1937.[6] He resided on Corfu, Rhodes, and Cyprus and travelled throughout Attica, the Peloponnese, and various Greek islands.

Ithaca is one version of Durrell's Arcady. Of course he knew that the island was Odysseus's home and the destination of his travels from Troy. Like Byron swimming across the Hellespont, Durrell may have enjoyed drawing parallels between himself and some of his literary predecessors. He cherished Greece, he pursued an Odyssean path across the Eastern Mediterranean, by accident or not, but the trajectory of his life was more Roman than Greek. He wasn't like his friend and fellow writer, Patrick Leigh Fermor, another philhellene, who divided his time between Kardamyli on the Mani Peninsula and Dumbleton, England.

Leigh Fermor and Durrell met in Cairo in 1942 and shared similar visions of Greece. In the 1930s, Henry Miller had previously befriended Durrell, and both had similar interests in the Greek experience. For all these writers, Greece became a private domain, but, unlike Byron and his historical approach, they based their vision on the present, as Edmund Keeley adduces, that is, on "what they could actually see".[7] Miller's *Colossus of Maroussi* (1941) and Leigh Fermor's *Mani* (1958) exemplify this method, as does Durrell's reification of Ithaca. The new vision, however, was not as phenomenological as it might seem. Peter Green describes Leigh Fermor as undertaking a "quest for the Earthly Paradise";[8] the same could be said of Durrell and Miller, albeit in their unique ways. As Green points out, James Hilton's novel *Lost Horizon* (1933) coincides with Leigh Fermor's "Great Walk" across Europe and Frank Capra's eponymous film released in 1937.[9] Durrell and Miller saw it repeatedly in Paris;[10] it fed their need to find "Shangri-La" in Greece or elsewhere. *Elsewhere* could mean either fantasy or place: either Durrell's mythical Tibet or Miller's Big Sur, California.[11]

Durrell and Virgil have much in common. Durrell's "rock" of pastoral is based on a personal vision of Greece and is as unsubstantial and

[5] *Virgilian Tradition*, p. 193.
[6] Chamberlin, *Durrell Log*, p. 31.
[7] Keeley, *Inventing Paradise*, pp. 121-22.
[8] P. Green, "Man of Gifts", p. 14.
[9] P. Green, "Man of Gifts", p. 15.
[10] Hodgkin, *Amateurs*, p. 17.
[11] For Tibet as myth, see *DML* 51-52, 76. For Big Sur as paradise, see Miller, *Big Sur*, pp. 24-26.

mythic as Virgil's invention. The two poets stand together on fictive turf and might be called *"Arcades ambo"* (Arcadians both [*Ecl.* 7.4]),[12] if we emphasize Arcadia as Arcady, that is, as an imagined place.

Virgil was an exile from his native Andes in Cisalpine Gaul, and Durrell was a refugee from a distant and obscure past. Born in India in 1912 during the British Raj, he was sent to England for schooling at age eleven. At sixteen he was left fatherless. He never returned to India. Durrell called himself an "expatriate"[13] and chose to live the last thirty-three years of his life in Provence (1957-1990), where he extolled that former part of the Roman Empire in his last book, *Caesar's Vast Ghost* (1990). He knew both the root meaning of *nostalgia* as the pain of a lost home[14] and its artistic implications, namely, the story of a man like Aeneas who is *fato profugus* (exiled by fate [*Aen.* 1.2]). The theme of a lost home resonates throughout the works of Durrell and Virgil. In the words of Brooks Otis, "[Aeneas] is a man without a true *nostos*, a man who is mainly kept from his goal by his own nostalgia and passion".[15]

The poetics of exile has its own *mise-en-scène*. Scholars usually characterize the pastoral landscape as an idealization replete with shepherds, swains, *loci amoeni*, and such topoi as Ernst Robert Curtius enumerates in *European Literature and the Latin Middle Age*. According to Curtius, "Its minimum ingredients comprise a tree (or several trees), a meadow, and a spring or brook. Birdsong and flowers may be added".[16] Virgil's pastoral, however, tends towards darkness as its defining feature. His bucolic scene typically begins during the heat of noon and ends in the shadows of evening. As in the conclusion to *Eclogue* 10, emphasis falls on *umbra* (shade, shadow). Erwin Panofsky famously describes "Virgil's ideal Arcady" as a "dissonance" between "human suffering and superhumanly perfect surroundings". It is "resolved in that vespertinal mixture of sadness and tranquility which is perhaps Virgil's most personal contribution to poetry. With only slight exaggeration one might say that he 'discovered' the evening".[17] Otis concurs: "Virgilian sadness or melancholy represented a new note in poetry: it was also an excellent preparative for epic".[18]

---

[12] Virgil, *Eclogues, Georgics, Aeneid*, p. 66 (*Ecl.* 7.4).

[13] L. Durrell, *Big Supposer*, p. 24.

[14] *OED* 3ʳᵈ s.v. *nostalgia*: "ancient Greek νόστος [nostos] return home + -ἀλγία -algia comb. form [< 'ἀλγος pain]".

[15] Otis, *Virgil*, pp. 311-12.

[16] Curtius, *European Literature*, pp. 195; 183-202.

[17] Panofsky, *Meaning in the Visual Arts*, p. 300.

[18] Otis, *Virgil*, p. 128.

With one qualification, those statements also apply to Lawrence Durrell, man and writer. His "surroundings" are not "superhumanly perfect". His pastoral is not easily defined. Its physical elements vary; water and foliage are usually present but not always. It is not a separate genre but free to appear anywhere and not confined to a specific locale. It can occur on an island, a seashore, a mountain, or elsewhere. Its time and season vary and are not restricted to noon or evening, spring or summer. It is a state of consciousness, one that engenders the freedom of the interior monologue. Shadows and darkness are usually its main emotive constituents.

Durrell likes to quote Latin. The short poem "In Cairo" (1948) integrates English and Latin, as these lines illustrate:

> Home for most is what you can least bear.
> *Ego gigno lumen,* I beget the light
> But darkness is also of my nature. (*CP* 203)

He highlights the Latin, "burgled" verbatim from an obscure alchemical text of the sixteenth century, *Rosarium Philosophorum*, and his next line is a translation of the Latin, unquoted and unattributed: "*tenebrae autem naturae meae sunt*".[19]

Durrell has many uses for obscurity, one of which is to conceal plagiarism, but it is also a major theme of his writings. Indeed, his very "nature" owes much to "darkness" (*tenebrae*) and links him directly to Virgil and the frequency of *tenebrae* in the *Aeneid*.[20] Durrell's counterpart to Virgilian *umbra* and *tenebrae* is *penumbra*, an unusual term denoting the gray periphery of a shadow.[21] The modern term normally connotes a hazy condition surrounding an object or emotion.[22] This is not Durrell's usage,

---

[19] *Rosarium Philosophorum* (Frankfurt, C. Jacob, 1550). Durrell's secondary source was probably C. G. Jung's *Psychologie und Alchemie* (Zürich, 1944). See Jung's *Psychology and Alchemy,* trans. R. F. C. Hull (New York: Pantheon Books, 1953). The Latin appears on p. 76, n. 33. Re plagiarism, Durrell admits to stealing other people's ideas: "I burgle ideas". See L. Durrell, *Conversations*, p. 105.

[20] See *Virgil's "Aeneid"*, p. 106, Word List III.

[21] *Penumbra* is not classical Latin, rather late Latin in origin. The *OED* 3rd records its first usage in 1604 and cites the German astronomer Johannes Kepler (1571-1630). The term denotes, in part, "The partially shaded region around the shadow of an opaque body".

[22] See the Thomas Hardy example of *OED* 3rd, s.v. *penumbra*, II, Extended uses, 3: "A faint intimation of something undesirable; a peripheral region of uncertain extent; a group of things only partially belonging to some central thing. [...] 1874. T. Hardy *Far from Madding Crowd* I. vii. 84[:] He fancied that he had felt himself in the penumbra of a very deep sadness when touching that slight and fragile creature".

however. His usage of *penumbra* suggests shadows and darkness, as will be argued below. Virgil "'discovered' the evening", as Panofsky rightly notes, but Durrell continues the tradition without acknowledging his Roman legacy. In his hands, dark pastoral comes to mean not only "dissonance" but also darkness in its most personal and gloomy sense which increases with age.

II. Dido, Aeneas, and Durrell

"tune ille Aeneas, quem Dardanio Anchisae
alma Venus Phrygii genuit Simoentis ad undam?"

"Are you that Aeneas whom gracious Venus bore to Dardanian Anchises by the wave of Phrygian Simois?"
—Virgil, *Aeneid* 1.617-18

"Cher maître, excuse me. [...] Be assured. Your anonymity is safe with me and with my wife. Nobody shall ever know that Lawrence Durrell is with us."
—Durrell, *Sicilian Carousel* (1977)

Dido's question pertains to identity and paternity. Those issues could also be asked of Lawrence Durrell, who often questions himself.

Like the dualism of Arcady and Arcadia, there were at least two Durrells: the writer known to the world as "Lawrence Durrell" and the person born with the name "Lawrence George Durrell". The former was partly fictive, the latter real. When Durrell the writer talks about himself or writes about himself, we are dealing with "Lawrence Durrell". When Durrell the man is considered, we are dealing with "Lawrence G. Durrell". It is often difficult to separate the two Durrells, no doubt as the author wished. In his poem "Paris Journal" (1939) (*CP* 68), he proclaims, "The absence of a definite self", and in "Alexandria" (1946) (*CP* 154), he adds "As for me I now move / Through many negatives to what I am". This is confusing, keeping the "negatives" straight (literal and figurative, philosophical

---

See also, Hofstadter, *Anti-Intellectualism*, p. 407: "Finally, the penumbra of sanctity with which the figure of the child was surrounded made it difficult to discuss with realism the role of democracy in education". Richard Hofstadter's *Anti-Intellectualism in American Life* was originally published in 1962, the same date as the publication of the Durrell's revised edition of *The Alexandria Quartet*. Hofstadter's standard usage of *penumbra* contrasts with Durrell's unique usage.

and photographic),[23] and it's impractical to insist on the distinction, but we should keep the ambiguity in mind. In brief, Lawrence Durrell avoids confronting his own identity.

On the other hand, Lawrence George Durrell had trouble with paternity in the literal and literary senses. In 1923, his father, Lawrence Samuel Durrell, sent him to England to get an education for the purpose of obtaining a degree from an Oxbridge college. But young Durrell left public school at fifteen and failed, perhaps "deliberately", his entrance examinations.[24] Then his father died and was buried in India. It's a common story. Not unlike many young men, Durrell rebelled against his father's wishes and was haunted by the trauma of an "absent father", whom he had disappointed. This pattern of refusal and denial bears a strong resemblance to Durrell's literary relationship with Virgil. For he disguises his debt and, with few exceptions, rarely mentions Virgil.[25]

Anxiety runs deep in Durrell's work; Richard Pine calls it the "overriding theme".[26] In *Sicilian Carousel,* a personal account of a tour of Sicily, the condition is both stratagem and undercurrent. Durrell's disclaimer at the beginning of the book makes clear that "all the characters in this book are imaginary". The warning surely includes the author himself, who alludes to a suggestive title, *The Man Who Never Was,* and who feels compelled to travel incognito (*SC* 17).[27] The Lawrence Durrell in this book is the fictive Durrell. He tells a story and portrays himself.

Aeneas begins his journey uncertain where the Fates will lead him ("*incerti, quo fata ferant*" [*Aen.* 3.7]). So Durrell's account begins in fear: "All my journeys start with a kind of anxious pang of doubt—you feel suddenly an orphan" (*SC* 21). Then, in Syracuse, a French diplomat

---

[23] Is Durrell referring to "negative" as a concept in apophatic theology, where only negative statements can be made of God? Or is he referring to photography and using "negative" as a metaphor for the self? In Egypt, Durrell studied Neo-Platonism. Plotinus and Proclus, both mentioned in *The Alexandria Quartet,* advocated the *via negativa.* In 1933 in London, Durrell and his first wife Nancy Myers had a studio called "Witch Photos" (Chamberlin, *Durrell Log,* p. 18).

[24] L. Durrell, *Big Supposer,* p. 29. Ian MacNiven, Durrell's authorized biographer, disputes this frequent assertion: "Quite possibly Durrell never attempted entrance examinations for Oxford or Cambridge". See MacNiven, *Lawrence Durrell,* p. 697, n. 71.

[25] Two exceptions in his poetry: "In the vale's Vergilian shade" ("At Epidaurus" [1941]) and "the blood of Virgil / Grew again in the scarlet pompion" ("To Argos" [1942]).

[26] Pine, *Mindscape,* p. 28.

[27] Ewen Montagu, *The Man Who Never Was: World War II's Boldest Counterintelligence Operation* (New York, 1953).

recognizes Durrell but promises to keep his secret (*SC* 61). Anonymity is
concealment. When the tour guide talks about "the *Aeneid* with its famous
cruise along [the Sicilian] coast", Durrell says, "to my shame I have never
read it" (*SC* 177). Such modesty is preposterous, given the rigour of the
British educational system. Durrell attended schools in London and
Canterbury.[28] The traditional curriculum would have included reading the
Aeneid in Latin.[29]

Why would Durrell deny the obvious? Perhaps to obscure a painful
memory. Virgil's description of Sicily in Book 3 provides an emotional
account of the death of Aeneas's father Anchises (*Aen.* 3.692-715). In a
sense, Anchises "abandons" his son; Otis calls the death a form of
desertion.[30] Durrell last saw his father in 1926. In 1928, his father suddenly
died, and he was left half an "orphan". But he never abandoned his father.
Like Aeneas carrying Anchises out of burning Troy (*Aen.* 2.707-804),
Durrell appears to struggle with the burden of a deceased father.

The Aeneas analogy originated early in Durrell's life. In 1942,
when he was in Egypt, Nancy Myers, his first wife, left him because of
physical abuse and fled to Beirut with their daughter Penelope Berengaria,
then two years old.[31] Durrell pursued the pair and unsuccessfully attempted
a reconciliation in November of 1943. Michael Haag believes that the two
never met.[32] Durrell then returned to Alexandria and composed a letter to
Penelope but never sent it (**Figure 9**).[33] Durrell and Myers were divorced in
1946.

---

[28] St. Olave's and St. Xavier's Grammar School (1924-1926) and St. Edmund's
School (1926-1927).
[29] See Ziolkowski, *Virgil and Moderns*, p. 101. Ziolkowski discusses the importance
of Virgil in the British curriculum after the First World War.
[30] Otis, *Virgil*, p. 264.
[31] For Durrell's physical abuse of his first wife, Nancy Myers, see Chapter Two
above.
[32] See Haag, *City of Memory*, p. 280: "But it seems that she refused to meet with him
face to face".
[33] My transcription of the text: "Dear Tschup Tschick[:] Just a short letter to wish
you every happiness. I spent all today with you at Baalbek: so it didn't matter you
not coming with me. Little things sometimes make big differences in our lives —
when they have become stale and empty and no longer lives. My name is LARRY
DURRELL[,] address Alexandria[,] British Information Office. One Rue Toussoum.
Telephone 27347. Bless you. Good bye. L[.]"

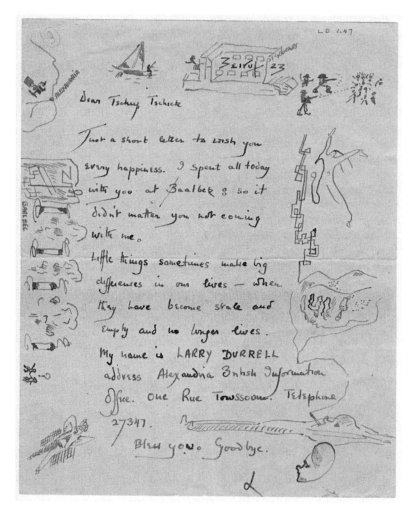

Figure 9: Letter from Lawrence Durrell to "Tschup Tschick", c. 1943 (published with permission of McPherson Library, University of Victoria [BC]; reproduced with permission of The Estate of Lawrence Durrell ©Lawrence Durrell)

The McPherson Library at the University of Victoria (BC) acquired the letter in 1966. The holograph has illuminations reminiscent of a medieval manuscript. These drawings are not idle doodlings. Durrell was an artist of considerable skill, who later exhibited Matisse-like paintings under the pseudonym of "Oscar Epfs". The letter was undated and addressed to "Tschup Tschick". The nickname probably refers to Penelope, although Nancy is another possibility. Durrell's pet name for Penelope was "Pinky" or a variant, as in the poem "To Ping-Kû, Asleep" (1942) (*CP* 103-04). The letter's childish tone, the infantile reduplication, the need to identify himself — all suggest Durrell is speaking to Penelope, a child barely cognisant of her own world, as he does in this poem addressed to her, "Invent a language where the terms / Are smiles".

Virgil and Durrell are subjective writers. Otis identifies Virgil's "subjective style" and analyzes how "[he] is constantly conscious of himself inside his characters".[34] Paul Alpers agrees and emphasizes Virgil's "self-representation" and "self-reflexiveness" in *Eclogues* 4, 5, 6, and 10.[35] Pastoral poetry moves from the ideal to the actual. So the *Eclogues* have numerous allusions to Octavian's policies and aspects of Virgil's own personal relationships. The milieu reflects William Empson's argument that "literature is a social process, and also an attempt to reconcile the conflicts of an individual in whom those of society will be mirrored".[36] While true in the main, that statement is not true of Durrell's treatment of literature, for he reverses the process by idealizing real-life situations. His starting point is opposite. This is not escapism — creating "a faraway land overlaid with the golden haze of unreality",[37] as Snell describes Virgil's Arcadia — rather a form of therapy. So Durrell confides in the first part of "Cities, Plains and People" (1946): "Until your pain become a literature" (*CP* 159).

Literature as pain concludes the first section of the poem. Beneath the title is a note, "Beirut 1943", which may be the approximate date of the letter to Penelope. The letter shows his imagination at work and provides an insight into his personality. If Haag is correct, Durrell and Myers never met in Beirut, and father and daughter never spent a day together "at Baalbek". The letter's content and marginalia are largely fantasy. The content is imaginary and valedictory, the marginalia dreamlike and surrealistic. As a character in *Sicilian Carousel* says (and it is worth repeating), "'We have been brought up to believe that facts are not dreams—and of course they are'" (*SC* 36).

The hotel scene at the top illustrates the central motif. The building and its archaic lettering recall Phoenician Beirut, north of Tyre, Dido's original home (*Aen.* 1.340). A woman on a balcony waves with outstretched arms at a figure sailing away. The scene evokes Carthage. As Haag points out, the depiction suggests the great departure episode near the end of Book

---

[34] Otis, *Virgil*, p. 49.
[35] Alpers, *Singer*, pp. 181, 221, 244-45.
[36] Empson, *Some Versions of Pastoral*, p. 19.
[37] Snell, *Discovery*, p. 282.

4 of the *Aeneid:* Aeneas abandoning Dido.[38]
    Durrell transforms Nancy Myers into another Dido. The physical similarities, though superficial, are intriguing. Both women are blondes, both regal and beautiful. Virgil's queen stands in her watchtower, watches Aeneas depart, and tears her hair:

> regina, e speculis ut primum albescere lucem
> vidit et aequatis classem procedere velis,
> litoraque et vacuos sensit sine remige portus,
> terque quaterque manu pectus percussa decorum
> flaventisque abscissa comas, "pro Iuppiter! ibit
> hic," ait, [...]

> Soon as the queen from her watchtower saw the light whiten and the fleet move on with even sails, and knew the shores and harbours were void of oarsmen, thrice and four times she struck her comely breast with her hand, and tearing her golden hair, "O God," she cries, "shall he go?" [...] (*Aen.* 4.586-91)

Dido's betrayal reverberates through time. In literature, Marlowe and Nashe wrote *The Tragedie of Dido Queene of Carthage* (1594). In music, there were operatic renditions, among them Purcell's *Dido and Aeneas* (1689) and Berlioz's *Les Troyen*s (1858). The ubiquity of Dido's story provides a precedence for Durrell dramatizing himself as another Aeneas. Whether or not Myers fits Virgil's Dido is beside the point. She certainly does not reach Dido's epic stature. What matters is how Durrell sees himself. He portrays her as Dido because he sees himself as another Aeneas. The comparison is double-edged, however: Aeneas is both hero and betrayer. And both roles fit Durrell himself. Moreover, his drawing gives truth to Otis's observation that Virgil's "sadness or melancholy [...] was also an excellent preparative for epic". A chastened Durrell returned to Alexandria and eventually wrote his epic, *The Alexandria Quartet* (1957-60). On 22 August 1944, subsequent to the Beirut episode, Durrell wrote Henry Miller and said, "I have a wonderful idea for a novel in Alexandria" (*DML* 174).

---

[38] I thank Michael Haag for showing me this letter and for mentioning the similarities to the *Aeneid.*

III. Pleasance

"mecum inter salices lenta sub vite iaceret;
serta mihi Phyllis legeret, cantaret Amyntas.
hic gelidi fontes, hic mollia prata, Lycori,
hic nemus; hic ipso tecum consumerer aevo."

"my darling would be lying at my side among the willows, and under the
creeping vine above—Phyllis plucking me flowers for a garland, Amyntas
singing me songs. Here are cold springs, Lycoris, here soft meadows, here
woodland; here with you, only the passage of time would wear me away."
—Virgil, *Eclogue* 10.40-43

A seminal passage of gemlike concision. As Robert Coleman comments,
Virgil's description encapsulates the *locus amoenus*: trees, meadows,
fountains, flowers, song. Gallus, Virgil's speaker, emphasizes its primary
features by repeating *hic* four times. The repetitions move from the ideal to
the real: the last demonstrative subjects the pastoral enclave to time and
decay. Gallus also alludes to abundant *umbrae*, for Coleman notes that
willows "provided too much shade and moisture for the grapes to ripen
properly".[39] Chiasmus intertwines the plucking of flowers and singing of
songs (*legeret, cantaret*) into another "garland of verse".[40] But beauty and
elegance are not enough. It is not enough, as Alpers argues, to identify an
"idyllic landscape" in terms of these features, for they are a "selective
emphasis determined by individual or cultural motives, of the central fiction
that shepherds' lives represent human lives".[41]

Durrell's contribution to the tradition was not a deliberate effort to
revive pastoral, to make an appeal to contemporary tastes, rather it sprang
from deeply personal needs. They were indeed "dark". His tone changed
over time, but the impetus remained strong. In 1939, a young man of twenty-
seven, he visited Shakespeare's home in Stratford-upon-Avon and wrote to
Henry Miller about the experience. He rhapsodized about the "radiance" of
the grounds and a "trim English garden where the house stood, with green
lawns, and shining little trees". There, sitting in that patch of pleasance,
Durrell had a revelation about Shakespeare. He found "THE KEY TO
EVERYTHING HE WROTE" (*DML* 126; original capitalisation). In 1975,
an elderly man of sixty-three, he travelled to Sicily and chanced upon the
"Fountain of Arethusa", a fixture of pastoral literature. No longer strident
and exuberant, Durrell left unsaid that Theocritus, Moschus, Virgil, and

---

[39] *Virgil: Eclogues*, p. 286.
[40] *Oxford Classical Dictionary*, p. 1745, s.v. *serta*.
[41] Alpers, *What Is Pastoral?*, p. 27.

Milton had made the fountain famous. Nor did the fountain inspire any revelations. Instead, he described the "jet" of the spring as still "strong" and remarked that the water was now disturbed by "a Coke bottle and a newspaper" (*SC* 83, 85-86). The comment was only slightly jarring; the Durrell of pastoral tendencies was not frustrated by a little litter. The litter, in fact, places him squarely in what Alpers calls "modern pastoral", a revision of Classical and Renaissance modes.[42]

Sicilian Carousel is Durrell's fourth island book and "recounts" an organized tour of Sicily. The "Carousel" is a "little red bus" (*SC* 39) that circles the island, clockwise, from Catania to Taormina. The name is also a metaphor for a circle. Durrell's last published poem is titled "Le cercle refermé" (1990). He tends to associates circles with dying. *Sicilian Carousel* concludes with a mock death or disappearance.

The book is Durrell's definitive work on pastoral, as it should be, for Sicily was the home of Theocritus and the traditional birthplace of bucolic poetry. Virgil situates the second *Eclogue* on the island (*Ecl.* 2.21). Durrell's book is supposedly a travel piece, but it's mainly a piece of fiction that incorporates several pastoral conventions. The narrative doesn't employ any shepherds, which Alpers considers requisite for Virgilian pastoral (Alpers 1996, 161), but Durrell maintains a steady dialogue with "Deeds", a fellow tourist, who functions as the author's conscience and sounding board. The friendly exchanges between the two companions resembles the "amoebaean contests" of *Eclogues* 3 and 7 and also serves to heighten the author's responsiveness to the island. Durrell's countryside has the conventional flora and fauna of the *Eclogues*: "these fastnesses of oak and beech" (*SC* 68) correspond to "*densas, umbrosa cacumina, fagos*" (the thick beeches with their shady summits [*Ecl.* 2.3]); "the drone of bees and the sharp stridulations of the cicada" (*SC* 53) echo "*sole sub ardenti resonant arbusta cicadis*" (the copses under the burning sun echo [...] the shrill cicadas [*Ecl.* 2.13]). Through old letters Durrell communicates with the ghost of a beautiful woman, Martine, whose presence hovers like a Virgilian shade, and at the end of the story, a travelling companion, Beddoes, fakes his suicide. Martine and Beddoes are possibly examples of the trope: *et in Arcadia ego.* More importantly, Durrell's dark ambience is Virgilian. He begins his Sicilian journey as the plane descends into an evening that "seemed to be rising from the ground like a faint grey smoke"; he ends it as dawn breaks over the Ionian Sea with a "strange watery moonlight" (*SC* 26, 218).

---

[42] Alpers, *What Is Pastoral?*, p. 248.

Much of Durrell's oeuvre lies between the "radiance" of Stratford-upon-Avon and the shadows of Sicily. The antinomies are not antagonistic. They coexist. Largely situated along the Mediterranean littoral, Durrell's bucolic adaptations make him a true descendant of Virgil and his twilight preferences.

Latin *umbra* (shade, shadow, ghost), as Fiona Cox points out, resounds throughout Virgil and influences Dante's *Inferno* and Hermann Broch's *Death of Virgil* (1945).[43] Latinate *penumbra* has a similar resonance in Durrell; he uses the term most notably as "penumbra of shadow". His first memoir, *Prospero's Cell,* completed in 1944 when he was thirty-two, begins with a hymn near the coast of Corfu:

> In the morning you wake to the taste of snow on the air, and climbing the companion ladder, suddenly enter the penumbra of shadow cast by the Albanian mountains. (*PC* 11)

His last book, *Caesar's Vast Ghost,* published shortly before he died in 1990, opens with a drive along the back roads of Provence:

> Swerving downs those long dusty roads among the olive groves, down the shivering galleries of green leaf I came, diving from penumbra to penumbra of shadow, feeling that icy contrast of sunblaze and darkness under the ruffling planes, plunging like a river trout in rapids from one pool of shadows to the next, the shadows almost icy in comparison with the outer sunshine and hard metalled blue sky. (*CVG* 1)

This psychic landscape, a pleasance in miniature, shivers and swelters, blazes and darkens. The confusion is intentional, not illogical. It is also characteristic of a mental state which balances opposing emotions. This state will be further discussed in section V.

On occasion Virgil varies his diction to include Latin colloquialisms and Greek proper nouns. Coleman says these "must have been very piquant to contemporary readers".[44] Durrell's diction has a similar "piquant" or odd flavour. As previously noted, the noun *penumbra* denotes "the partially shaded region around the shadow of an opaque body" (*OED* 3rd). The first recorded instance of the term is in 1604, when Kepler uses it in an astronomical context. This is not, however, the primary sense of Durrell's usage. He often uses the term to mean "shadow" in the broadest sense — a nebulous condition suggestive of a state of mind. Patrick Leigh Fermor also

---

[43] Cox, "Envoy", p. 330.
[44] *Virgil, Eclogues*, p. 110.

uses *penumbra* in this context when describing his exhaustion after travelling in the Mani.[45] Thus, Durrell's "penumbra of shadow" marks the beginning and the end of his travel literature. The repetition indicates a deliberate rounding of the genre. The usage is redundant — but effective — and not unlike Ezra Pound's redundant "cadaverous dead" in Canto I. Both poets exploit the sonority of Latin at the expense of good sense.

IV. *Hortus Conclusus*

> I think of Melissa once more: *hortus conclusus, soror mea sponsor.*
> —Durrell, *Justine* (1957)

> Unlike the rose garden of the Virgin Mary, the *locus conclusus* of chastity untrammeled and protected, the *locus amoenus* of the pastoral carries with it no symbolic overtones, no weight of significance.
> —Thomas G. Rosenmeyer, *The Green Cabinet*

Thomas Rosenmeyer's statement is true of the classical tradition but not of Lawrence Durrell. Although Durrell's idea of pleasance owes much to classical antecedents, his special sense of *penumbra* also characterizes his approach to pastoral and its subset the *hortus conclusus*, the enclosed garden. Durrell's garden does have "symbolic" or psychological "overtones".

When Darley, one of Durrell's *alter egos*, thinks of his mistress Melissa as a *hortus conclusus*, he indulges in a lot of irony, the levels of which are uncertain. The confusion, however, is consistent with Durrell's method. First, Darley's memory is faulty.[46] The noun should be *sponsa*, not *sponsor*. Durrell had the opportunity to correct this mistake in the revised 1962 edition of *The Alexandria Quartet* — he did not.[47] The Latin verse is

---

[45] Leigh Fermor, *Mani*, p. 299: "Lying in a bed again, vaguely shrouded like a corpse on the brink of resurrection, seemed an incomparable, almost a guilty luxury. The penumbra was pierced by a thin blade of afternoon light falling from the junction of the two shutters".

[46] I thank Michael Haag for pointing out this error.

[47] The phrase *mea sponsor* is ungrammatical. Is the mistake intentional? If so, Durrell imitates a grammatical error akin to Rimbaud's famous declaration, *"Je est un autre"*. Durrell composed a poem of that same title in 1942. In his unpublished Note to the 1958 edition of *Balthazar,* he wrote, "My topic is an investigation of love; the bisexual psyche". But in the published Note he wrote, "The central topic of the book is an investigation of modern love". *Mea sponsor* suggests bisexuality: unorthodox grammar suggests unorthodox sexuality. Bisexuality in pastoral, as Robert Coleman mentions, is "normal and natural" (*Virgil*, p. 10). For the unpublished quotation, see Pine, *Mindscape*, p. 90.

from the *Vulgate* version of *The Song of Songs*; it correctly reads, "*hortus conclusus soror mea sponsa*" (AV: "A garden inclosed is my sister, my spouse").[48] Second, Melissa is a cabaret dancer and prostitute. She is neither an "enclosed garden" (in Rosenmeyer's sense of being chaste and protected), a "sister", nor a "spouse". As Ariel Bloch and Chana Bloch explain, "'sister'" in Hebrew poetry "suggests intimacy".[49] Third, whether Durrell was aware of these possibilities is problematic. What isn't doubtful is that incest is one of his persistent themes,[50] and Melissa is quite possibly being co-opted, however inappropriately, into a complex pattern of incestuous behaviour. Durrell's use of pastoral is often messy.

Messiness leads to obscurity. In *Sicilian Carousel*, Durrell acknowledges the Homeric origin of the "Greek garden" and quotes an unidentified translation of Alcinous's garden that includes "vineyard", "row of trees", and "garden plots" (*Od.* 7.113ff.). Then he speculates: "In the culture which followed each plant and flower had its story, its link with the mythopœic inner nature of man" (*SC* 70). The orderly layout of this garden is similar to Calypso's (*Od.* 5.63ff.). As Norman Austin notes, her garden "is a carefully constructed ideal landscape set in concentric balance".[51] This is not Durrell's garden, ideal or real. His *hortus conclusus*, like his use of *penumbra*, relies on a lack of definition or what Stephen Booth calls "indefinition" in his discussion of Shakespearean tragedy.[52] Durrell's idea of pleasance is basically disorderly, unruly, and rundown and often conveys a feeling of limitless desolation. It is imbued with a sense of chaos.

Examples of Durrell's garden proliferate throughout his oeuvre. A typical description appears in *Clea* (1960), the last novel of *The Alexandria Quartet*:

> An old house […] its cracked and faded shutters tightly fastened […] The gardens desolate and untended. Only the little figures on the wall move their celluloid wings — scarecrows which guard against the Evil Eye. The silence of complete desuetude. But then the whole countryside of Egypt shares this melancholy feeling of having been abandoned, allowed to run to seed, to bake and crack and moulder under the brazen sun. (*Quartet* 686-87)

---

[48] *Biblia Sacra*, p. 999 (*Canticum Canticorum* 4:12).

[49] *Song of Songs*, p. 175.

[50] Fertile, "Meaning of Incest", p. 105.

[51] Austin, *Archery*, p. 149.

[52] Booth, *Indefinition*, p. 94: "[*Macbeth*], as play, has definition—a beginning, a middle, and an end—but its materials, even those that are used to designate its limits, provide insistent testimony to the artificiality, frailty, and ultimate impossibility of limits. A sense of limitlessness infuses every element of the play".

And another in *Monsieur* (1974), the first novel of *The Avignon Quintet*:

> It is through this little garden with its kitchen herbs that one can reach the
> more extensive formal gardens of the chateau — for so long fallen into
> disrepair. […] It is difficult to imagine how they must have looked in their
> heyday. Ever since I knew them they have remained overgrown and
> unweeded, full of the romantic melancholy of desuetude. (*Quintet* 46)

These are not literary exercises. They also describe Durrell's own garden in
Sommières, France. In 1975, Ian S. MacNiven, the author's future
biographer, visits the home in Provence. In his "search for the real Lawrence
Durrell", he draws the following parallel:

> Garden is not the right word: Enchanted Forest better describes the
> surroundings of Durrell's Castle Perilous. Readers of *Prospero's Cell* may
> recall that on Count D's property "the walks are unkept and the trees
> unpruned," and Durrell—Count Durrell—too has let nature run wild.
> Brambles ten feet tall and other secondary growth have taken over what
> was once a formal garden with paths, boxwood hedges, plots of palm trees,
> mimosas, ferns, and statuary.[53]

MacNiven doesn't use "melancholy" and "desuetude", common terms of
Durrell's garden *topos*, but he notes that Durrell "lives in perpetual twilight"
and concludes, "I picture him in the gloomy house and tangled, bird-infested
garden".

Durrell dwells on "melancholy" and "desuetude" and opens himself
(or his persona) to the charge of sentimentality or a macabre sensibility. He
anticipates the objection by calling his usage "romantic", although "Gothic"
is more accurate. The real question, however, is why he dwells on these
emotive terms and scenes. They clearly appeal to his love of the exotic and
Latinate diction. They also have a particular context, and underlying them
is the sense of abandonment without hope of relief. That is the force of the
passage taken from *Clea*, where the narrator extends the "silence of complete
desuetude" and the "melancholy feeling of having been abandoned" to
encompass an entire Egyptian "countryside".

In the *Quartet*, Durrell rarely describes Upper Egypt. He situates
his imagined landscapes in the Delta, which, unlike the Nile Valley and its
escarpments, has no prominent boundaries. Lower Egypt is flat, limitless,
and monotonous. Long ago Herodotus recognized Egypt as the "gift of the
river" and emphasized the sharp contrast between the Upper and Lower
regions (*Hdt.* 2.5-8).

---

[53] MacNiven, "Durrell and Nightingales", pp. 235, 239.

The Nile Valley and the Delta may have had a decisive effect on Durrell's psychology and reinforced his Manichaean tendencies, the tension between light and darkness. Furthermore, as Otis says about Virgil, Durrell's language is ultimately subjective. It inevitably leads to his statement about the "mythopœic inner nature of man", even though we must grant him his own method of mythmaking, a form of which is his preference for abandoned gardens. Recall the various uses of *abandon*: Anchises abandons Aeneas, Aeneas abandons Dido, Durrell abandons Penelope, and Lawrence S. Durrell abandons his son Lawrence G. Durrell.

V. *Otium*

"O Meliboee, deus nobis haec otia fecit."
"O Meliboeus, it is a god who gave us this peace."
        —Virgil, *Eclogue* 1.6

It is not peace we seek but meaning.
        — Durrell, "The Reckoning" (1971)

Otium is a staple of Latin pastoral. Rosenmeyer calls it both "condition" and "ethos", and it is usually glossed as "leisure" or "peace". The opposite of labour, *otium* is a state of being at rest, as Thomas Rosenmeyer explains.[54] In Virgil's *Eclogues*, the shepherds enjoy this condition which enables leisure and calm reflection.

Otium, however, is not a staple of Durrell's pastoral. Indeed, peace seems alien to his world, and he looks for a substitute, either through some kind of spirituality or equanimity, which is a balance of conflicting emotions. "The Reckoning" is not a pastoral lyric, but it provides a comment on a rare word in Durrell's vocabulary — *peace* as peacefulness. Undoubtedly, the absence of peace prompts his statement — which sounds like sour grapes — and that condition exists from the beginning of his poetic career.

In 1890, when W. B. Yeats was a man of twenty-five, he published "The Lake Isle of Innisfree", a pastoral lyric, which describes the poet building a cabin in a lush "bee-loud glade" (l.4). The island retreat soothes and softens: "peace comes dropping slow" (l. 5), and bright light either "glimmer[s]" or "glow[s]" (l. 7).[55] In 1931, Durrell, a brash youth of nineteen,

---

[54] Rosenmeyer, *Green Cabinet*, pp. 67-68.
[55] Yeats, *Collected Works*, p. 39. For first date of publication, see *Major British Writers II,* p. 790.

published "Pioneer", his detailed subversion of Yeats's poem.[56] There the young poet builds his house in an "arid" and rocky "wilderness" (ll. 12). In that mountain retreat, the tranquillity of Yeats's "deep heart's core" (l. 12) becomes "Only a living strife / Calling me back from this core of desolation" (ll. 12-13). These two locales provide a stark contrast in pastoral psychology: Yeats's "core" is peaceful, whereas Durrell's is desolate.

If not *otium*, then *ataraxía*. The closest that Durrell gets to peace is the kind of calm associated with Epicurean tranquillity (*ataraxía*). The Greek philosopher Epicurus (341-270 BC) had his garden, and his school in Athens was called "the Garden". Virgil studied under the Epicurean philosopher Siro.[57] Latin *otium* is defined positively, by direct reference to a certain condition, but Greek *ataraxía* is defined negatively, by indirect reference to what it is not.[58] It is the absence of pain and emotional disturbance. Like the meaning of *ataraxía*, Durrell's sense of peace is difficult to define. It is easier to say what it is not than what it is. It is certainly not peacefulness, nor is it a "core of desolation". It is something in-between.

Durrell's stay on Cyprus typifies his struggles. In 1953, Cyprus was British territory. Durrell went to the island in search of a quiet place to live and write; instead, he became enmeshed in political and emotional turmoil. *Enosis*, the movement to join the island with Greece, erupted into open conflict, and his position as Director of Information Services of the Cyprus (British) Government damaged his friendship with the poet George Seferis and other Greek intellectuals. The rebellion required that he carry a pistol; Greek terrorists bombed his garage. As events deteriorated, his second marriage to Yvette Cohen neared dissolution, and a third relationship with Claude-Marie Vincendon Forde began in earnest. The political situation eventually forced him to leave the island in 1956. He wrote about some of those experiences in *Bitter Lemons* (1957), perhaps his most famous memoir. Even under these circumstances, he still wrote poetry and fiction: *The Tree of Idleness and other poems* (1955), *White Eagles over Serbia* (1957), an espionage novel, and *Justine* (1957), first novel of the *Quartet*. This extraordinary productivity suggests that unrest is sometimes an essential precondition for creativity. But irony and loneliness pursued

---

[56] *CP* 17. "Pioneer" parodies "The Lake Isle of Innisfree" with respect to the latter's imagery. Moreover, Durrell mocks Yeats's experiments in magic and occultism. His subversive lines include: "Proof against occult art or wizardry" (l. 3), "Here I kept silence" (l. 7), and "No eloquent shadows" (l. 11).

[57] *Virgil, Ecologues*, p. 6; *Virgilian Tradition*, p. 365.

[58] *OED* 3rd, s.v. *ataraxía*: "Greek ἀταραξία impassiveness, < ἀ privative [negative affix] + ταράςςειν to disturb, stir up".

him. Durrell bought a house and lived for a while in a village outside Kyrenia called Bellapaix (beautiful peace). But *otium* was impossible. The short poem "Bitter Lemons" (1955) serves as his coda to the island retreat on Cyprus:

> In an island of bitter lemons
> Where the moon's cool fevers burn
> From the dark globes of the fruit,
>
> And the dry grass underfoot
> Tortures memory and revises
> Habits half a lifetime dead
>
> Better leave the rest unsaid,
> Beauty, darkness, vehemence
> Let the old sea-nurses keep
>
> Their memorials of sleep
> And the Greek sea's curly head
> Keep its calms like tears unshed
>
> Keep its calms like tears unshed. (*CP* 238)

As in much of Durrell's poetry, darkness competes with light, obscurity with comprehension, and what is "unsaid" with what is said. The antinomies are balanced, and the result is a moment of poetic *ataraxia*. The condition resembles the previously discussed beginning of *Caesar's Vast Ghost*, where a "trout in rapids" jumps from light to darkness, "from one pool of shadows to the next". Durrell's trout is "in rapids" because, like the poet himself in "Bitter Lemons", it swims in a watery turmoil and seems to seek some kind of balance.

"Bitter Lemons" is a great poem and deserves close analysis. The lyric concludes a book about political upheaval and broken friendships, but the poem itself is quiet and anonymous. No sounds of warfare in the background, no names divulged, no details given. It is not an example of Imagism and lacks the "precision" and "hitting power" Durrell saw in T. S. Eliot's and Ezra Pound's poetry and wrote about in *A Key to Modern British Poetry* (*Key* 126). The poem's power lies elsewhere and relies on a darkening of Virgilian pastoral: night instead of day, aridity instead of verdure, seascape instead of landscape, sorrow instead of melancholy, and loneliness instead of companionship.

Durrell situates his pastoral scene on unnamed Cyprus, the "island of bitter lemons", and places an unidentified speaker on an unidentified headland overlooking the Mediterranean, misidentified as "the Greek sea". The time is not the usual noontime of pastoral, when *otium* prevails, rather it is night with a luminous moon and eerie phenomena. We may ask how the "moon's cool fevers" can "burn", and we may wonder how lemons, which should be bright yellow in moonlight, can be "dark globes".

Strange things happen under the influence of Durrell's moon. His moon is uncanny. In *Sicilian Carousel*, a young, naked blonde takes a late-night stroll in "white milky light" (*SC* 173). In *Balthazar*, the moon is maleficent: "Each of us, like the moon, had a dark side — could turn the lying face of 'unlove' towards the person who most loved and needed us" (*Quartet* 297). The analogy is ambiguous and inaccurate. Durrell's moon is supernatural and defies science, for earth and moon have synchronized rotations, and the "dark side" of the moon never turns to face the earth. "Unlove" is unusual and serves as a euphemism for hate. Why it has a "lying face" is unclear. Or why should moonlit grass "torture memory"?

We may also inquire about the identity of the "old sea-nurses". The Sirens lived by the sea, but they were not the nurturing type; more likely, the nymphs are the Nereids, who could subdue rough seas, but they were not wizened, if that's what "old" means, nor were they known to "keep / Their memorials of sleep". All these changes suggest that the speaker "revises" a great deal. Then there are the big abstractions — "Beauty, darkness, vehemence" — which hang disembodied in the air like Virgil's "*tristes umbrae*" (*Aen.* 5.734), the gloomy shades of Tartarus. Although it is nighttime, the weird situation resembles, as Rosenmeyer remarks about pastoral, "the belief that supernatural beings are most likely to be encountered during the noon hour".[59]

The ambiguity of "Bitter Lemons" is a subterfuge; it avoids directly confronting unpleasantness. And it is apotropaic; it wards off evil much as "the little figures" on the garden wall of the house in the Egyptian Delta "guard against the Evil Eye". Virgil mentions it in *Eclogue* 3.103, and Durrell's references to the superstition proliferate throughout his oeuvre. He usually describes the evil eye in terms of protective devices, blue or green objects, such as beads or amulets. These occurrences are not simply evidence of ethnographic curiosity, for Durrell was superstitious. In *Justine*, he describes the "blue imprints of juvenile hands" on the walls of a brothel as a "talisman" against the evil eye (*Quartet* 42), and the illustration on the dust jacket of the 1957 Faber edition consists of the imprint of a blue hand.

---

[59] Rosenmeyer, *Green Cabinet*, p. 89.

Another form of apotropaic behaviour is to avoid talking about something for fear of "jinxing it". Figuratively speaking, Durrell's "Bitter Lemons" avoids eye contact; it averts its gaze and eschews direct associations. To unlock the code we must look into Durrell's life.

"Beauty, darkness, vehemence" allude to Yvette Cohen, Durrell's second wife, whom he called Eve.[60] At the end of his book on Rhodes, *Reflections on a Marine Venus* (1953), he recapitulates his friendships on the island and acknowledges "the dark vehement grace of E.". Yvette was indeed dark, passionate, and beautiful. Durrell dedicated *Justine* to her: "To / EVE / these memorials of her native city". Memorials are usually thought of as monuments to the dead, and the poem's "memorials of sleep" has morbid connotations.

The music of "Bitter Lemons" lulls and calms. The rhymes are sweet, seductive, and repetitive: keep/sleep/keep/keep offset by dead/unsaid/head/unshed/unshed. In a phonetic transcription, the vowels swing from high-front [i] to mid-front [ε] and come to final rest on the dead/unshed rhyme. The last two lines replicate the sound of waves and locate the situation at the seashore: "Keep its calms like tears unshed / Keep its calms like tears unshed". The balance between "keep" and "unshed" suggests a similar equanimity in the poet himself, who stands poised on a headland above the immense deep, either Virgil's *"vastum maris aequor"* (*Aen.* 2.780) or Horace's *"ingens aequor"* (*Carm.* 1.7.32). But the calm is only momentary, for the "Greek sea's curly head" will not keep its "calms" forever, and Durrell himself, as happens so often in his life and work, seems on the verge of a leap into a vast unknown.

VI. Dark Pastoral

"omnia vel medium fiat mare. vivite silvae:
praeceps aërii specula de montis in undas
deferar; extremum hoc munus morientis habeto."

"Nay, let all become mid-ocean! Farewell, ye woods! Headlong from some towering mountain peak I will throw myself into the waves; take this as my last dying gift!"
— Virgil, *Eclogue* 8.58-60

The sad little island of Lefkas (or Santa Maura) has little to interest the modern traveller at its northern end, where its position *vis-à-vis* the mainland suggests a vermiform appendix.
— Durrell, *The Greek Islands* (1978)

---

[60] I thank Michael Haag for pointing out this connection.

Three points need to be emphasized. First, Durrell's version of Virgilian pastoral is "dark" because of what it conceals. He uses darkness as a cover or screen. Images and paradoxes such as "dark crystal", "dark globes", "dark side" of the moon, or "penumbra of shadow" are sometimes deliberate, always repetitive, and occasionally redundant. Repetition is a major aspect of his style. Second, his explanations are often contorted, ingenious, and unconvincing. His contortions reveal the real substance of his arguments. Third, he makes mistakes, either errors of fact or errors of omission. His mistakes are as important as his explanations, perhaps more so.

"The sad little island" is where Sappho died, according to tradition, and a "vermiform appendix" is little and uninteresting, until it ruptures and causes death. "Little things sometimes make big differences", as Durrell says in his letter to Tschup Tschick.

Virgil's distraught Damon alludes to Sappho's leap off a cliff on Lefkas. Her suicide is the classical paradigm for Durrell's obsession with suicide or self-extinction. In *The Greek Islands* he visits the island of Lefkas in the Ionian, which is a true "Greek sea", apparently stands on the "White Cliffs", and relates part of the legend of "the Sapphic jump" (*GI* 38). He avoids mentioning, either deliberately or unconsciously, the reason for her suicide — her love of Phaon.

Durrell reprises numerous versions of this leap in his poetry and fiction. They usually have four elements in common: they appear at a critical point in the story; they have a pastoral or wilderness setting; they occur on some kind of a promontory; and they terminate with a plunge or voyage into darkness or the deep blue. The usage is deliberate. In *Sicilian Carousel*, Durrell spoofs the trope when Beddoes, a character with all the charm and attractiveness of a death's head (*SC* 41, 216), avoids the police by faking his suicide. He plans to "jump" into the caldera of Mount Etna (*SC* 217). Three other examples follow.

In the poem "Matapan" (1943), Durrell recounts his wartime flight from Greece to Crete and to an unknown future in Egypt. Matapan is the southernmost projection of mainland Greece, a jumping-off point into the Sea of Crete. His ship passes by the tip of the wild Mani peninsula and proceeds down a "corridor of darkness" (*CP* 116). In *The Greek Islands* he recalls that journey: "Cape Matapan (ancient Taenaron) was the very last toe-hold on the peninsula; after that the black bitumen of the night sea which took us to Cythera" (*GI* 106). "Black bitumen" is as redundant and nonsensical as "white snow". Bitumen is a form of petroleum and has many uses, one of which the Ancient Egyptians employed as an ingredient in mummification. Durrell "loathed" his stay in Egypt (*DML* 320), and it's reasonable to assume he considered it an "Egyptian Death", analogous to the "English Death" he makes famous in *The Black Book* (1938).

In the allegorical novel *The Dark Labyrinth* (1947), Durrell traps a group of British tourists in a labyrinth on Crete and subjects them to various fates. One of these characters is Campion, an artist who resembles Durrell himself. Campion is on a mission to paint the graves of British military on the island. His only escape from the labyrinth is to jump with his companion, Virginia Dale, from a ledge several hundred feet above the sea. They strip naked, jump together, and Campion "felt himself turning over and over as his body was poured down the ladder of blueness" (*DL* 215). Then Campion/Durrell literally disappears from the narrative. Virginia Dale survives the fall. An abbot reports that a novice sees "'a woman falling out of the sky'" but no one else (*DL* 261). Campion leaps and vanishes into "blueness". Blue is Durrell's favourite colour (so begins *Prospero's Cell:* "Somewhere between Calabria and Corfu the blue really begins"), and, at his wake in 1990, he was laid out in a "blue jacket".[61] Jumping into "blueness" suggests absorption into an infinite unknown.

White Eagles over Serbia (1957) is a thriller in the manner of John Buchan's novels. During the early years of the Cold War, British Intelligence dispatches Methuen to Yugoslavia to aid a Royalist band called "The White Eagles". The rebels are hiding in the "fastnesses" of the Balkan mountains. Methuen joins the band and becomes involved in transporting a treasure. At a mountain pass, Communist troops ambush the White Eagles. Methuen escapes down the wall of a canyon and watches the rebels tumble into the lake below:

> It was strange to see how slowly objects seem to fall as they reached the level of the ledge upon which he stood, turning over and over and giving the impression of trying to unfold in space as they travelled towards the dark below.[62] (*WES* 170).

Later he recalls the incident: "Once more in his mind's eye he saw those toppling, turning figures spinning slowly down into the icy fastness of the great lake [...] and ignominious death in the fastnesses of Serbia" (*WES* 192-93).

These two passages are odd in form, content, and purpose. *Fastness*, as "the quality or state of being difficult to attack or otherwise access; safety, security," the *OED* 3rd considers "somewhat *archaic*" (s.v.

---

[61] MacNiven, *Lawrence Durrell*, p. 688.

[62] In the Penguin/Peacock paperback edition to *White Eagles* (1980), Susan Hunter has an excellent depiction of this scene. Her cover illustration attests to the power of Durrell's description of the plunge into the lake.

fastness, 5). Durrell's diction is odd. Aside from the dubious paradox of death being "ignominious" yet insuring "icy fastness", both shameful and secure, the simulation of slow-motion cinematography reveals an unusual preoccupation with falling and dying. These passages also, as well as the previous examples, contrast markedly with the intent to avoid confronting some obscure fear.

Why fixation? Why avoidance? These obvious questions lead to another classical paradigm — the Medusa. Durrell's use of the myth is another key to his use of Virgilian pastoral.

In *The Greek Islands* Durrell offers an extensive interpretation of the Medusa pediment in the Corfu Museum (*GI* 31-35). He confronts the Gorgon, stands "face to face" with the monster — "the insane grin, the bulging eyes, the hissing ringlets of snakelike hair, the spatulate tongue" — and struggles to explain the origin of the myth. His is a "free interpretation", as he admits, but he doesn't acknowledge that he again "revises" something to suit his own needs.

He commits two flagrant errors. Medusa was not "the mother of the Gorgons", as he claims; she was one of three sisters known by that name. He is also wrong about her early history and gives a misleading version of the account in Hesiod's *Theogony*: "In Hesiod's poem, [Medusa] fell in love with the rippling blue hair of Poseidon and gave herself to him in the depths of the sea". The paraphrase flows seductively, but Hesiod actually says "With her alone the dark-haired one [Poseidon] lay down in a soft meadow among spring flowers".[63] Durrell has a fondness for the colour blue and watery immersion. "Blue hair" may approximate "dark-haired", but "depths of the sea" does not equal "soft meadow". He doesn't recount; he darkens.

Durrell studied Freudian theory and was surely aware of the psychoanalytic interpretation of Medusa's severed head as a manifestation of the "castration complex". But he alters the usual psychoanalytic interpretation. The snakes on her head are not Freud's "multiplication of penis symbols".[64] Instead, he interprets the Medusa as a representation of madness: "On the distorted face of the Gorgon we see something like an attack of acute schizophrenia. (She foundered in the ocean of the subconscious as symbolized by her love affair with Poseidon)". Durrell knew well that look of "acute schizophrenia", for Yvette Cohen was diagnosed as schizophrenic in January of 1953.[65] He also repeats the error about Poseidon's affair with Medusa and introduces another element — the "subconscious".

---

[63] Hesiod, *Theogony*, p. 25 (ll. 270-79).
[64] Freud, *Collected Papers*, p. 105.
[65] Chamberlin, *Durrell Log*, p. 95.

These alterations raise other questions. As Margaret Homans has shown in her discussion of *Wuthering Heights*, an author may repress some aspect of reality or "something else" that he or she finds threatening. Ultimately, that "something else" may be "inherently unnamable".[66] An "unnamable something" haunts Durrell's writings. Does he repress and sublimate? Exactly what? Does he commit a "Freudian slip" and use Poseidon as a screen for himself and the Gorgon as one for Yvette Cohen? And if Yvette is Medusa, Durrell's "mother of the Gorgons", does that make their daughter Sappho Jane a Gorgon? We know this for certain — Sappho Jane was highly unstable. She had at least two nervous breakdowns and hanged herself in 1985 at the age of thirty-three. Father and daughter had a troubled relationship, and Sappho sought psychiatric help.[67] She objected to his mistreatment of women and identified too closely with her father's works, where incest and suicide are prominent themes. In her journal she even accused him of "committing a kind of mental incest".[68] Since schizophrenia is potentially hereditary, Durrell may have thought of Sappho (unconsciously or not) as a "Gorgon", in the sense that she inherited her mother's mental illness and that he found her threatening.

Durrell deflects such questions by offering a bizarre interpretation of the Medusa myth — a failed religious experience causes Medusa's "schizophrenia". The snakes represent Yogic enlightenment gone awry: "The hissing hair symbolizes a short circuit, a discharge of electricity — ideas which have overwhelmed her mind". Medusa's head represents an attempt to "yoke [...] two primordial forces", which are undefined. On the decapitation, he says "Perseus, head turned away, performs a clumsy act of exorcism"; nevertheless, "the old fear of madness is still there, still rivets us; the glare of a lunatic still turns us to stone". Durrell even manages to bring in the evil eye and apotropaic blue beads: "Can we see her [Medusa] then as something like our modern charms against the Evil Eye — the blue beads we find affixed to the dashboard of taxis or the prams of small children?" He concludes: "The old Gorgon reminds us of the [...] dangers which must be faced in order to achieve full selfhood". However ingenious, his explanation is pure lunacy and a good illustration of what he explains — avoidance, fixation, and exorcism as literature. Durrell had his demons. Richard Pine may have had this method in mind when he comments on Durrell reading his own poetry: "Apprehension is the keynote; schizophrenia the suggestion".[69]

---

[66] Homans, "Repression and Sublimation", p. 16.
[67] Chamberlin, *Durrell Log*, p. 178.
[68] S. Durrell, "Journals and Letters", p. 70.
[69] Pine, *Mindscape*, p. 172.

VII. Farewell Arcady

ite domum saturae, venit Hesperus, ite capellae.

Get home, my full-fed goats, get home—the Evening Star draws on.
                            — Virgil, *Eclogue* 10.77

> Then the long wait by a strange watery moonlight until an oven lid started to open in the east and the "old shield-bearer" stuck its nose over the silent sea. […] I reflected how lucky I was to have spent so much of my life in the Mediterranean—to have so frequently seen these incomparable dawns, to have so often had sun and moon both in the sky together.
> — Durrell, *Sicilian Carousel*

Robert Coleman says that Virgil's last words in *Eclogue* 10 are his "farewell to the genre".[70] The poet's departure is final. He leaves on a "despondent note", Coleman suggests, yet he conveys satiety and quietly recedes into the *umbrae* of evening. Durrell, on the other hand, never abandons his various uses of the genre. His farewell is a final farewell from an unruly garden in Sommières, the "last goodbye" of "Le cercle refermé" (*CVG* 205).

In 1977, he concludes his book on Sicily by welcoming another day of struggle. The sun as "old shield-bearer" may be the God of Psalm 84:11 — the God of protection and conflict, "the Lord of hosts". Relief comes with the concurrence of "sun and moon both in the sky together". He is happiest or luckiest during moments of ambiguity, suspended opposition, when he is like a trout "diving from penumbra to penumbra of shadow".

Durrell's moments of peace occur fitfully. Virgil concludes his final *Eclogue* in the guise of a shepherd, withdraws peacefully into the evening, and goes on to other endeavours, as his legendary epitaph records: "*cecini pascua rura duces*" (I sang of pastures, fields, leaders).[71] Virgil's progression is linear (or so it seems), Durrell's is circular. "Le cercle refermé" is the title of his last poem; it serves as his epitaph and appears at the end of his last book, *Caesar's Vast Ghost* (1990). The poem does not convey a sense of final fulfillment; it does not refer to literary accomplishments, rather to shadowy details of his own *vita*. It begins in Benares with "Boom of the sunset gun", the holiest city of India and a place he probably never visited, refers to cremations and "Corpses floating skyward", portrays himself as "Caressed by my heliocentric muse / With lunar leanings", and ends (presumably) in Sommières:

---

[70] *Virgil, Eclogues*, p. 297.
[71] *Virgilian Tradition*, p. 404.

Love-babies nourished by the sigh,
With little thought of joy or pain,
Or the spicy Kodak of the hangman's brain
A disenfranchised last goodbye,
                    Goodbye.

The "love-babies" could be his two daughters. The "spicy Kodak" could be a metaphor for photography and memory (e.g., "photographic memory").[72] "Spicy" suggests an allure of some kind, piquant or provocative — but why that is the case remains unclear. The "hangman's brain" may refer to suicide — Sappho Jane's or thoughts of his own. Or it could refer to "The Hanged Man" in the Tarot and the subject of an early poem, "The Hanged Man" (1939). We can never be certain what Durrell intends. This imagery may be a prime example of what Michael Haag calls, "Saying yet not saying".[73] Namely, it is part of a private code, a way for Durrell to reveal yet hide his innermost feelings.

"Disenfranchised" recalls a scene from *Mountolive*, the third novel of *The Alexandria Quartet*. Mountolive's father has abandoned his family and lives as a Buddhist scholar in an Indian monastery. He dutifully sends to his wife in England copies of his "work". In the preface to his translation of a "Pali text", he writes:

> "For those of us who stand upon the margins of the world, as yet unsolicited by any God, the only truth is that work itself is Love." (*Quartet* 467)

As the son remarks, the statement is "odd", without explaining why, for eloquence conceals something questionable: the rationalization that work substitutes for love and that "Love" itself is an abstraction. The father's books are really an offering, an apology to an abandoned wife and son. This is not unlike Durrell's poem of farewell and his "disenfranchised last goodbye". "Le cercle refermé" may be a sad apology from an absent and marginalized father: an *apologia* to one surviving daughter, Penelope Berengaria, to a deceased daughter, Sappho Jane, and, possibly, to his readers and admirers.

---

[72] For the role of the Kodak camera in shaping modern memory, see N. West, *Kodak*, p. 1: "The central argument of this book is that Kodak taught amateur photographers to apprehend their experiences and memories as objects of nostalgia". In 1933, Durrell and his first wife Nancy Myers briefly establish a photography studio in London called "Witch Photos" (Chamberlin, *Durrell Log*, pp. 18-19).
[73] See Chapter Six above.

That apology, if it is one, is Virgilian in tone: concise, modest, devoted. *Pius*, if you will, pious or dutiful, as in *"pius Aeneas"* (*Aen.* 1.305), and imbued with the nebulousness of *"sunt lacrimae rerum"* (there are tears of things) (*Aen.* 1.462). This is not necessarily the Virgil of literary deeds, but more like the legendary Virgil, true or not, who on his deathbed requested that the manuscript of his unfinished *Aeneid* be burned. This is Hermann Broch's Virgil. On his bier, Durrell wore a "slight smile", his inevitable "blue jacket", and Sappho Jane's scarf "knotted about his neck".[74] "Above all, Virgil is European" says George Steiner and further comments that Virgil is a major predecessor of Modernism and that Broch (1886-1951) is one of its major exponents.[75] Durrell belongs in this tradition.

Was Virgil's artistic development linear? Was he simply a perfectionist and didn't want anything less than a perfect *Aeneid*? He of course had the advantage of biographical impoverishment. Unlike Lawrence Durrell, he didn't give over one hundred interviews and have two full-scale biographies written about him — with a third underway.[76] Still, we know much but understand little. Which comes back to Virgil. Even if we must concur with Theodore Ziolkowski "that Broch knew little and cared less about the historical Virgil, using him merely as a figure upon which to impose his own views and concerns",[77] it's pleasing to pretend, as Broch does, that Virgil was deeply troubled. He too had doubts about himself and the worth of his accomplishments.

No matter Broch's views of Virgil and the projection of his personal philosophy on the Roman poet, the mood and ambience of *The Death of Virgil* are Virgilian and consistent with Durrell's vision of a "dark pastoral". Broch's novel begins by entering a crepuscular world of Virgilian *umbrae* and never leaves until perhaps twenty-four hours later.[78] "Steel-blue and light" (*"Stahlblau und leicht"*) are the first words of the novel. They describe the colour and serenity of the Adriatic but also characterize the half-light of the approaching evening, where, we learn later, "the mirror of sky and the mirror of sea [are] merging to a single essence".[79] Those same

[74] MacNiven, *Lawrence Durrell*, p. 68.
[75] Steiner, "Homer and Virgil and Broch", pp. 10-11.
[76] For interviews, see L. Durrell, *Conversations*, p. 10. Major biographies include Gordon Bowker's *Through the Dark Labyrinth: A Biography of Lawrence Durrell* (1998) and Ian S. MacNiven's *Lawrence Durrell: A Biography* (1998). Michael Haag (1943-2020) died before completing his long anticipated biography.
[77] Ziolkowski, *Virgil and the Moderns*, p. 220.
[78] Arendt, "Achievement of Hermann Broch", p. 481.
[79] Broch, *Death of Virgil*, p. 477; Broch, *Tod des Vergil*, p. 449.

words — "steel-blue and light" — recur near the conclusion.[80] Broch's
Virgil spends his last hours in perpetual twilight. The novel ends by circling
back to the beginning ("the end was the beginning"; "*das Ende war der
Anfang*")[81] and so anticipates Durrell's "*le cercle refermé*" and his last
book's "penumbra of shadow". Although Durrell would surely have felt
uncomfortable with Broch's final vision of the unity of all things, with its
Christian overtones and composure, both writers have a common
sensibility. Broch's Virgil progresses through stages of understanding. At
the end, he sees the "crystal of unity" ("*Kristall der Einheit*") at the heart of
the cosmos, and then he sees that crystal become "just the darkest radiation"
("*sondern nur noch dunkelste Strahlung*"). His vision, as transformed
through a Hindu or Buddhist "third eye" ("*er bestand nur mehr aus Auge,
aus dem Auge in seiner Stirn*"), becomes the experience of "the seeing
blindness" ("*die sehende Blindheit*").[82] Durrell could agree with that. His
"dark crystal" is similar, although much darker.

[80] Broch, *Death of Virgil*, pp. 11, 480; Broch, *Tod des Vergil*, pp. 11, 453.
[81] Broch, *Death of Virgil*, p. 481; Broch, *Tod des Vergil*, p. 453.
[82] Broch, *Death of Virgil*, pp. 477-79; Broch, *Tod des Vergil*, pp. 450-51.

CHAPTER NINE

ANCIENT EGYPT
AND *THE ALEXANDRIA QUARTET*

Ego gigno lumen, I beget the light
But darkness is also of my nature.
— Lawrence Durrell, "The Anecdotes. II: In Cairo" (1948)

He considered himself a poet first and after that a seeker of truth.
— Anthea Morton-Saner, Lawrence Durrell's literary agent (2020)

I. Durrell and Egypt

In *Ptolemaic Alexandria,* P. M. Fraser comments on the Roman designation
for Alexandria: "Its official nomenclature was 'Alexandrea ad Aegyptum'",
or "'Alexandria by Egypt', not 'Alexandria in Egypt'". The Romans saw
the city as administratively and culturally distinct from the rest of the
country. Fraser further notes, "The modern city, with its once large European
population, was not usually regarded as characteristically Egyptian".[1] These
comments could apply to Lawrence Durrell's *Alexandria Quartet* (1957-
60), both in terms of the work itself and the critical response. The *Quartet*
does not seem situated in Egypt proper, and its author would seem to pay
scant attention to three thousand years of ancient Egyptian history.

This view is a justifiable oversight, for Durrell obscures,
deliberately or not, his debt to ancient Egypt. A few scholars have explored
the *Quartet*'s Egyptian matrices. Carol Peirce examines Durrell's use of
Plutarch's *Isis and Osiris* in the portrayal of incest,[2] and Michael V. Diboll
analyzes Osirian themes of "death and re-birth".[3] Diboll's emphasis,
however, is not on myth, rather the "socio-historical" culture of modern

---

[1] Fraser, *Ptolemaic Alexandria*, vol. 1, pp. 107, 109.
[2] Carol Peirce, "Plutarch", pp. 82-83.
[3] Diboll, *Egyptian Contexts*, p. 227.

Egypt.[4] Modernity as the Alexandria of Forster, Cavafy, and Durrell is the key for Michael Haag and his reconstructions of the city, based upon photographs, witnesses, documents, and material culture.[5] While these critics make valuable contributions, I focus on Durrell's use of ancient Egyptian paintings, their conventions and iconography, and pharaonic traditions, specifically in reference to the Narmer Palette and the role of dwarfs. This usage is like Durrell's treatment of King Narmer's catfish — it hangs in the shadows.

    The influence of classical or native art on western artists is well known. In 1817, John Keats saw an exhibit of the Elgin or Parthenon Marbles in London,[6] and this inspired two of his poems: "On Seeing the Elgin Marbles" (1817) and the "Ode on a Grecian Urn" (1819). In the Grecian urn ode, the influence is direct: the scene of cattle being led to sacrifice (slab XL of the Marbles in the British Museum) appears at the beginning of the poem's fourth stanza ("Who are these coming to the sacrifice?"). Similarly, in 1907, Pablo Picasso came under the influence of African art,[7] and this led to his radical painting, *Les Demoiselles d'Avignon* (1907), and to Proto-Cubism. In this painting, the faces of women appear as stylized African masks. As of the writing of this essay, no such documentation exists for Lawrence Durrell, who was both writer and painter, but the influence of ancient Egypt on his art can nonetheless be inferred by studying *The Alexandria Quartet*.

    Finally, I would like to emphasize that my viewpoint is presumptuous and attempts to see ancient Egyptian art and culture as Durrell might have seen it. I am not making any contribution to current scholarship in Egyptology. I shall mention and cite current research in the area, but I do so to present context and to make comparisons. I believe this approach is legitimate because it opens up an area for discussion previously closed or unconsidered.[8]

---

[4] Diboll, *Egyptian Contexts*, pp. 4-5.

[5] Haag, *City of Memory*, p. 10.

[6] Bate, *John Keats*, p. 146.

[7] Stein, *Writings*, p. 510.

[8] A word of re-emphasis. My dates for ancient Egyptian history, which are contentious and often disputed, are taken from Toby Wilkinson's *Thames & Hudson Dictionary of Ancient Egypt* (2008).

II. Durrell in Egypt

Lawrence Durrell (1912-90) lived in Egypt from May 1941 until July 1945. As the German army advanced into the Balkans, he fled Corfu, then Greece, and ended up in Egypt. He first worked as a press officer for the British Embassy in Cairo. In November 1942, he transferred to Alexandria where he served as Public Information Officer. On Corfu, he called himself a "Hellene" (*PC* 23); later in France, he claimed he "loathed Egypt" (*DML* 320). Whatever the truth of his claim, what is true is that Durrell's Egyptian experiences had a profound affect on his personal development. Those would lead to *The Alexandria Quartet.*

Unlike Hamlet's predicament, a "defect" need not be fatal, and some flaws are insignificant. Durrell was not a serious student of Egyptology. So Ian S. MacNiven, Durrell's authorized biographer, comments in a personal communication: "My own opinion is that LD was opportunistic in his research: whatever drifted into his ken and caught his fancy was apt to be dumped into his fictional hopper. He did, however, count many Old Hands in Egypt among his friends [...] and I am sure they loaned him books that would not appear in his library. And he talked a good deal about haunting the Patriarchal Library in Alexandria".[9]

Carelessness also contributes to the confusion of the "fictional hopper". In *Justine,* Darley, Durrell's *alter ego,* spends two years in Upper Egypt, whose vastness stretches from south of Cairo to Aswan, about 500 miles. The Nile Valley of Upper Egypt has a narrow floodplain and variable escarpment; the Nile Delta of Lower Egypt is broad and flat. Darley transposes Valley and Delta. He describes his southern landscape as "flat rich fields", stresses its "flatness", and has its river "moving corpulently through the Delta" (*Quartet* 185-86). Durrell travelled to Aswan in 1943; yet, he confuses Egyptian geography.

The influence of geography on culture is a major aspect of Lawrence Durrell's poetic and critical thinking. He calls it "the spirit of place" and uses the Latin tag, *deus loci.* For example, in *Prospero's Cell* (1945), Durrell describes the olive poetically, as the very embodiment of Mediterranean culture in all its diversity:

> The whole Mediterranean—sculptures, the palms, the gold beads, the bearded heroes, the wine, the ideas, the ships, the moonlight, the winged gorgons, the bronze men, the philosophers—all of it seems to rise in the sour, pungent taste of these black olives between the teeth. A taste older than meat, older than wine. A taste as old as cold water. (*PC* 96).

---

[9] Email 29 September 2014.

Then later, in *Sicilian Carousel* (1977), he refines the idea, compresses it, and defines Mediterranean culture in terms of the geographical distribution of the olive:

> What we mean when we use the word Mediterranean starts there, starts at that first vital point when Athens enthrones the olive as its reigning queen and Greek husbandry draws its first breadth. (*SC* 65)

Ultimately the idea of *Mediterranean* becomes monistic. Diversity yields to unity, to oneness.

Deus loci could also apply to the land of Egypt. Some Egyptologists see a correspondence between the divergent landscapes of Upper and Lower Egypt, known in pharaonic times as the "Two Lands", and the Egyptian tendency to dualism, to see the world in terms of contrasting but complemental pairs. The concept of duality was "fundamental in Egyptian thought"[10] and was well known among Egyptologists such as Henri Frankfort (1897-1954).[11] John A. Wilson (1899-1976), another prominent Egyptologist, was a contemporary of Durrell. In *The Burden of Egypt* he argues, "Perhaps the duality of 'the Two Lands' was a stronger factor in producing the dualism of Egyptian psychology".[12] However appropriate to his theories of landscape and human psychology, Durrell never discusses Egyptian geography in terms of duality — perhaps because he prefers Oneness. It is the old philosophical problem of "the One and the Many" or Monism and Pluralism.[13] It was a problem for which Durrell had his own solution.

Furthermore, Durrell does not mention Wilson's work and shows no interest in the ancient Egyptian worldview and its preoccupation with social stability. Durrell's worldview presumes instability and impermanence — social, physical, and psychological (*EB* 7-8). He does not introduce essential concepts like *maat* (truth), "the cosmic force of harmony, order, stability, and security", as Wilson explains.[14] The goddess Maat appears often in the Egyptian *Book of the Dead*, a book Durrell read, and the truth she embodies could have provided a dramatic contrast to a notorious paradox in *Balthazar*: "Truth is what most contradicts itself in time" (*Quartet* 216). Durrell's "truth" exists elsewhere, beyond the Heraclitean

---

[10] T. Wilkinson, *Dictionary*, p. 70.
[11] Frankfort, *Kingship*, pp. 19-20.
[12] J. Wilson, *Burden*, p. 17.
[13] R. Hall, "Monism and Pluralism", p. 363: "How many things are there? Or how many kinds of thing? Monism is the doctrine that the answer to one or others of these questions is 'Only one.' Opposed to monism is the doctrine of pluralism, which is that there are many kinds of thing, or that there are many things".
[14] J. Wilson, *Burden*, p. 48.

world of flux and change.

The evidence for Durrell's written sources on Egypt is substantial. William Leigh Godshalk reveals that Durrell "declared himself 'deficient in true scholarship'" but "prides himself on both the diversity and the obscurity of his reading".[15] MacNiven identifies the major materials:[16] Anthony de Cosson's *Mareotis* (1935); E. M. Forster's *Alexandria* (1922); R. Talbot Kelly's *Egypt Painted and Described* (1903); Edward William Lane's *Modern Egyptians* (1836); S. H. Leeder's *Desert Gateway* (1910), *Modern Sons of the Pharaohs* (1918), *Veiled Mysteries of Egypt* (1915); Joseph W. McPherson's *Moulids of Egypt* (1940); and Mary Louisa Whatley's *Ragged Life in Egypt* (1863).

I believe Durrell was also familiar with Forster's other book on Alexandria: *Pharos and Pharillon* (1923), with its essays on Lake Mareotis and C. P. Cavafy, both prominent topics in the *Quartet*.

Forster's and Lane's books are classics. The other sources are perishable literature, illustrating the authors' stated aims. In 1960, Durrell explained that he sought to reproduce the "color of Egypt": "I had to have enough 'color' [sic] to support four long volumes without boring".[17] His syllabus reflects that programme. At times, his "color" paints romantic squalor: "Flies and beggars own it today", says Darley of Alexandria (*Quartet* 17), recalling Whatley's *Ragged Life in Egypt*. On one occasion, he plagiarizes Kelly's *Egypt Painted and Described*: "We saw, inverted in the sky, a full-scale mirage of the city [...]" (*Quartet* 211).[18] And at other times, descriptions of the Delta allude to Predynastic and Ptolemaic Egypt.[19] So we have Durrell's "Harpoon Men" (*Quartet* 209) and the allusion to Forster's "Mareotic civilisation".[20]

IIIa. The Painter's Eye

The relationship between literature and painting is an old one. It is at least as old as Horace's formula in his *Ars Poetica*: "Ut pictura poesis" (as painting is, so is poetry) (*Ars P.* 361). Horace (65-8 BC) probably refers to the descriptive similarities of the two arts and their effects on the viewer and the reader (or listener). Van Gogh acknowledges this reciprocal relationship when he writes to Theo, "There's something of Rembrandt in Shakespeare

---

[15] Godshalk, "Some Sources", p. 158.
[16] MacNiven, *Lawrence Durrell*, pp. 386, 391-92, 431.
[17] L. Durrell, *Conversations*, p. 62.
[18] Godshalk, "Some Sources", pp.170-71, n. 57.
[19] Haag, *City of Memory*, pp. 76-77.
[20] Forster, *Alexandria*, p. 242.

and something of Correggio or Sarto in Michelet".[21] In his *George Eliot and the Visual Arts*, Hugh Witemeyer has written a whole book on the influence of paintings on George Eliot's writings. Witemeyer writes, "From the time she received her first illustrated book and painted her first water colors of floral arrangements, she had an abiding interest in the visual arts".[22] A similar statement could be said of Durrell's interests in paintings. His interests, however, were closer to what Mariella Guzzoni says of Van Gogh's intensive readings in literature: "In the books he read Vincent sought himself, and in his most beloved texts even saw himself, as if mirrored in them, finding sympathy in the ideas and sentiments therein".[23] As in much of his oeuvre, written and painterly, Durrell was continually seeking himself, looking for other ways to express himself, and finding ways to integrate the two disciplines in the pursuit of his interests. He found an outlet for the latter in various forms of art, ancient and modern, Western and Eastern.

Lawrence Durrell was a talented painter, although he modestly called himself a "dauber".[24] He signed some of his early paintings with his own name; his later works used the pseudonym "Oscar Epfs", a deliberate joke which Durrell claimed was either unpronounceable in French or the sound of flatulence.[25] "Oscar Epfs" was clearly a form of personal concealment reminiscent of his pseudonym "Charles Norden", which he used for some of his early publications.[26] In 1964, an exhibition of Oscar Epfs's artwork was held in Paris. Durrell attended the affair but was not identified as the artist. The exhibition was largely a joke.

Durrell's paintings are not easily accessible. They are held by his estate or by private collectors, but some have appeared in books such as Alan G. Thomas's collection of Durrell's essays in *Spirit of Place: Letters and Essays on Travel* (1969); *The Big Supposer: Lawrence Durrell, a Dialogue with Marc Alyn* (1974); Corinne Alexandre-Garner's collection, *Lawrence Durrell: Dans l'Ombre du Soleil Grec* (2011); and Richard Pine's two-volume collection, *Lawrence Durrell's Endpapers and Inklings, 1933-1988* (2019).

Durrell's style is Post-Impressionistic, flat and two-dimensional, and often reminiscent of Matisse's use of cool colours, such as green and blue. Blue was Durrell's favourite colour. At the beginning of *Prospero's*

---

[21] Gogh, *Life in Letters*, p. 26.
[22] Witemeyer, *George Eliot*, p. 9.
[23] Guzzoni, *Vincent's Books*, p. 12.
[24] L. Durrell, "Art of Fiction", p. 50.
[25] MacNiven, *Lawrence Durrell*, p. 538.
[26] Chamberlin, *Durrell Log*, pp. 31, 34, 55.

Cell (1945), he announces, "Somewhere between Calabria and Corfu the blue really begins" (*PC* 11). Durrell's medium varies — either oil, charcoal, gauche, or watercolour. The subject matter may be nature, the human figure, or still life. Of those paintings I have seen, I find his distinctive mode to be a landscape in close association with a body of water: the sea, a harbour, or possibly a marshy lake.

As far as I can determine, Durrell did not paint *en plein air*, as many of the Impressionists and Post-Impressionists did, such as Cézanne, Renoir, and Van Gogh. He painted from memory, imaginatively. His method was similar to Turner's, whose paintings also influenced Durrell's style of writing. J. M. W. Turner (1775-1851) was an English painter of Romantic landscapes, and Ian MacNiven reports that Durrell "developed a passion for Turner's landscapes" during the early 1930s in London.[27] Durrell was in the right place to satisfy his passion, for the Tate Gallery in London holds the largest collection of Turner's paintings in the world.[28]

Durrell mentions Turner many times in his oeuvre. In *Sicilian Carousel*, he makes a positive comparison between a "display" of "clouds of whiteness" seen on a beach and Turner's use of light "worthy of a nervous breakdown" (*SC* 127). The emphasis is on creativity as the distortions of an altered state. As with Durrell, water plays an important role in Turner's art. It is almost always nearby, even in one of his most famous paintings: *Rain, Speed and Steam* (1844).[29] The landscape shows the blurry image of a locomotive emerging from mists and traversing a bridge over water. The power of this extraordinary painting defies any full description. Its effect is overwhelming, even menacing, largely because Turner's watery world is one of indefinition. It is a world of light, emergence, and confusion. Turner travelled widely in Britain and Europe, drew his sketches in the field, and later returned to his London studio "to paint more elaborate versions of the same composition".[30] Durrell's method of painting was similar. After his travels, his studio was his home and private study; his sketchbook was apparently his own rich but distorted memory.

As a writer, Durrell had a painter's eye for the urban landscape of Alexandria and its surrounding countryside. In the *Quartet*, one of his favourite idioms is "my mind's eye". So we are invited to see: "In a flash my mind's eye shows me a thousand dust-tormented streets" (*Quartet* 17). Or: "In my mind's eye the city rose once more against the flat mirror of the green lake and the broken loins of sandstone which marked the desert's

[27] MacNiven, *Lawrence Durrell*, p. 86.
[28] Brown, *Turner in the Tate Collection*, p. 7.
[29] Warrell, *Turner's Sketchbooks*, p. 152.
[30] Warrell, *Turner's Sketchbooks*, p. 10.

edge" (*Quartet* 216).

Durrell's mind's eye, however, is deeply indebted to the eye of other artists. His book on Cyprus, *Bitter Lemons* (1957), which is roughly contemporary with the writing of the *Quartet*, opens with a view of Venice as seen from a ship departing at dawn. Durrell describes the city as

> Venice wobbling in a thousand fresh-water reflections, cool as jelly. It was as if some great master, stricken by dementia, had burst his whole colour-box against the sky to deafen the inner eye of the world. (*BL* 15)

This is Turner's smoky Venice of suffused light (e.g., the watercolour, *Venice: The Giudecca from the Lagoon* [1840])[31] and not the exact, illusionistic paintings of Canaletto's Venice (e.g., the oil, *The Bacino di San Marco* [c. 1738-39]).[32] Nor, for that matter, is this the Venice of clear and sharp contours that I have personally experienced. Later in the same memoir, Durrell describes a mosque on a headland at sunset:

> But when I looked back the Mosque still blazed in sunlight, vertical and emphatic, echoing those ancient discoveries in space which still haunt our architecture—the cube, the sphere, the square, the cylinder. (*BL* 241)

This is Paul Cézanne's geometric treatment of his native landscape around Aix-en-Provence, in particular his oil of 1904-1906, *Le Mont Sainte-Victoire vu des Lauves*.[33]

Durrell's eye is similar but different from those of his predecessors. His "inner eye of the world" is really the mind's eye he shares with other artists, some modern and some ancient. Among the moderns are Turner and Cézanne; the ancients are the unknown artists of Egyptian tombs. In Alexandria, Durrell surely observed the technique of Hellenistic sculpture known as *sfumato*, the softening of facial features.[34] Durrell the writer delights in the painterly aspect of *sfumato*, especially the dim light of dawn or dusk, but he also suffers from synesthesia, a kind of altered state. He mixes the senses of sight and sound — his vision "deafen[s]" and "echo[es]".

---

[31] Brown, *Turner in the Tate Collection*, plate 110.

[32] Beddington, *Venice*, plate 22.

[33] Athanassoglou-Kallmer, *Cézanne and Provence*, frontispiece.

[34] Daszweski, "Hellenistic Polychrome of Sculptures", p. 141; Stewart, "Alexandrian Style", pp. 240-41.

Synesthesia characterizes Durrell's palette, which is a mixture of blended colours and sensory experiences. Near the beginning of the *Quartet*, in a striking example of Horatian *ut pictura poesis*, he paints the city's landscape:

> Notes for landscape-tones. . . . Long sequences of tempera. Light filtered through the essence of lemons. An air full of brick-dust — sweet-smelling brick-dust and the odour of hot pavements slaked with water. Light damp clouds, earth-bound yet seldom bringing rain. Upon this squirt dust-red, dust-green, chalk-mauve and watered crimson-lake. In summer the sea-damp lightly varnished the air. Everything lay under a coat of gum. (*Quartet* 18)

Durrell is literally preparing his palette before the reader's eyes. The diction is painterly ("tempera", "squirt", "varnished", "gum") and sensuous ("odour", "slaked", "damp"). An underlying "coat of gum" is a method of forming pastels with a binder of gum. It creates chalky tones and has a "cooling" effect ("chalk-mauve and watered crimson-lake"). Despite the heat of summer, Durrell's image of Alexandria is as refreshing as pastels or the liquid "essence of lemons".

This Alexandrian landscape reappears at the beginning of *Balthazar*. Only this time Durrell's palette is pure colour:

> Landscape-tones: brown to bronze, steep skyline, low cloud, pearl ground with shadowed oyster and violet reflections. The lion-dust of desert: prophets' tombs turned to zinc and copper at sunset on the ancient lake. It huge sand-faults like watermarks from the air; green and citron giving to gunmetal, to a single plum-dark sail, moist, palpitant: sticky-winged nymph. Taposiris is dead among its tumbling columns and seamarks, vanished the Harpoon men ... Mareotis under a sky of hot lilac. (*Quartet* 209)

"Bronze", "pearl", "oyster", "lion-dust", "zinc", "copper", "lilac", "citron", "gunmetal", "plum-dark" — all these are Durrell's poetic terms for the colours of his paint box. So Balthazar admonishes Darley, who is another of Durrell's *alter ego*s, "You have been painting the city, touch by touch, upon a curved surface — was your object poetry or fact?" (*Quartet* 213). The object is poetry — which may or may not apply to Pursewarden's novel of three or four dimensions (*Quartet* 198, 386). "Landscape-tones" apply to a two-dimensional surface, one in which a "steep skyline", an indication of perpendicularity, usually pertains to a plane, for example, to a flat canvas.

IIIb. The Fish-Drive

Durrell's Mareotis, now called Lake Mariut, is a shallow, brackish backwater of the Nile, full of reeds and papyrus sedge. It is located in the Nile Delta. The lake is large and within sight of Alexandria, as Darley mentions: "Mareotis glinted here and there between the palm-tops, between the mud huts and the factories" (*Quartet* 188). Ubiquitous references to the lake suggests a preoccupation with the enduring presence of ancient Egypt as an aspect of its Nilotic environment (*Quartet* 38, 43, 50, *et passim*; twenty-seven references *in toto*). In the *Quartet*, Egyptian history as an embodiment of its pyramids, Sphinx, and tombs warrants an occasional comment, but the Nile as wetland receives the most serious and extended attention. Durrell is famous for his set-piece descriptions. Two of those are the "duck-shoot" near the end of *Justine* and the "fish-drive" at the beginning of *Mountolive* (*Quartet* 168-78; 397-402). Both of those occur at either dawn or dusk and within the marshy reaches of Mareotis.

I shall consider the scene in *Mountolive* first, for its Egyptian elements are prominent. The set-piece in *Justine*, however, is cryptic and requires elaboration. A few artistic principles need stating, however obvious. As the Egyptologist Cyril Aldred (1914-1991) and others have noted,[35] ancient Egyptian art presents a two-dimensional depiction of the world, and, as Aldred emphasizes, this art aims towards timelessness (the "eternal verities") and the impersonality of the artist (the "non-perspectival vision"). The first two apply to the fish-drive but not the third.

The fish-drive takes place in the dark after sunset and involves small boats or "punts" forming a large "semicircle" and slowly tightening the circumference (*Quartet* 397). The prows of the punts hold carbide lamps, thus illuminating the teeming life below the surface of the water. As the circle tightens, the fish inside concentrate *en masse*, and fishermen gather them into nets. The description of the event is long, detailed, and sensuous. The narrator begins by saying "The land had become dense as tapestry in the lilac afterglow" (*Quartet* 397), his protagonist finds "the rotting smells of the estuary" pleasurable (*Quartet* 398), and the final narrative builds to a visual climax accompanied by "drumming and singing" (*Quartet* 400).

Durrell's narrator describes the fish-drive as two-dimensional "bas-reliefs upon a screen of gold and violet" (*Quartet* 397), occurring within the context of "forgotten Pharaonic frescoes of light and darkness" (*Quartet* 402). Time exists — "'Time'", Nessim emphatically calls out

---

[35] Aldred, *Egyptian Art*, p. 15; Schäfer, *Principles*, pp. 78ff; Robins, *Art*, p. 21.

(*Quartet*, 399) — but it seems suspended within the long descriptive moment. Narrative time is overwhelmed by what the scientific writer John McPhee calls the "deep time" of geology[36] — and by what Durrell's narrator describes as "the soft cracked mud of prehistoric lake-faults, or the bituminous mud which the Nile drove down before it on its course to the sea" (*Quartet* 399). Lake Mareotis rests upon a muddy bed of immense time.

All this is seen through the eyes of the young British diplomat, David Mountolive, and his point of view is not objective in the least. It is passionate and incurably Romantic. He sees Egypt with a lover's eyes: "'Egypt' he said to himself as one might repeat the name of a woman. 'Egypt'" (*Quartet* 398). The incantation of *Egypt* is more than just a name; it personifies a real woman. On the occasion of the fish-drive, Mountolive is also having a love affair with Leila Hosnani, "the dark swallow" of Alexandria (*Quartet* 408), who is a Copt and one of the "true descendants" of the "ancient Egyptians" (*Quartet* 421-22).

Some Egyptian depictions of Nilotic scenes had another aspect. From at least the Old Kingdom onward (c. 2658-2135 BC), they describe a violent encounter between man and nature, which scholars often interpret as an attempt either "to eliminate a potential danger to people and fields", to subdue the forces of "chaos", or to destroy "potential enemy forces".[37] So the hunt of the hippopotamus, the crocodile, and wild birds. In this context, the fish-drive in *Mountolive* is both violent and dangerous. Flocks of birds descend on the fishermen in a wild feeding frenzy. In this frenetic mêlée, some men have faces slashed or eyes gouged out (*Quartet* 400), while others are wounded in "cheek" and "thigh" (*Quartet* 402). Men fight birds, and "blood" is shed (*Quartet* 402). Bloody violence is an integral part of Durrell's vision in the *Quartet*. The mayhem also contains a tinge of sexuality as suggested by Mountolive's youthful infatuation, by the narrative's inevitable climax, and by the birds' "terrifying cupidity" (*Quartet* 402).

Durrell's use of *cupidity* is ambiguous. It can mean "greed", which is probably the primary sense, or it can mean "lust", which is the context of Nessim's maxim in *Balthazar*: "Love is a wonderfully luxuriant plant, but unclassifiable really, fading as it does into mysticism on the one side and naked cupidity on the other" (*Quartet* 389).

Nessim's mother is Leila Hosnani, whom Mountolive loves. The maxim is about love, but it also encapsulates the atmosphere of the fish-drive: luxuriant vegetation, dim light, vague emotions, and naked brutality.

---

[36] McPhee, *Basin*, p. 108.
[37] Malek, S*hadow of the Pyramids*, p. 42; Robins, *Art*, p. 69; Parkinson, *Nebamun*, p. 132.

IIIc. The Duck-Shoot

Among the many treasures in London's British Museum are ten paintings taken from the Theban tomb of Nebamun in Upper Egypt. Nebamun was a minor official serving the temple of Amun at Karnak (his name means "My lord is Amun"). He lived during the Eighteenth Dynasty, possibly during the reigns of either Thutmose IV (1400-1390 BC) or Amenhotep III (1390-1353 BC).[38] The museum acquired the paintings in 1821 and first displayed them in 1835. The paintings have long been famous and have appeared in many publications, most notably in Nina M. Davies's *Ancient Egyptian Paintings* (1936).

The most famous of the ten is the painting of Nebamun known as *Fowling in the Marshes* (**Plate 5**; British Museum EA 37977). The scene is not unique in Egyptian paintings; similar scenes stretch back to the Old Kingdom.[39] Davies considers the depiction of the cat in that painting as one of the "masterpieces" of Egyptian painting.[40] The same could be said of the entire painting. Richard Parkinson, a curator of Egyptian antiquities at the British Museum, chose *Fowling in the Marshes* for the cover and frontispiece of his book on the paintings cited in this essay.

In the early 1930s, Lawrence Durrell spent a lot of time in the Reading Room of the British Museum.[41] Largely an autodidact, Durrell was pursuing a programme of intensive self-study. I have not been able to confirm that he visited the museum's Egyptian collection, but that seems likely, for Durrell, while on Corfu in 1937, wrote Henry Miller that he had acquired a copy of the ancient Egyptian *Book of the Dead* (*DML* 67). Richard Pine, a prominent scholar of Durrellian studies, has a "hunch" that Durrell began studying the *Book of the Dead* during his time spent in the British Museum.[42] I assume that Durrell was familiar with the painting of Nebamun hunting and fishing in the marshes and that it played a role in his creation of the duck-hunt episode at the end of *Justine*.

Parkinson describes some of the salient features of *Fowling in the Marshes* as follows.[43] "Nebamun" stands on a skiff in the act of launching a throw-stick. He dominates the scene and is naked except for a kilt. Among the papyri are various waterfowl; one of the species is "perhaps a pintail duck". A cat assists in the hunt and has caught birds in its jaws and claws.

---

[38] Parkinson, *Nebamun*, pp. 32, 39-41.
[39] Nina Davies, *Paintings*, p. xxvii.
[40] Nina Davies, *Paintings*, p. 174.
[41] MacNiven, *Lawrence Durrell*, p. 86.
[42] Email 3 November 2020.
[43] Parkinson, *Nebamun*, pp. 122-38.

On the prow of the boat stands a goose, "an animal sacred to Amun". Between Nebamun's legs sits his naked "young daughter" holding her father's leg with one hand and clasping a lotus blossom with the other. Behind Nebamun stands his beautiful wife "Hatshepsut" in reduced stature. She poses in formal attire with an incense cone atop her head. The "unguent cone" and pleated dress are appropriate for a typical "banquet scene".[44] She also holds a sistrum in one hand. The rattle is associated with Hathor, "the goddess of sexuality and fertility". We know the names of Nebamun and Hatshepsut because they are identified by hieroglyphic inscriptions. The caption to the painting in the British Museum would presumably transliterate the names of husband and wife.

As many Egyptologists have noted, paintings such as *Fowling in the Marshes* are rich in symbolic meaning normally connected to sexuality as a form of rebirth in the afterlife.[45] Every detail in the painting has special significance: the boat, the throw-stick, the birds, the cat, the plant life, even the dress or nakedness of Nebamun and his family. The painting was not intended to be realistic and governed by conventional notions of time and space. Although the scene occurs in daylight, the actual time is "the permanent time of the afterlife",[46] where all forms of life are fixed in a timeless moment. The physical location of the scene is generic and not specific to a particular locale, which could be almost anywhere along the Nile, although the Delta seems most likely. Moreover, no cat could perch itself on a papyrus stalk; no wild goose would decorate the prow of a boat; and no wife dressed for a banquet would accompany her husband on a hunting expedition.

Lawrence Durrell was probably unaware of the painting's sexual symbolism, which has taken Egyptologists decades to decode, but his painter's eye probably retained a memory of the broad composition of the scene. As seen in his appreciation of Turner and Cézanne, Durrell had the ability to isolate the essentials of a painter's style. Those essentials in the painting of Nebamun would have been the theme of *Fowling in the Marshes* and the positioning of the central characters as an embodiment of that theme.

Durrell's duck-shoot occurs at dawn near the end of *Justine* (*Quartet* 172). He opens the section with a description of the lake during the migratory season of winter: "The migrants multiplying on the shallow reaches of Mareotis. Waters moving from gold to grey, the pigmentation of winter" (*Quartet* 168).

---

[44] Hartwig, *Tomb Painting*, pp. 92, 99.

[45] For example: Manniche, *Sexual Life*, pp. 39-40; Hartwig, *Tomb Painting*, pp. 103-06; Parkinson, *Nebamun*, p. 132; Baines, *High Culture*, p. 41.

[46] Hartwig, *Tomb Painting*, p. 126.

Just *what* is "moving"? The "waters" are not in themselves changing colour. Water reflects light; it is not itself light. What is actually "moving" are the "pigments" perceived by the painter's eye. As in many other instances, Durrell's eye acts like a brush painting the scene. After the scene is set, the novel's main characters converge for a final gathering which brings the story to a climax.

The stars tell time. *Justine* opens on an unidentified Greek island. During "the midst of winter", roughly mid-January of 1940-41,[47] Darley says that the bright star "Arcturus" illuminates the night sky (*Quartet* 17). His statement is accurate.[48] Now, near the end of the novel, the story circles back to winter. The waters of Mareotis become a flat star chart, anticipating the description of the "the flat mirror of the green lake" (*Quartet* 216): "The water is full of stars, Orion down, Capella tossing out its brilliant sparks" (*Quartet* 172). The description is not mere colour. The reflection of the stars on the surface of Lake Mareotis also reflects ancient Egyptian beliefs in the afterlife and the Nilotic basis of their calendar.

Stars rise and fall along the plane of the ecliptic as the earth orbits the sun. They provide a vague sense of time in Durrell's world. The ancient Egyptians were also stargazers. In the Old Kingdom Pyramid Texts, the constellation Orion and its companion Sirius, the Dog Star, played important roles in defining the king's immortality among the imperishable stars. The Egyptologist I. E. S. Edwards quotes one of the texts' magical spells: "O king, thou art this great star [Sirius], the companion of Orion, who traverses the sky with Orion".[49] Sirius's heliacal rising around the middle of July coincided with the start of the Nile's annual inundation and marked the beginning of the Egyptian calendar.[50] The expression "Orion down" — perhaps signifying that the constellation and Sirius are low on the horizon at dawn — suggests winter, the time of the duck-shoot. Durrell's star chart is accurate in another respect, for Capella, a star of the first magnitude, the first order of brightness, appears with "its brilliant sparks" in the Northern Hemisphere during winter.[51]

The structure of the shoot itself closely resembles *Fowling in the Marshes*. Both Darley and Nebamun are participating in bird hunting in the marshes: Darley on Lake Mareotis in the Delta, Nebamun in a Nilotic type

---

[47] Kaczvinsky, "Darley in Alexandria", p. 594.
[48] I rely on the following computer program to determine the approximate position of stars mentioned in the *Quartet*: StarMap 3D (version 3.11.0), Ed Sanville programmer, 22 August 2020.
[49] Edwards, *Pyramids*, p. 285.
[50] Breasted, *History of Egypt*, p. 33.
[51] R. Allen, *Star Names*, p. 89.

scene. Both figures dominate their respective scenes.

Two broad correspondences between Nebamun and Darley are obvious, but the last two noted below are less so. Thus, Nebamun stands on a skiff; Darley sits in a "punt" (*Quartet* 172). Nebamun wields a fancy throw-stick with a serpentine head; Darley fires an expensive and high-quality shotgun, a "beautiful stout twelve by Purdey" (*Quartet* 169). Less obvious are two other details. Nebamun has a large cat as his hunter and retriever; Darley has the Egyptian "gun-bearer" Faraj (*Quartet* 172), who behaves sullenly and fetches slain ducks. In-between his duties, Faraj "yawns heavily and scratches himself" like a cat (*Quartet* 173). On the prow of Nebamun's skiff sits a goose; alongside Darley's punt "one silly duck settles for a moment" (*Quartet* 174). Whether or not Durrell deliberately copied all these aspects of the Egyptian painting is open to debate. But the similarities are striking and nevertheless there.

Special attention should also be paid to the comparative roles of Justine and Hatshepsut in their respective representations. Both wear unusual clothing. At the beginning of the duck-shoot, Darley describes Justine as appearing in a "velveteen costume": she wears a coat, a "schoolgirl's hat", and "leather jack-boots" (*Quartet* 169). Her attire is ambiguous, both feminine and masculine. At the beginning of *Justine*, Darley describes Justine as "her legs crossed in a mannish attitude", and he later notes she has a "husky speaking-voice" (*Quartet* 31, 56). Throughout the *Quartet*, Justine, the *femme fatale* of the novels, has androgynous qualities. And so Durrell's famous formulation: "The symbolic lovers of the free Hellenic world are replaced here by something different, something subtly androgynous, inverted upon itself" (*Quartet* 18).

Hatshepsut, Nebamun's wife, on the other hand, appears provocatively feminine in her diaphanous gown. Nonetheless, her very name immediately conjures other associations to anyone remotely familiar with Egyptian history. Since the early days of Egyptology at the beginning of the twentieth century, Queen Hatshepsut has been famous — and notorious — for her extraordinary accomplishments as a ruler of Egypt during the Eighteenth Dynasty.[52] Whatever the circumstances of her ascendency to kingship, she ruled a world normally ruled by men.[53] Hatshepsut assumed the role, regalia, and appearance of a male pharaoh. Her mortuary temple at Deir el-Bahri, one of Egypt's most recognizable landmarks, is located on the west bank of the Nile opposite Thebes.

---

[52] Breasted, *History of Egypt*, pp. 266-88.
[53] *Hatshepsut*, pp. 3-4.

Durrell knew the story of Queen Hatshepsut. In 1978, he refers to "that violent young queen" and mentions her mortuary temple in his *New York Times* article, "Egyptian Moments".[54] Thus, in Durrell's mind, Justine, another dominant woman, could be easily conflated with Hatshepsut, either as Queen of Egypt or wife of Nebamun — or both. Even their relative sizes are comparable, for Justine has reduced importance in the duck-shoot (she appears briefly and then abruptly disappears). And Hatshepsut in *Fowling in the Marshes* stands diminutively next to Nebamun. As Parkinson says, she is "respectfully standing behind her husband".[55]

Another relevant feature of Nebamun in the marshes is the image of his daughter sitting between his legs, clinging to him out of affection or for protection. She also clutches a lotus blossom, a symbol based on the Egyptian creation myth of rebirth. At night the lotus closes its blossom but opens it at dawn — thus, the deceased is reborn after death. So, a wood carving in the Cairo Museum shows King Tutankhamun's head emerging from a lotus blossom (**Figure 10**). The myth is also another aspect of the Egyptian solar myth.[56] Chapter 81 of the *Book of the Dead*, which Durrell may have begun reading in the British Museum, has a spell for the deceased related to the lotus and the creation myth ("I am the lotus pure coming forth from the god of light".)[57] Furthermore, Nebamun's daughter is a child, and, unlike her parents, she is unnamed. Her youth is indicated by her nakedness and "sidelock" of hair.[58]

The *Quartet* reflects the basic components of this complex image. At the beginning of *Justine*, Darley has left Alexandria and retreated to an unnamed island in the Mediterranean, possibly one of the Cyclades. He brings with him an infant girl and explains, "I have escaped to this island with a few books and the child — Melissa's child" (*Quartet* 17). Melissa, the infant's mother, has died of tuberculosis in Alexandria, where "she lies buried deep as any mummy in the shallow tepid sand of the black estuary" (*Quartet* 19). The infant's father is Nessim, not Darley, who acts as a surrogate parent, both teacher and protector (*Quartet* 188). On the unidentified Greek island, Darley raises the child and creates for her a "fairy story" around her father Nessim and stepmother Justine (*Quartet* 660). In effect, he creates a myth facilitating the child's paternal reunion or rebirth,

---

[54] *EB* 371, 376. In the *From the Elephant's Back* edition, Durrell's original title, "Egyptian Moments", is retitled and anthologized as "With Durrell in Egypt". The original title appeared in *The New York Times* on 11 June 1978.

[55] Parkinson, *Nebamun*, p. 124.

[56] T. Wilkinson, *Dictionary*, p. 139.

[57] Budge, *Book of the Dead*, p. 182.

[58] Parkinson, *Nebamun*, p. 127; T. Wilkinson, *Dictionary*, pp. 229-30.

once the two of them return to Alexandria.

Figure 10: King Tutankhamun emerging from a lotus flower (Wikimedia Commons)

In an ancient Egyptian context, the return may also be interpreted as a resurrection of Melissa from a mummified state. She returns to life through her unnamed daughter. The "child" remains unnamed throughout the four novels and is continually referred to as simply "the child" (*Quartet* 211, 280, 671). Not giving the girl a name allows a maternal identification — she could be another Melissa, whom Durrell in "Workpoints" calls a "patron of sorrow" (*Quartet* 197). Her sorrowful life turns then into a kind of postmortem happiness. So, "the child" remains a child enveloped within a mysterious "myth" of rebirth or, as Darley expresses it, "the poetry of infant uncertainty" (*Quartet* 661).

IV. Landscape and Orientalism

In Durrell's world, topography, national character, and iconography are all related, the latter being a way to represent the former two. In an important essay entitled "Landscape and Character" (1960), he writes,

> I have evolved a private notion about the importance of landscape, and I willingly admit to seeing 'characters' almost as functions of a landscape. [...] Yes, human beings are expressions of their landscape. [...] For they exist in nature, as a function of place. (*SP* 156, 157, 163).

Durrell was a poet, and his ideas often have a poetic basis. He thinks metaphorically in terms of concrete images, where, in this instance, landscapes become iconic representations set in stone. They are either "the great stone omphalos" of Delphi, the "Mena House pyramid" on the Giza Plateau, or the monoliths of "Stonehenge" on Salisbury Plain (*SP* 158-59). In Durrell's mind, all of these were lithic landmarks, artifacts of iconography, representing the different "characters" of Greece, Egypt, and England.

Durrell did not consider himself a "travel-writer" of colourful prose. *Colour* could mean reflections on Egyptian ruins such as Shelley's "Ozymandias" (1817) or writings like the Arabian romance of T. E. Lawrence's *Seven Pillars of Wisdom* (1926). E. M. Forster provides historical colour in *Alexandria: A History and a Guide* (1922) and *Pharos and Pharillion* (1923). R. Talbot Kelly's *Egypt: Painted and Described* (1903), a book Durrell was familiar with, is also in this tradition. As previously noted, Durrell so admired Kelly's book that he plagiarized some of his prose.

Egypt with its long history and exotic culture readily lent itself to versions of this orientalist treatment. In the nineteenth century, "Orientalism" became an international school of art, as seen in the paintings of the

Frenchmen Eugène Delacroix (1798-1863) and Jean-Léon Gérôme (1824-1904), the Scotsman David Roberts (1796-1864), and the American Frederick Arthur Bridgman (1847-1928). Bridgman's *Cleopatra on the Terraces of Philae* (1896) illustrates this wistful style in a pharaonic context (**Plate 6**). Orientalism in art was a testimony to the widespread appeal of Egypt, which would coincide, as Ronald H. Fritze describes, with "the rise of mass Egyptomania" after the discovery of Tutankhamun's tomb and its treasures in 1922.[59]

Orientalism surely had an influence on Durrell, and he was not above its romantic tendencies, however ironically he may have treated the topic. So, David Mountolive's lovesick sigh of "Egypt" during the duck-shoot was probably addressed to Leila Hosnani (*Quartet* 398), the Coptic "dark swallow" of *Mountolive* (*Quartet* 408), but it could have been equally addressed to a woman like Bridgman's Cleopatra, a legendary woman of far greater allure.

In *Alexandria: City of Memory* (2004), Michael Haag has little to say about the *Quartet*'s topographical descriptions, particularly those associated with the Delta and Lake Mareotis. In an earlier chapter on E. M. Forster, Haag limits himself to a few well-chosen quotations from *Pharos and Pharillon*,[60] where Forster meditates on the lake's "spirit of the place":

> Year after year she [Mareotis] has given this extraordinary show [of flowers] to a few Bedouins, has covered the Mareotic civilisation with dust and raised flowers from its sherds. Will she do the same to our own tins and barbed wire? Probably not, for man has now got so far ahead of other forms of life that he will scarcely permit the flowers to grow over his works again. His old tins will be buried under new tins. This is the triumph of civilisation, I suppose.[61]

Haag's quotations from Forster create "colour", irony, and historical depth. The effect is Shelleyan and recalls "the lone and level sands" of "Ozymandias".

Rose Macaulay (1881-1958), author of *Pleasure of Ruins* (1953), was another writer in a historical vein. In 1953, she visited Durrell on Cyprus, and they toured Gothic ruins together.[62] Macaulay's views on ruins, by her own admission, tend towards "picturesqueness".[63] The Canadian

[59] Fritze, *Egyptomania*, p. 222.
[60] Haag, *City of Memory*, pp. 76-77.
[61] Forster, *Alexandria*, pp. 240, 242.
[62] MacNiven, *Lawrence Durrell*, p. 393.
[63] Macaulay, *Pleasure*, p. xv.

artist Roloff Beny (1924-1984) provided the design and photographs for a lavish book based upon *Pleasure of Ruins*. In Beny's photographs, ruins are not ruins — they are another form of art engendered by time. They are like the lofty poetry of Shelley's *Prometheus Unbound*, which provided the title and epigraph for his first book of Mediterranean photographs, *The Thrones of Earth and Heaven* (1958). Beny's photographs enable "the soaring of the imagination into the high empyrean where huge episodes are tangled with myths and dreams".[64] Beny and Macaulay shared similar views on art and history. In *Bitter Lemons*, her visit to Cyprus prompted Durrell to ask himself, "Does time itself confer something on relics and ruins which isn't inherent in the design of the builder" (*BL* 96)?

That "something" was more than romantic pleasures in the passage of time. For Durrell's notion of the "spirit of place" reflected much deeper interests, religious or philosophical, as Ray Morrison argues with respect to Taoism.[65] These passions go beyond mere "colour". Part of Durrell's abiding concern remained uncovering the ethos of a place and its monumental "relics" (*SP* 156). Ian McNiven previously noted Durrell's pursuits at self-education in Egypt: a private tour of an Egyptian tomb, conversations with "Old Hands", and "haunting" the Patriarchal Library. All these activities indicate Durrell's interest in some basic aspects of ancient Egyptian culture. Durrell's topography is not always topography. It involves "spirit of place". It also involves, as Durrell says at the beginning of *Prospero's Cell*, "the discovery of yourself" (*PC* 11).

Va. The Narmer Palette

One theme common to the fish-drive and the duck-shoot is Durrell's depiction of violence. The fish-drive ends up as a bloody affair; the duck-shoot is inherently violent. These activities are unremarkable in themselves because they are an assault on nature and the environment, both commonly treated as human property or playthings. Man the hunter is an accepted and long-honoured role; it has even been normalized as sport. But a most disturbing, indeed horrifying, kind of violence is the assault on other human beings, no matter how justifiable warfare may be. And so we have the Narmer Palette and its celebration of ritualized mayhem (**Figures 11 and 12**). Violence in its most gruesome aspect is an integral part of that foremost monument of Predynastic Egyptian history.

---

[64] Beny, *Roloff Beny Interprets*, p. 28.
[65] Morrison, "City and Ontology", pp. 57-58.

Figure 11: Narmer Palette verso (Wikimedia Commons)

Figure 12: Narmer Palette recto (Wikimedia Commons)

I will argue that Durrell chose his influences carefully and
discreetly and used whatever information provided by MacNiven's
authorities on Egypt, one of whom was the famous Egyptologist George
Andrew Reisner (1867-1942). Durrell and Reisner had a short but important
relationship in which Durrell as student gained various insights into ancient
Egyptian culture. So, he reinterpreted Egyptian history and iconography as
they pertained to his artistic interests. Time and space were two of those,
and the timeless Narmer Palette was a prime vehicle for that process. The
palette is another distinctive stone monument like those just enumerated in
Durrell's article, "Landscape and Character".

Narmer's ceremonial palette has had an enormous impact on
ancient Egyptian historiography. Its great importance cannot be underestimated
— a fact which Durrell must have known. Although the palette marks the
violent inception of the Egyptian state, the unification of Upper and Lower
Egypt, the beginning of the story was quiet, as David O'Connor recounts:

> Round about 3000 BC, King Narmer, one of Egypt's earliest rulers,
> dedicated to the temple of the god Horus at Hierakonpolis a cosmetic
> palette richly decorated on both faces with representations in low relief.[66]

The artifact is large (25″ x 17″). Its "greenish-grey" stone is composed of
hard greywacke.[67] Discovered by James Edward Quibell (1867-1935)
during the 1897-98 excavation at Hierakonpolis, Upper Egypt, in the "Main
Deposit",[68] the palette holds a prominent position in the Cairo Museum of
Egyptian Antiquities, where it represents the beginning of Egyptian history.

Vb. Palette as Metaphor

How did the palette influence the *Quartet*? I propose unravelling a series of
linked metaphors: watch key, harpoons, glyphs, and heraldry. All connect
to Narmer's palette. Like Sigmund Freud, whom he studied, Durrell tends
to concatenate the imagery of his narrative. Darley at the beginning of
Justine struggles to understand his past by returning "along the iron chains
of memory" (*Quartet* 17). The image occurs in Freud's "Aetiology of
Hysteria" as "chain(s)", "associative chains", "linkage of the chains", or
(commonly) "chains of memory" (*Erinnerungsketten*).[69] Freud's analysis of

[66] O'Connor, "Narmer Palette", p. 145. Figs. 14 and 15.
[67] Stevenson, "Palettes", p. 1.
[68] Quibell, *Hierakonpolis*, p. 10, plate XXIX.
[69] Freud, *Standard Edition*, vol. 3, pp. 198-200, 202; Freud, *Gesammelte Werke*, vol.
1, p. 435.

dreams depends on the principle of association. In *A Key to Modern British Poetry* (1952), Durrell comments on Freud's method, "Our test of the dream, as of the modern poem, is the law of association. [...] The more you examine it, and the more you learn of the associations which surround each symbol, the richer and more varied the content becomes" (*Key* 57, 59).

The statement also describes a major aspect of Durrell's poetics. In "The Heraldic Universe" (1942), a note written in Egypt, he calls poetry an "associative approach [...] transcending logic" and then elaborates that "this Universe" is an entity "where for every object in the known world there exists an ideogram" (*EB* 103-04). During the writing of the *Quartet* in 1958, Durrell restates his ideas of the "*heraldic ideogram*" as a "set of associations" and "image making" (*DML* 308; original italics).

Watch-key: In *Justine,* Balthazar, medical doctor and astute commentator, keeps as a memento his father's "gold pocket-watch". It is wound with a key shaped like an *ankh* (☥), the Egyptian hieroglyph for life. Durrell's "ideogram" is iconic — *ankh* and key coincide — and conforms to Charles Sanders Peirce's definition of *icon* as the "resemblance" between "the sign and its object".[70] Iconicity is an aspect of Egyptian hieroglyphics,[71] as well as the poetics of Durrell's Heraldic Universe.

Balthazar loses the key and searches along the "rain-swept Corniche", as Lake Mareotis "crouched among the reeds, stiff as a crouching sphinx" (*Quartet* 80). The scene is quite mysterious. Its sphinxlike mystery, however, exceeds or "transcends" its role in the plot. The key complicates human relationships, but why did Durrell choose the *ankh*? If the key to life is time, then what is the nature of time? Durrell's answer appears to be an appropriation of Cartesian space, extension: "the unbound time which flowed through his body and mine" (*Quartet* 80). The suggestion is that time has physicality or substance and therefore extends through space. In the iconography of the *Quartet*, Durrell's imagery of ancient Egypt spans time like a bridge.

Harpoons: *Balthazar* opens with references to the Ptolemaic and Predynastic periods: "Taposiris is dead among its tumbling columns and seamarks, vanished the Harpoon Men ... Mareotis under a sky of hot lilac" (*Quartet* 209). The images of Mareotis link and extend the lake's associations, but the other proper nouns are obscure. In *Balthazar* and *Clea*, subsequent visits to Taposiris suggest Hellenistic ruins near the western end

---

[70] Charles Peirce, *Essential Peirce*, p. 226.
[71] Loprieno, *Ancient Egyptian*, p. 13.

of the lake (*Quartet* 369, 660). Plutarch translates "Taposiris" as "the tomb of Osiris".[72] E. M. Forster and Anthony de Cosson refer to the site as the "Temple of Osiris".[73] In either case, the myth of Osiris features mutilation, death, and resurrection — elements relevant to the final harpoon episode.

The final reference to the "Harpoon Men" occurs many years later in *Clea*, the last novel of the *Quartet*. During an outing by sailboat, along the Mediterranean coast, Balthazar grows drowsy and drifts into reverie: "[He] talked discursively (half asleep) of the Vineyard of Ammon, the Kings of the Harpoon Kingdom and their battles" (*Quartet* 846). The meditation conjures ancient Egyptian prehistory, and the "Harpoon Kingdom" manifests itself in the narrative as a synecdoche, "the old harpoon gun of Narouz" (*Quartet* 847). Not long afterwards, Clea is harpooned, mutilated, almost killed, and revived near "ancient Taposiris" (*Quartet* 829; 849), thus re-enacting the Osirian myth. In Durrell's fiction, the past exists as archaeological ruins or as a "gold pocket-watch" and its watch-key in the shape of an *ankh*. The past does not "vanish" like the "Harpoon Men".

The "Harpoon Kingdom" refers to a Predynastic area, probably east of Alexandria, which Durrell situates near Taposiris Magna, today's Abusir. "Harpoon Kingdom" is not glossed in many histories.[74] The designation has long had dubious validity, and it is doubtful that any authoritative source would have given it much credence when Durrell was writing *Balthazar*.

"Kingdom of the Harpoon", however, appears in de Cosson's *Mareotis,* a copy of which Durrell underlined extensively:[75]

> East of the land of Tehenu was the Kingdom of the Harpoon. Many years ago, Professor Newberry, in an article on "The Petty Kingdom of the Harpoon and Egypt's Earliest Mediterranean Port," pointed out that the slate palette of Nar Mer [sic] in the Cairo Museum proved that about 3400 B.C. the north-west of Egypt (west of the Canopic Nile) was inhabited by a settled pre-dynastic people. Their country was known as the Kingdom of the Harpoon because the harpoon was the hieroglyphic sign for this district, the cult object of the inhabitants, and their common weapon for killing fish in Lake Mareotis. [...] The celebrated slate palette shows Nar Mer (Menes) smiting *(i.e.* conquering) the King of the Harpoon, thus bringing the whole of Egypt under the dominion of the Pharaoh.[76]

---

[72] Plutarch, *De Iside et Osiride*, p. 151.
[73] Forster, *Alexandria*, p. 154; de Cosson, *Mareotis*, p. 109.
[74] Breasted, *History of Egypt*; Gardiner, *Egypt of the Pharaohs*; T. Wilkinson, *Rise and Fall*.
[75] MacNiven, *Lawrence Durrell*, p. 392.
[76] De Cosson, *Mareotis*, pp. 19-20.

The text includes an illustration of the palette's recto, where Narmer assumes the classic smiting pose. De Cosson was an amateur archaeologist; his source, Percy E. Newberry (1868-1949), was a highly reputable professor of Egyptology in the United Kingdom.[77] Nevertheless, Newberry's article is outdated. Still, de Cosson's "Kingdom of the Harpoon", text and illustration, encapsulates a mode of representation that undoubtedly appealed to Durrell's imagination, namely, the mysterious glyphs and images of the Narmer Palette.

Glyphs: Representations of the Narmer Palette are ubiquitous. Any standard history of ancient Egypt has depictions of its two sides. But the purpose of the palette is controversial. The following is a small selection of a large body of scholarship. Like Newberry, Alan Gardiner (1879-1963) interprets the recto as situated in the Delta and sees the verso as "commemorating the very events" that led to conquest and unification, although he acknowledges the uncertainty of identifying Narmer as Herodotus's Min (Menes), the legendary first pharaoh.[78]

The details of the scenes, the factuality of the "events", and the meaning of the glyphs are disputed. John Baines rejects factuality and calls the depictions "tokens of royal achievement", that is, "ritual incorporated events and thus gave them full meaning, so that there was no necessary distinction between events and the celebration of the achieved order of the world".[79]

Despite the controversy, the importance of the palette remains indisputable. Cyril Aldred calls the votive artifact "the most important single monument" of the early dynastic period.[80] Orly Goldwasser says it marks the "'turning point' from pre-state to state, from proto-history to history, from pre-canonical to canonical art" and sees it as a "poetic accomplishment".[81] It has become, then, a collection of tantalizing metaphors that invite continual speculation.

Durrell's view surely matched de Cosson's and Newberry's. He could not have known about the later debate. But he anticipated some of the main issues, especially with respect to Baines's observations about ritual. Moreover, his and Goldwasser's uses of the palette are similar and link to what he calls his "Heraldic Universe".

---

[77] Newberry, "Petty Kingdom", p. 17.
[78] Gardiner, *Egypt of the Pharaohs*, p. 404.
[79] Baines, *Visual and Written Culture*, p. 294.
[80] Aldred, *Egypt*, p. 44.
[81] Goldwasser, "Narmer Palette", pp. 68, 79.

Unlike historical events, which can be and are meant to be dated, cultural rituals are, in a sense, timeless. Like the Catholic Mass, they rely upon symbols to celebrate an undated or mythic "event". In her controversial study, *Arrest and Movement* in ancient Near Eastern art (1951), the Dutch archaeologist H. A. Groenewegen-Frankfort (1896-1982) analyzes the Narmer Palette in terms of its symbols. She comments, "But from the Narmer Palette coincidence and contiguity [i.e., time and space] are barred and the king's more violent gesture has therefore the peculiar static quality of a symbol. King Narmer's is a timeless act".[82]

Time and space were two of Durrell's major interests when *Arrest and Movement* was first published in the early 1950s, and he may have been aware of Groenewegen-Frankfort's book. The two authors shared, perhaps not coincidentally, the same publisher, Faber and Faber in London. The Dutch archaeologist's methodology, however, was subjective, idiosyncratic, and open to serious criticism from some of her colleagues in archaeology who favoured an objective, impersonal interpretation of ancient art.[83]

Archaeologists sometimes think of their discipline as a "science", so Richard H. Wilkinson refers to "Egyptology as it is actually practiced [today] as a modern scientific discipline".[84] It isn't one. Archaeology is not restricted to pure scientific objectivity. From my experiences of working on a "dig" in Israel, I can say that Israeli archaeology, no matter how rigorous and meticulous its methodology, depends upon a considerable amount of subjective interpretation of Canaanite material culture, which is often sparse, incomplete, and fragmentary. This is largely true throughout the

---

[82] Groenewegen-Frankfort, *Arrest and Movement*, p. 21.

[83] See Jacquetta Hawkes's contemporary review of *Arrest and Movement* and John Baines's much later review of a republication of the same book. Hawkes was an archaeologist and author of *Dawn of the Gods* (1968), a provocative study of Mycenaean and Cretan cultures. Baines was Professor of Egyptology at the University of Oxford and author of many books on his subject. Hawkes finds that Groenewegen-Frankfort's style lacks clarity ("the good manners of simplicity and clear writing") and that her definition of "monumental art" is arbitrary: it is "devised to suit her purpose" (Hawkes, "Review of *Arrest and Movement*", p. 368). Baines echoes the charge of subjectivity: "My own assessment of the descriptive part [of the book] is that it is largely subjective" (Baines, "Review of *Arrest and Movement*", p. 275). These two reviews offer mixed appraisals. Many archaeologists and art historians admired *Arrest and Movement* when it was first published in 1951, and Harvard later recognized the need to republish a paperback edition thirty-six years after its initial appearance. But today Groenewegen-Frankfort's ideas about ancient Near Eastern art are probably not in the mainstream of her profession. John Baines's review is probably representative of current critical thinking.

[84] R. Wilkinson, *Egyptology Today*, p. 1.

archaeological remains of many ancient societies, however "scientific" the interpretation of those remains may be.[85] In her recent book, *The Etruscans*, the archaeologist Lucy Shipley comments on archaeology as "science":

> Archaeological interpretations [...] are as fallible, as subjective, as a written source, in that they are produced by people, and people are the products of their experience. Even when pure science enters the picture, whether it is genetics or pollen sampling, it is still interpreted by a person. A person with an unavoidable, internalized agenda.[86]

Yes, I believe Lucy Shipley is correct.

All of which is relevant to Lawrence Durrell and H. A. Groenewegen-Frankfort. For he was a poet, and she had the sensibilities of a poet. Their outlooks were similar, highly personal, and subjective. Time is one of the most subjective of human experiences. Thus, as her subtitle indicates, Groenewegen-Frankfort's various observations introduce time as an important aspect of Egyptian art.

Egyptian Time: The Egyptologist Jan Assmann argues that the ancient Egyptian concept of time was essentially static. It had two main components: *neheh* (cyclical time) and *djet* (noncyclical time). *Djet* was not linear time, however; rather, it meant "becoming" or "that which has become" — a state of "immutable permanence" or "the suspension of time". Assmann summarizes this concept by saying, "*Djet* is time at a standstill. Only in *neheh* does time move".[87] These ideas are not far removed from Durrell's use of time in his oeuvre, whether or not he was exposed to the concepts of *neheh* and *djet*. Durrell's idea of time, on the few occasions he expresses it, is either a negation of time or a kind of cyclical process, a return to origins.

A conventional view of Egyptian history is that Egyptian time has stopped or that it is constantly repeating itself. One of the most striking features of ancient Egyptian civilization is that it does not appear to change very much in over three thousand years. The Archaic Period (Dynasties 1-2) at the beginning of its history (c. 2950 BC) seems much the same as the Late Period (Dynasties 26-30) at its end (343 BC). Dynasties come and go, wars and conquests happen, and centuries of dynastic interruptions occur,

---

[85] So the Scientific American Library has a large collection of scientific titles ranging from *The Discovery of Subatomic Particles* (1983) to *Consciousness* (1999). Among those titles is Jeremy A. Sabloff's *The New Archaeology and the Ancient Maya* (1990).

[86] Shipley, *Etruscans*, p. 20.

[87] Assmann, *Mind of Egypt*, pp. 18-19.

but the uniqueness of Egyptian art and culture remain recognizably Egyptian. So, many of the conventions of the Narmer Palette are readily identifiable throughout Egyptian history.

Durrell was fully aware of this commonplace of ancient Egyptian civilization, which often falls under the rubric of "Eternal Egypt". The cliché is ubiquitous in popular culture and can be closely associated with "Egyptomania", as Ronald Fritze's usage suggests.[88] The phrase *eternal Egypt* also serves as the title of many books, no matter how scholarly and excellent the treatment, art books such as Edna R. Russmann's impressive *Eternal Egypt: Masterworks of Ancient Art from the British Museum* (2001).

In his essay "Egyptian Moments" (1978), Durrell deliberately avoids the cliché of Egyptian timelessness. His account rejects the historic setting of Egypt's most famous monuments, where in 1798 Napoleon told his soldiers before the Battle of the Pyramids, "From the top of those pyramids, forty centuries are contemplating you".[89] Befitting his reputation, Napoleon's declaration was both grand and pompous. It was a type of rhetorical graffito. Egyptian monuments are covered with graffiti. Ever since the sixth century BC when Greeks mercenaries first came to Egypt,[90] foreign travellers have scrawled their marks on Egyptian ruins and attempted to share in a kind of ersatz immortality. Tourists do such things; they like to deface the past.

In 1977, Durrell was a tourist returning to Egypt after an absence of over thirty years. He was on assignment with the BBC for a film project directed by Peter Adam. The film was about Durrell's return to Egypt and was titled, *Spirit of Place: Egypt*. When in Cairo, Durrell and the film crew stayed outside the city at Mena House on the Giza Plateau. The hotel is one of the most luxurious and historic in Egypt. Churchill hosted Roosevelt there during the Cairo Conference of 1943.

Adam has the eye of a good film director. In his account of their stay at Mena House, he sets the scene in its majestic splendour: "Together we watch the great Egyptian cliché, the sun setting behind the pyramids from the terrace of my room".[91] In Durrell's essay of the journey, he does not mention the scene on the terrace. Rather, he notes that at dawn his travelling companions go horseback riding in the desert, which was another touristy thing to do, clichés notwithstanding. Instead of accompanying them "in the shadow of the ancient Pyramids", Durrell preferred another kind of private experience:

[88] Fritze, *Egyptomania*, p. 17.
[89] Roberts, *Napoleon*, p. 172.
[90] Milne, "Greek and Roman Tourists", p. 76.
[91] Adam, "Alexandria Revisited", p. 401.

> For my part, I had discovered the small haunting call of the rock doves—
> my room opened on the desert pure—and some of the forgotten rhythm of
> Egyptian time, which is like no other. One enters the slow blood rhythm
> of the Nile water flowing softly, unhurriedly down to the sea. (*EB* 372)

In his notes, Durrell elaborates on this passage: "that wonderful feeling of
stillness that Egypt always conveys: the slow, green blood-time of the
Nile".[92] "Egyptian time" has a special meaning for Durrell — it surely flows
through his blood as his imagery encapsulates a long history — but the
phrase *eternal Egypt* does not appear in this travel piece nor in *The
Alexandria Quartet*.

As "Egyptian Moments" shows, Durrell's primary impulse is to
look for the timelessness of a poetic moment, to find a small element
emblematic of a whole. In the landscape poem "Deus Loci" (1950), the
"small sunburnt *deus loci*", perhaps a small "specimen" of "dust", evokes a
philosophy of place (*CP* 214). In the love poem "A Portrait of Theodora"
(1955), "a freckle of gold / In the pupil of one eye" evokes a woman as one
of the "champions of love" (*CP* 245). And in this instance, the "small
haunting call of the rock doves" evokes the ethos of Egypt in time and
history. Richard Pine eloquently discusses this tendency in the context of
the "moment" in Durrell's "Heraldic Universe".[93]

Earlier in "Egyptian Moments", Durrell discovers a similar image
embodied in the "simple, eternal, ancient mud brick of Egypt" (*EB* 371).
Alluvial mud is the life of Egypt, and mud bricks are its commonest building
material. In the context of Durrell's essay, the "little brick" suggests both
social change and the richness of its history (*EB* 376). In a wider ancient
Egyptian context, the mud brick, as Luiza Osorio G. Silva argues,
symbolizes "creation and life cycles". Mud is intrinsically "mundane and
ephemeral",[94] but it is also the eternal stuff of life from beginning to end in
ancient Egypt. Mud bricks assisted women in childbirth who "crouched on
top of four bricks stacked in pairs";[95] in mortuary rituals, birthing bricks
reappeared to signify rebirth in the afterlife.[96] Durrell's "little brick", then, is
above all an image of an imperishable moment in time. It is both quiet and
unobtrusive. It is also an aspect of Egyptian *neheh,* time as "cyclicality",[97]
which is also the title of Durrell's last poem, "Le cercle refermé".

---

[92] Adam, "Alexandria Revisited", p. 410.
[93] Pine, "Lawrence Durrell's 'Heraldic Universe'", pp. 229-30.
[94] Silva, "Myth of the Mundane", p. 181, 182.
[95] Silva, "Myth of the Mundane", p. 187.
[96] Roth and Roehrig, "Magical Bricks", pp. 134-35.
[97] Silva, "Myth of the Mundane", p. 191.

Groenewegen-Frankfort defines "monumental art" as follows: "The criterion of monumental art should, in fact, lie in a tension between the ephemeral and the lasting, between concrete event and transcendent significance".[98] This definition aptly characterizes Durrell's usage of imagery. Moreover, emblems, metaphors, and timelessness form the basis of his "Heraldic Universe".

Heraldic Universe: I take Durrell's Heraldic Universe as a poetic version of Plato's Theory of Forms, where ideas or "universals" exist in some extra dimension beyond the mundane world.[99] There are at least three ways to discuss Durrell's idea of the Heraldic Universe. The first is by looking at his own words and noting how he develops the idea. The second is by looking at the works themselves and studying how the idea manifests itself in those contexts. And the third is a combination of the first two. I choose to emphasize the second approach. I trust Durrell's praxis more than his theory.

My discussion first requires a short excursus in literary history. Durrell gives great significance to his idea, as he writes to Henry Miller sometime in August 1936:

> Art nowadays is going to be real art, as before the flood. IT IS GOING TO BE PROPHECY, in the biblical sense. What I propose to do, with all deadly solemnity, is to create my HERALDIC UNIVERSE quite alone. The foundation is being quietly laid. I AM SLOWLY BUT VERY CAREFULLY AND WITHOUT ANY CONSCIOUS THOUGHT DESTROYING TIME. (*DML* 18; capitalisation in original)

Durrell's heraldic edifice exists in space as some kind of timeless, abstract entity, which relates directly to poetic creativity. Balthazar's "gold pocket-watch" illustrates the timelessness of heraldic creativity. The watch is a poetic symbol with a key shaped like the Egyptian hieroglyph of life, the *ankh*. Balthazar loses the "small key" as he walks along the Corniche, so the watch extends through space but will no longer tell time unless the key is found (*Quartet* 80-81). The symbolism is approximate and pointed as it

---

[98] Groenewegen-Frankfort, *Arrest and Movement*, p. 22.
[99] See A. E. Taylor on Plato's Theory of Forms or Ideas: "Plato inferred that the objects which science defines, and about which she undertakes to prove universally valid conclusions, cannot be the indefinitely variable things of the sensible physical world. There is therefore a supra-physical world of entities, eternal and immutable, and it is these unchanging entities, called by Plato 'Ideas,' which are the objects with which the definitions and universal truths of exact science are concerned" (Taylor, *Mind of Plato*, p. 39).

conforms to Einstein's theory of "time dilation".

Stopping time is a major component of Durrell's Heraldic Universe. In the early twentieth century, two men were closely associated with the great debate on time, a philosopher and a physicist: Henri Bergson (1859-1941) and Albert Einstein (1879-1955). Einstein's theory of relativity predicated that time would slow down or stop as it approached the speed of light. Time and space are directly related. The process became known as "time dilation".[100] Bergson's idea of time as "duration" (*la durée*) differs from Einstein's elastic concept of time. In *Time and Free Will* (1910), Bergson argues that time is experienced as a flow of continuous and heterogeneous moments.[101] It is not a spatial concept.

After Einstein's theory of special relativity appeared in 1905 and was confirmed in 1919, "space-time" (three dimensions of space and one of time) and Bergson's "duration" were widely discussed and debated among the arts and sciences.[102] In a famous essay "Spatial Form in Modern Literature" (1945), Joseph Frank argues that the modern novel of Joyce and Proust arrests time and treats it as space.[103] Durrell's Heraldic Universe is his unique contribution to the debate on time. But, as the psychologist Ciarán Benson points out, Durrell came under various influences in the 1930s, and his ideas were very much a product of his times, for good and bad.[104] As will be discussed soon, Benson also points out that Durrell's ideas on time were "idiosyncratic" and "mistaken".[105]

One of Durrell's major influences was the artist and critic Percy Wyndham Lewis (1882-1957), who had a notoriously prickly personality.[106] Based upon his reading of Lewis's *Time and Western Man* (1927), Durrell would probably reject any comparison of his work with Joseph Frank's observations on the modern novel. In his Note to the 1958 edition of *Balthazar*, later attenuated in the 1962 omnibus edition, he says the following about his method: "This is not Proustian or Joycean method—for they illustrate Bergsonian 'Duration' in my opinion, not 'Space-Time'" (L. Durrell 1958, 7). Durrell's source for this idea owes much to *Time and Western Man* (1927) and its polemic against Bergsonian time in favour of Einsteinian space-time.[107] As Lewis explains, Bergson conceives of time as

[100] Canales, *Physicist & Philosopher*, p. 11.
[101] Bergson, *Time and Free Will*, p. 110.
[102] Canales, *Physicist & Philosopher*, pp. 6-7.
[103] Frank, *Idea of Spatial Form*, pp. 21, 26-27.
[104] Benson, "Metaphor of 'Place-Time'", p. 247.
[105] Benson, "Metaphor of 'Place-Time'", p. 254.
[106] Meyers, *Enemy*, pp. 55-56.
[107] Lewis, *Time and Western Man*, p. 86.

a mental construct,[108] whereas Einstein treats it as pure physics. Lewis wants to de-emphasize time and replace it with space: "But the Time conception of Bergson seems to us entirely to misrepresent the rôle of Space". He later continues: "If we have any preference, it is for Space. [...] Regarding mind as Timeless, it is more at home, we find, with Space".[109]

Durrell thought so highly of Percy Wyndham Lewis that he turned him into one of his *alter egos* in the *Quartet*. Jeffrey Meyers, one of Lewis's biographers, notes that Durrell "modelled aspects of Pursewarden" on Lewis.[110] Meyers doesn't elaborate on his observation, but Pursewarden's acerbic personality is certainly one of those aspects. Darley calls him habitually "surly" (*Quartet* 114). Another is Pursewarden's full name — Ludwig Pursewarden — which resembles Lewis's. So Balthazar comments on Pursewarden's given name, which does not appear until *Balthazar*, the second novel of the *Quartet*:

> Yes, his real name was Percy and he was somewhat sensitive about it because of the alliteration, I suppose; hence his choice of Ludwig as a signature to his books. He was always delighted when his reviewers took him to be of German extraction. (*Quartet* 289)

Indeed. The mistaken identity was probably intended as one of Durrell's private jokes. The mistake in one sense was not a mistake. Between the two world wars, anyone of "German extraction" probably elicited hostile feelings from the British public. Such was certainly the case after 1914, as A. N. Wilson notes in his biography of the Poet Laureate, John Betjeman (1906-1984).[111] Durrell was also the perennial outsider who felt compelled to create his own audience in the epigraph to *Quinx* (*Quintet* 1176), and that Durrell surely felt "delighted" to go against the British grain.

But why the choice of the very Germanic and un-English "Ludwig"? Possibly because of Durrell's great affection for the music of Ludwig van Beethoven, which he enjoyed while living on Corfu (*DML* 18). Of Beethoven's Fourth Piano Concerto, he writes in a letter of 1935: "I know it now—every stitch of it—more intimately than I know Nancy [Myers]. I've got it in my bowels" (*SP* 34). Later, in Provence in 1982, he compares the contradictions of Taoism to "the madman's idiom and the A

---

[108] Lewis, *Time and Western Man*, p. 419.

[109] Lewis, *Time and Western Man*, p. 427-28.

[110] Meyers, *Enemy*, p. 182.

[111] "Britain, which had been so fervently pro-German in the last years of Queen Victoria's reign, developed an insane anti-Hun mania from almost the moment the war broke out in 1914. Much-loved German bakers' shops were torched. It became unpatriotic to like Beethoven" (A. N. Wilson, *Betjeman*, 26).

minor Quartet", that is, to one of Beethoven's late quartets, the String Quartet no. 15 (*SME* 88). Durrell admired rebels and innovators like Beethoven, Wyndham Lewis, as well as others such as D. H. Lawrence, and he later demonstrated his admiration for these types of artists through the characterization of Ludwig Pursewarden, who was presented as a radical and a provocateur. By early 1936, Durrell was reading Lewis's nonfiction (*DML* 11), and, in 1952, he acknowledges his indebtedness to *Time and Western Man* in *A Key to Modern British Poetry* (*Key* xii).

Durrell had a profound aversion to time. "Mere time", he belittles it in his last poem, "Le cercle refermé". Brewster Chamberlin discreetly states the problem in his chronology of Durrell's life: "Caution is advised when LD dates anything".[112] A few more examples follow. First, there is the avoidance of time. Most of his letters were undated, and I assume that omission was deliberate.[113] In his Preface to the 1962 edition of the *Quartet*, Durrell pointedly rejects "the time-saturated novel of the day" (*Quartet* 9). As a result of this injunction, time in the *Quartet* is hard to uncover. It lies concealed. As in many of his letters, Durrell does not provide dates for events. The temporal framework of events leading to and during the Second World War is secure, but, as Donald P. Kaczvinsky notes, "The dates of Darley's first stay [in Alexandria] are difficult to assess".[114] (Kaczvinsky 1991, 592). It takes considerable attentiveness and ingenuity on Kaczvinsky's part to reconstruct a plausible, if artificially imposed, chronology on the *Quartet*.

Time in these four novels is hidden — or deliberately suppressed. Kaczvinsky concludes that Durrell had a definite chronology in mind: "Durrell, keeping close to historical events in the region, has computed the time, and we can as well".[115] This programme presupposes that Durrell wanted his chronology "computed" and made manifest through careful analysis. Kaczvinsky suggests that Durrell was trying to "fool" or trick the reader about the passage of time.[116] I don't believe any trickery was involved. The suppression was deliberate for personal reasons. It may well be that Durrell didn't want to have revealed or computed any clock-time or calendar-time in his novels.

I am first suggesting that Durrell the novelist and Durrell the philosopher (the "seeker of truth", as Durrell was described by his former

---

[112] Chamberlin, *Durrell Log*, p. 62, n. 32.
[113] For a small sample of Durrell's undated letters, see *DML* 2, 3, 8, *et passim*; *SP* 29, 30, 31, *et passim*; and *Aldington-Durrell Correspondence,* pp. 2, 5, 6, *et passim*.
[114] Kaczvinsky, "Darley in Alexandria", p. 592.
[115] Kaczvinsky, "Darley in Alexandria", p. 594.
[116] Ibid.

literary agent, Anthea Morton-Saner) were at odds with one another. As a novelist, much like Henry Fielding in *Tom Jones* (1749), Durrell had the need to create a cohesive plot for the events in the *Quartet*.[117] But, as a philosopher of time in the manner of Wyndham Lewis, he also had the need to de-emphasize time. The result is a story without temporal markers on its surface but with a loose chronology in its substratum.

Second, the title of Durrell's 1962 note on Rainer Maria Rilke's novel, *The Notebooks of Malte Laurids Brigge* (1910), was translated into German as "*Alle Uhren stehen [Still]*" (All Clocks Stopped) (L. Durrell, "Uhren"). The note then praises Rilke for working and creating his "poetic vision" in a darkly enclosed and timeless space.

Finally, when Durrell's third wife Claude-Marie Vincendon died on 1 January 1967, Ian MacNiven reports that he "stopped the hands of the wall clock at 7.10, the time of Claude's death, and would never restart it".[118] Thus, in these examples, Durrell treated time as an adversary, something to be opposed, suppressed, and ultimately "stopped".

Durrell's notion of time as subsidiary to space is hard to justify, particularly in the context of his own writings. His narrator in *The Black Book* says, "I live only in my imagination which is timeless" (*BB* 56). Wyndham Lewis says something similar when he regards the "mind as Timeless".[119] In terms of the human personality, however, Ciarán Benson emphasizes that to deny time is to deny memory.[120] And, as an extension of Benson's point, it is hard to conceive of the human "imagination" — or more broadly, the human "self" — as existing without memory.

Darley, another of Durrell's *alter egos*, calls Alexandria "the capital of Memory" (*Quartet* 152). The foundation of *The Alexandria Quartet* is indeed memory, as seen in *Justine* when Durrell dedicates the

---

[117] See R. S. Crane's classic essay on the plot of *Tom Jones*. For Crane, cohesion in fiction means a plot's "probable or necessary connections". So: "It is in nothing short of this total system of actions, moving by probable or necessary connections from beginning, through middle, to end, that the unity of the plot of *Tom Jones* is to be found" (Crane, "Concept of Plot", p. 77). A "probable" chronology in Durrell's *Quartet* would be one of those "necessary connections". On the importance of chronology in the novel, allow me to submit an anecdote of an anecdote. One of my teachers at the University of California, Berkeley was Ralph W. Rader, a scholar of the early English novel. If I recall correctly, Rader once mentioned in class that Fielding had a clock before him when plotting out an incident in *Tom Jones*. Fielding wanted to make sure that the incident was temporally accurate. I have not found the source of Rader's anecdote.

[118] MacNiven, *Lawrence Durrell*, p. 553.

[119] Lewis, *Time and Western Man*, p. 428.

[120] Benson, "Metaphor of 'Place-Time'", p. 254.

novel to Yvette Cohen, his second wife: "To / EVE / these memorials of her native city" (*Quartet* 16). And what is a memorial? It is nothing more than a form of remembrance. It is the reification of memory. This is Bergsonian "duration". It is, in the words of the French scholar Suzanne Guerlac, Bergson's "project" of "thinking time concretely".[121] Moreover, Durrell's last book was *Caesar's Vast Ghost* (1990), and the last poem in that book is entitled "Le cercle refermé", which is a brief summation of his life. There, Durrell the poet — "jaunty as a god of the bullfrogs" — jumps through time, from his beginning in India to his end in Provence (*CVG* 205). So, for Durrell to deny the importance of time in his own oeuvre is self-defeating and, in some sense, a denial of his own genius. At the end of this essay, I will offer a suggestion as to why Durrell chose this odd description of his Heraldic Universe as the negation of time.

"Heraldic" appears five times in the *Quartet* (*Quartet* 367, 759, 772, 773, 792). All the references are made by or attributed to Darley or Pursewarden, both of whom are Durrell's *alter ego*s. "Heraldic" implies some poetic or imaginative dimension, but Durrell's meaning is unclear. In *A Smile in the Mind's Eye* (1980), he says, "[Heraldic] means simply the 'mandala' of the poet or of the poem. It is the alchemical sigil or signature of the individual; what's left with the ego extracted. It is the pure nonentity of the entity for which the poem stands like an ideogram" (*SME* 86).

Mandala, sigil, ideogram: all these are forms of symbolic or iconic representation, where time disappears and space remains as "the pure nonentity of the entity". Durrell proclaims himself a "*Taoist*" in *A Smile in the Mind's Eye* (*SME* 49). He delights in Taoist "apophasis" or "self-negating language", as Morrison comments,[122] but his choice of figures reinforces what he described earlier in his letter: the emphasis on metaphor (as heraldry) and the emphasis on space (as absence of time). These characteristics readily apply to the Narmer Palette, particularly as Durrell would have responded to the artifact in the context of his previously declared intentions.

Vc. Palette and *Quartet*

Violence is a prominent element of the creation myths of ancient Egyptian and other cultures.[123] It is also essential to the development of Durrell's aesthetic, and the palette readily serves as a template of ritualized mayhem

---

[121] Guerlac, *Thinking in Time*, p. 3.
[122] Morrison, "City and Ontology", p. 63.
[123] Bryan, "Episodes of Iconoclasm", p. 363.

in the creation of the Egyptian state. In creating his "Heraldic Universe",
Durrell does not simply eliminate time — he emphatically "DESTROY[S]"
it (*DML* 18; capitalisation in original). The diction is not casual.

The palette traditionally commemorates King Narmer's unification
of the Two Lands — Upper and Lower Egypt — and the birth of the "whole
of Egypt", as de Cosson puts it.[124] On the recto, Narmer wears the White
Crown of Upper Egypt, on the verso, the Red Crown of Lower Egypt. Like
a human birth, the event is painful and bloody. O'Connor sees the total
symbolism of the palette as representing "the daily (re-)birth of the sun god
Re".[125] Current scholarship further analyzes the colour symbolism of these
crowns. Katja Goebs, for example, associates red with "sunrise" and
"blood".[126] O'Connor expands Goebs's analysis and sees the Red Crown as
a "symbol of blood, slaughter, and destruction".[127] Durrell could not have
known these analyses; nevertheless, they coincide with his predilections.

Narmer's Horus name appears as the glyphs of a horizontal catfish
above a vertical chisel. Baines says the name "signifies something like
'Mean Catfish'";[128] Goldwasser translates it as "Cleaving Catfish";[129] and
Toby Wilkinson argues the name is not a name but "a symbolic association
of the king with the controlling animal force represented by the catfish".[130]
In any case, the name connotes aggression. On the top register of the verso,
the king wears the Red Crown and approaches ten decapitated prisoners. As
O'Connor notes, "each has his head neatly placed between his legs, and each
head — save one — is neatly topped by its owner's severed penis".[131]
Narmer is the dominant figure in a procession led by four standard bearers.
His towering size defines his importance, much as Nebamun's depiction
does, both of which are in accordance with the conventions of Egyptian
art.[132] Behind Narmer is his sandal bearer, before him what is probably a
small priestly figure wearing a large wig or headdress.[133]

On the central register of the recto, the king adopts the "smiting
pose", which depicts him in the act of wielding a piriform mace. This classic

---

[124] De Cosson, *Mareotis*, p. 20.
[125] O'Connor, "Narmer Palette", p. 150.
[126] Goebs, *Crowns*, pp. 163, 204-05.
[127] O'Connor, "Narmer Palette", p. 151.
[128] Baines, *Visual and Written Culture*, p. 289.
[129] Goldwasser, "Narmer Palette", p. 68.
[130] T. Wilkinson, "What King Is This", p. 25.
[131] O'Connor, "Narmer Palette", p. 148. See also Davies and Friedman, "Narmer Palette", pp. 243-46.
[132] Schäfer, *Principles*, p. 233.
[133] Aldred, *Egyptian Art*, p. 34; Baines, "Origins", p. 120.

display of pharaonic power endures on temple walls and ornamental objects beginning with the Predynastic period and continuing into Roman times.[134] In this context, "Narmer" may signify "Striking Catfish". Near the head of the prisoner is the glyph of a harpoon and above that an image of papyrus stalks personified as the defeated enemy. Space prevails over time: the metaphors situate the scene in the marshy Nile Delta.

Whether by plan or accident, the Narmer Palette's scenes, images, and metaphors correspond to themes, actions, and characterizations in *The Alexandria Quartet*. Durrell never directly mentions the palette, but the correspondences are provocative. They lurk in the shadows. When Darley and Clea visit "Narouz' island" on the Mediterranean coast, they swim underwater and discover seven "faceless" corpses in canvas sacks on the seafloor. Darley says mysteriously, "Once I thought I saw the flickering shadow of a great catfish moving among them but I must have been mistaken" (*Quartet* 829, 833-34). The noun *catfish* occurs only once in the *Quartet*. Is it a sly allusion to Narmer's name and the decapitations on the verso of his palette? Probably. What would a freshwater fish — perhaps a Nile catfish of the genus *Clarias*[135] — be doing in saltwater?

Durrell transposes Predynastic depictions to fit his artistic ends, just as he turns a place name, the Harpoon Kingdom, into a physical object, an old harpoon gun. The palette as emblem of unification transforms into the spiritual problem of the artist uniting his or her being with the cosmos. In *Justine*, Balthazar describes this process as "enlisting everything in order to make man's wholeness match the wholeness of the universe" (*Quartet* 85). At the end of the *Quartet*, Darley concludes the story with these words: "I felt as if the whole universe had given me a nudge" (*Quartet* 877). "Whole" may be a play on *whole* as totality and *whole* as completion or unification. "Whole" may also be a pun on *hole* and the Taoist idea of emptiness underlying the universe. Morrison calls wholeness as being "at one with this vision of Tao".[136] Durrell's ending is celebratory, commemorative, and another example of his search for wholeness or oneness.

Durrell's idea of wholeness, however, presupposes the trauma of parturition and the exploitation of violence. He even claimed that he could remember the details of his own birth: "a forceps delivery, botched".[137] Gothic violence permeates the *Quartet*. Camels are butchered publicly (*Quartet* 56, 488), circumcisions are mentioned regularly (*Quartet* 228, 302,

---

[134] E. Hall, *Pharaoh Smites*, pp. 4, 44.
[135] Hollis, *Tale of Two Brothers*, p. 121.
[136] Morrison, *Smile in His Mind's Eye*, p. 465. Cf. Morrison, "City and Ontology", p. 59.
[137] MacNiven, *Lawrence Durrell*, pp. 13-14.

303, *et passim*), "circumcision caps" are kept as mementos (*Quartet* 689, 698), mutilations are part of a religious festival (*Quartet* 866). The plot hinges on rape, accidental "death", suicide, and murder (*Quartet* 69, 176, 312, 360). The frequent references to circumcision afford it special status. Scobie, a comical character, remarks, "The Amalekites used to collect foreskins like we collect stamps. Funny, isn't it?" (*Quartet* 304). Not really. The humour recalls Narmer and his ten castrated captives.

Clea is the paradigm for Durrell's version of "forcible rebirth" (*Quartet* 852) — ironically — loss precedes unity. For the painter to become a whole and productive artist, she must undergo the trauma of having her right hand hacked off (*Quartet* 849-50). Although she acquires a prosthesis – "IT can *paint!*" she exclaims (*Quartet* 874) — losing her hand is equivalent to castration. Durrell confirms the "castration scene" in an interview.[138] In another interview, he defends the scene's brutality as "poetic realization" and reasserts, "It hurts to realize".[139] The justification seems more like obfuscation. Why? Because the ordeal is excessive, disproportionate, and unwarranted. Castration or mutilation, real or metaphorical, goes far beyond the platitude — realization is painful — which sounds Freudian. For Freud, a patient reliving infantile experiences feels "distress" and reproduces the trauma "with the greatest reluctance".[140] And Freud himself cites the "axiom", which sounds more moral than clinical, that an "effect [e.g., realization] must be proportionate to its cause [e.g., mutilation]".[141]

Two of Durrell's pivotal characters resemble Narmer's dual roles as king of Upper and Lower Egypt. The brothers Nessim and Narouz Hosnani are Copts. Their father instructs David Mountolive, a young British diplomat, that the Copts are the original Egyptians: "*Gins Pharoony.* Yes, we are *genus Pharaonicus* — the true descendants of the ancients, the true marrow of Egypt. We call ourselves *Gypt* — ancient Egyptians" (*Quartet* 421-22).

Lawrence George Durrell does not bestow names lightly. They are often iconic and contain hidden referents. Darley is the main narrator of the *Quartet*, and his initials are L. G. D., the same as Durrell's (*Quartet* 281). The proper nouns Nessim and Narouz contain all the letters of Narmer, and the former two are, figuratively speaking, two-syllable allophones of the latter. All three names begin with the phoneme /n/. The text encodes *N* as

---

[138] L. Durrell, *Conversations*, p. 121.

[139] L. Durrell, *Conversations*, p. 244.

[140] Freud, *Standard Edition*, vol. 3, p. 204.

[141] Freud, *Standard Edition*, vol. 3, p. 217.

unique. A "crude N" is carved on a "granite boulder" and identifies "the little island of Narouz" (*Quartet* 828-29) — or so Clea thinks. The letter could allude to Narmer, whose catfish swims nearby. The Hosnani family is wealthy and belongs to an elite class of Coptic powerbrokers, "the brains of Egypt" (*Quartet* 422). They are the rightful heirs of pharaonic royalty.[142] The elder brother has the "nickname" of "'prince' Nessim" (*Quartet* 29).

Nessim is the public face of the Hosnani family. He lives and works in Alexandria and manages the family's financial interests. Handsome, suave, educated, his conduct is serene, aloof, decorous, and not unlike the regal and ceremonial portrait of Narmer on the verso of his palette. Narouz, on the other hand, lives in the Delta and oversees the family estate. He represents the underside of the Coptic family — its brutality — as it corresponds to the recto of the palette. A religious fanatic, he preaches Coptic nationalism and religion (*Quartet* 489-91). He is also the family protector, which accords with O'Connor's explanation of the secondary face: "It is the one that shields and protects the primary face from that potential pollution and chaotic, negative force".[143]

Deformed, gauche, sadistic, Narouz has a harelip and relishes violence. Narmer's weapon of choice is the mace, and he uses it to smite a captive. Another form of execution in ancient Egypt was impalement; a glyph graphically depicted this method of punishment.[144] The method will have subsequent relevance when Narouz kills Toto de Brunel by driving a "hatpin" into his temple. When not defending the family honour (*Quartet* 360, 373-74), Narouz's preferred weapon is a "hippopotamus-hide whip". He uses it to mutilate animals and foes alike (*Quartet* 255, 651). In these contexts, mace and whip are symbols of public roles. Further, the two roles have an uncanny resemblance, for Narmer also has a connection with a hippopotamus. According to the Ptolemaic priest Manetho, "[Menes] was killed by a hippopotamus".[145]

Did Durrell read Manetho? Probably not. But, if I may conjecture, casual conversation accounts for the acquisition of such knowledge. George Andrew Reisner, an "Old Hand in Egypt", renowned for his stories and "imagination",[146] could have told Durrell the anecdote. And so Narouz is buried with the "great bloodstained", hippopotamus-hide whip beneath his head (*Quartet* 651). If Nessim is the "prince", then Narouz is the "smiter".

---

[142] MacNiven, *Lawrence Durrell*, p. 392.
[143] O'Connor, "Context", p. 21.
[144] Muhlestein, *Violence*, p. 54, fig. 7.1.
[145] *Berossos and Manetho*, p. 131.
[146] J. Wilson, *Signs & Wonders*, pp. 150, 166-69.

VI. Dwarfs

For someone unfamiliar with the conventions of ancient Egyptian art, the "priest" on the Narmer Palette could be mistaken for a dwarf. The figure is much smaller than the king, and the wig makes his head seem disproportionately large. The headdress resembles the "'bouffant' coiffure" of the ivory statuette of a female dwarf found at Hierakonpolis, in the same "Main Deposit" as Narmer's palette.[147] Two other dwarfs with similar wigs were also found in that deposit.[148] All three now reside in the Ashmolean Museum, which Durrell could have visited in 1951 during his stay in Oxford.[149] I am not suggesting the "priest" is a dwarf. As noted previously, Durrell is capable of profound confusion. I am suggesting he confuses the appearance of dwarfs with a representation on the palette.

Dwarfs play an important role in the history of art. In 1957, Erica Tietze-Conrat published *Dwarfs and Jesters in Art*, in which she briefly discusses Egyptian dwarfs and the related Bes deity, along with photographs of the latter.[150] Durrell was undoubtedly aware of this long tradition, and his Egyptian experiences reinforced his awareness. This is speculation, however.

I assume dwarfs had personal significance for Durrell — a stigma that became an obsession. He was diminutive, perhaps "five foot two" inches.[151] In his *Black Book* (1938), a novel of "self-discovery", a character declares "My disease is the disease of the dwarf" (*BB* 9, 186). The confession seems painful, although the author himself was not a dwarf in the clinical sense. Durrell did not suffer from achondroplastic dwarfism, the most common type and a hereditary condition with a specific diagnosis.[152] He was not "short-limbed" and was not bandy-legged. But he had a head too large for his body and believed it was misshapen at birth.[153]

In public, Durrell exuded the positive attributes of dwarfs. He was entertaining and powerful: he amused and dominated. A born performer, he played the piano in a London nightclub and composed his own songs. MacNiven quotes a source who describes Durrell entering a room of people: "It's as though someone had uncorked a bottle of vintage champagne".[154] In private, he portrays himself as engaged in "biblical" prophecy and later

---

[147] Patch, *Dawn of Egyptian Art*, pp. 120-21.
[148] Dasen, *Dwarfs in Ancient Egypt*, p. 108.
[149] Dasen, *Dwarfs in Ancient Egypt*, p. 338; Chamberlin, *Durrell Log*, pp. 90-91.
[150] Tietze-Conrat, *Dwarfs and Jesters in Art*, pp. 9-10.
[151] MacNiven, *Lawrence Durrell*, p. 101.
[152] Dasen, *Dwarfs in Ancient Egypt*, pp. 8-10.
[153] MacNiven, *Lawrence Durrell*, illus. 8 and p. 14.
[154] MacNiven, *Lawrence Durrell*, pp. 85-86, 280.

confides that he is a "*religious*" writer (*DML* 18, 227).

Dwarfs were valued and respected in ancient Egypt. Their representations in tombs and statuary, along with written accounts of their importance (e.g., the Old Kingdom "Autobiography of Harkhuf"), proliferate throughout Egyptian history. This commonplace was well known among Egyptologists from at least the early twentieth century. In 1909, James Henry Breasted (1865-1935) writes "These uncouth, bandy-legged creatures were highly prized by the noble class in Egypt".[155] In 1938, Warren R. Dawson notes that the ancient Egyptians distinguished between pygmies and dwarfs and reaffirms Breasted's observation that dwarfs were occasional members of the pharaonic court, where they could be retainers or, as in the case of Seneb, both official and "Prophet of Cheops and Buto".[156]

The Egyptian Museum in Cairo was closed during the war.[157] Durrell could not have seen the original Narmer Palette nor the various representations of dwarfs, unless he did so furtively (and he had influential connections). But he accessed other Egyptian monuments and antiquities.

In September 1941, Durrell took a private tour of an Old Kingdom tomb at Giza and had as his guide the famous Egyptologist George Andrew Reisner, who was almost blind and near death.[158] Theodore Stephanides, Durrell's close friend, was a member of the party and mentions that Reisner was a good storyteller.[159] The archaeologist undoubtedly shared with his guests some of his vast knowledge of Egyptology. Stephanides enthusiastically describes the artwork: "These *paintings* were made in great detail and in colours. [...] They were beautifully done and one could see fishermen on the Nile, weavers at their looms, potters at their wheels, housewives at their housework and all the other scenes of a busy world".[160]

Stephanides believes they visited a queen's tomb located in "one of the tiny pyramids which surround the three great ones". His memory errs. All the pyramids at Giza were undecorated. Almost certainly, Stephanides visited the nearby mastaba-chapel of Queen Mersyankh III, which Reisner discovered in 1927.[161] Hers is the only tomb of a royal lady that approximates the description. The paintings in the tomb of Mersyankh III

---

[155] Breasted, *History of Egypt*, pp. 139-40.
[156] Dawson, "Pygmies and Dwarfs", p. 187, n. 6.
[157] MacNiven, *Lawrence Durrell*, p. 245.
[158] Bierbrier, *Who Was Who in Egyptology*, pp. 388-89.
[159] Stephanides, *Autumn Gleanings*, p. 82.
[160] Stephanides, *Autumn Gleanings*, pp. 81-82.
[161] Dunham and Simpson, *Mastaba of Queen Merysankh III*, p. v.

depict several dwarfs. In the Main Room, South Wall, the fifth register has "a dwarf (large head and body on very short legs)".[162]

MacNiven writes that Durrell was "spellbound" during his tour and already "familiar" with "Wallis Budge's *Egyptian Book of the Dead*".[163] "Familiar" is an understatement. Stephanides does not use "spellbound", but MacNiven's usage is entirely justifiable. In 1937, Durrell tells Miller that he was "tremendously moved by the hymns to Ra as he comes forth" in *The Book of the Dead* (*DML* 67). The location of Durrell's copy of Budge's translation is unknown. Under Budge's biographical entry, M. L. Bierbrier lists five editions between 1895 and 1920.[164] I use the Dover reproduction of the 1895 edition. It appeals to the general reader and has a good introduction, an interlinear translation, and some of the vignettes from the papyri. It may be a coincidence, but Durrell uses the "interlinear" metaphor for the narration of *Balthazar* (*Quartet* 213).

Durrell read *The Book of the Dead* for its verbal imagery and jokes about his own lineage as derived from the goddess Nut, the god Thoth, and the Bennu bird, the mythic heron of Heliopolis (*DML* 67). In his introduction, Budge defines the god "Ptah-Seker-Ausar" (now spelled Ptah-Sokar-Osiris) as a solar deity and describes him "as a dwarf standing upon a crocodile, and having a scarabæus upon his head".[165]

While in Egypt, Durrell was planning his own "Book of the Dead".[166] Sixteen years later in 1957, Durrell's project turned into *Justine*, originally intended as a single novel and later expanded into a tetralogy.[167] In the "Consequential Data" (later renamed "Workpoints") at the end of the British edition of 1957, he tantalizes his reader: "Aurelia beseeching Petesouchos the crocodile god ..."[168] Then in 1958, Michael Haag argues that "Durrell made another set of corrections and alterations" where "Narouz" follows the ellipsis.[169] According to Haag, the "remark" originates from "a series of [Durrell's] impressions of the Graeco-Roman Museum in Alexandria" and serves to introduce Narouz into the story.[170] Thus, Narouz enters the *Quartet* at the same time as the Narmer Palette and the Harpoon Men. Petesouchos the crocodile deity is ugly and dangerous but not

---

[162] Dunham and Simpson, *Mastaba of Queen Merysankh III*, pp. 16-17.

[163] MacNiven, *Lawrence Durrell*, p. 243.

[164] Bierbrier, *Who Was Who in Egyptology*, p. 77.

[165] Budge, *Book of the Dead*, p. cviii.

[166] MacNiven, *Lawrence Durrell*, p. 247.

[167] Haag, "One Volume to Four", p. 65.

[168] L. Durrell, *Justine*, p. 250.

[169] Haag, "One Volume to Four", p. 64.

[170] Ibid.

dwarfish. Narouz the smiter is not a dwarf, although he is "bandy-legged" and becomes a prophet or *"preacher"* (*Quartet* 640, 491). He is equally malformed and deadly with his harelip and whip. Durrell replaces iconographic malformation with physical deformity.

Dwarfs or small men figure prominently in *The Alexandria Quartet*: Mnemjian, Toto de Brunel, Capodistria, Memlik Pasha, and homunculi. Like the three main types of Egyptian dwarfs, Durrell's dwarfs alternate between entertainers, powerbrokers, and (loosely) prophets — sometimes embodying all three.

Mnemjian first appears in *Justine*. He is a genuine "dwarf" and a man of many talents: barber, gossip, "Memory man", "oracle", and sexual curiosity. He attributes his sexual appeal to his "hump", which "excites" the women of Alexandria (*Quartet* 36, 55). As Véronique Dasen remarks, "dwarfs were strongly associated with birth and regeneration".[171]

"Poor little Toto de Brunel" dies in *Balthazar* (*Quartet* 218). He is an amusing homosexual, who flits about Alexandrian high society like a court jester. During the carnivalesque set piece, Toto masquerades as Justine and is mistakenly murdered with a "hatpin" thrust through his temple, "pinning him like a moth" (*Quartet* 360). What warrants such a bizarre act? One possibility is Egyptian justice. Toto is in effect impaled, and impalement was a form of execution in ancient Egypt.[172] So, Narouz is the executioner. After he metes out justice, he cries *"Justice!"* (*Quartet* 355), a play on *Justine*.

Durrell's characterizations of Capodistria and Memlik Pasha are the most interesting of his adventures in dwarfism. These are powerful figures. Capodistria is introduced near the beginning of *Justine*. His sexual prowess gives rise to the nickname: *"Da Capo"*. He is "more of a goblin than a man. [...] The flat triangular head of the snake with the huge frontal lobes. [...] A whitish flickering tongue is forever busy keeping his thin lips moist. He is ineffable rich" (*Quartet* 33-34). Goblins are, by definition, dwarfish.

In *Mountolive,* Memlik is the Egyptian Minister of Interior: "His blood was haunted by an Albanian father and a Nubian mother. [...] Physically too [he resembled his Nubian mother], the long silky head-hair with its suggestion of kink, the nose and mouth carved flatly in dark Nubian sandstone and set in bas-relief upon a completely round Alpine head" (*Quartet* 598). "Nubian" could refer to the Nubian people of Upper Egypt,

---

[171] Dasen, *Dwarfs in Ancient Egypt*, p. 152.
[172] T. Wilkinson, *Dictionary*, p. 58.

but the term harbours an ancient reflex: *Nubia* is an archaic toponym of Graeco-Roman origin,[173] hence a reference in *Balthazar* to "the forgotten Nubian race" (*Quartet* 247). Perhaps Durrell chooses "Nubian" because a famous pygmy in the Egyptian "Autobiography of Harkhuf" comes from Nubia,[174] perhaps he chooses "bas-relief" because it is a technique of Egyptian art, and perhaps he chooses "Alpine" because Memlik's head, like the author's, is too large for his body. Memlik needs a "damask footstool" to sit properly (*Quartet* 600). At the end of *Clea,* he accompanies Justine like a "toad" or "poodle" (*Quartet* 876).

These two characterisations recall ancient Egyptian representations of Bes, although the *Quartet* makes no direct reference to the deity. Allusions suffice to make the connections; the correspondences are suggestive, not exact.

Bes is a minor spirit, a dwarf, a popular household god with apotropaic and procreative powers (**Figure 13**). The "Bes-image", as James F. Romano implies,[175] originates in the Middle Kingdom (c. 1975-c. 1650 BC) and extends into the Ptolemaic-Early Roman Period (332 BC-1st century AD). It may have leonine features: bow legs, exposed genitals, and "beardlike mane".[176] As in Figure 13, an image of Ptolemaic or Roman origin, Bes is occasionally depicted holding a snake and sword; an erect phallus would have fit into the hole in his groin. Sympathetic magic is an essential element of the deity. James P. Allen emphasizes "prevention through magic", namely, "[Bes's] gruesome figure was thought to deter the approach of malevolent gods or hostile spirits of the deceased".[177] Another trait stands out. Dasen notes that, from the Third Intermediate Period on (c. 1069-c. 664 BC), Bes exposes (perhaps comically or provocatively) "a large tongue protrud[ing] beneath a row of menacing teeth".[178]

[173] Hillelson, "Nubian Origins", p. 142.
[174] Lichtheim, *Ancient Egyptian Literature*, p. 23.
[175] Romano, "Origin of Bes Image", pp. 39, 44.
[176] Romano, "Origin of Bes Image", pp. 39-56.
[177] J. Allen, *Art of Medicine*, p. 10; E. Thompson, "Dwarfs", p. 97.
[178] Dasen, *Dwarfs in Ancient Egypt*, p. 59.

Figure 13: Stela of the God Bes (reproduced by courtesy of the Metropolitan Museum of Art, Rogers Fund, 1922)

Thus, Bes is sexual, powerful, and comical — attributes shared by Capodistria and Memlik. Ugliness or gruesomeness, however, is the deity's distinctive feature. In late depictions, the dwarf's conspicuous tongue corresponds to the serpentine imagery of Capodistria's portrait. Durrell fixates on orality. Da Capo's "flickering tongue" and "moist" lips foreshadow the ugliest and most violent figure in the *Quartet* — bandy-legged and whip-wielding Narouz Hosnani and his perpetually "wet" harelip (*Quartet* 252).

Where did Durrell see Bes? Stone carvings and faience amulets of the deity proliferate from the New Kingdom through the Roman periods. Durrell possibly came across originals or reproductions of Bes in either the Ashmolean Museum in Oxford, the Graeco-Roman Museum in Alexandria, or the souks of Cairo.

One of the strangest episodes in the *Quartet* occurs near the end of *Clea*, when Capodistria takes "the Luciferian path" and plunges into "Black Magic" (*Quartet* 807). Da Capo sends a long letter to Balthazar, refers to Paracelsus, the Renaissance alchemist, who even merits an authorial note (*Quartet* 808, 884), and relates a story about the generation of dwarfs or homunculi. The bizarre tale is told tongue-in-cheek, but it seems a freakish sideshow and begs the question: How does it fit in?

Clea reads the letter aloud in a cemetery. The histrionics are elaborate: mysterious persons perform occult rites in a wintry setting. Homunculi materialize in the amniotic fluid of alembics: "They were exquisitely beautiful and mysterious objects, floating there like seahorses" (*Quartet* 809). These homunculi are not only fantastic creatures — they also prognosticate. After various mishaps, they are consumed in "all the flames of hell" (*Quartet* 810, 812).

Strip away the Poe-esque melodrama, and three elements remain: magic, prophecy, and violence — all dear to Durrell. Magic also characterizes Capodistria as he leaves the *Quartet*. His strange story reminds the reader that his true nature seeks fulfillment as a dwarf magician, as another avatar of Bes. Capodistria, the "goblin", is no longer baking "in sensuality like an apple in its jacket". He finally chooses "the Dark Path towards my own light" (*Quartet* 197, 812).

Whatever "Dark Path" means to Da Capo, it has another meaning for Lawrence Durrell — obscuring his debt to ancient Egypt – and obscurity, as the poet confides, was part of his Cairene experiences: "darkness is also of my nature" (*CP* 203). Durrell acknowledges Paracelsus as a source, yet fails to acknowledge two major influences: the role of dwarfs in Egyptian society and the significance of the Narmer Palette. Why obscurity? I suggest that aspects of Durrell's personality are relevant. Citing Paracelsus imparts erudition and eminence, whereas divulging Freudian "linkage[s]" to a short stature and violent disposition do not. Those are sensitive subjects for Durrell. In literature, he circumvents such problems through plot and characterization; in interviews, he obfuscates.

At the peak of his fame in 1959, Durrell grants an interview to *The Paris Review*. He discusses his relationship to art and concludes, "I use [the artist] to try and become a happy man, which is a good deal harder for me. I find art easy. I find life difficult".[179] The admission dissembles. Durrell wrote quickly, but art was not "easy" for him. His *Black Book* begins as an "agon" (no mere trope); his *Quartet* is more than sixteen years in the making; and he leaves unanswered the obvious question — why he finds "life difficult". Addressing that problem would have illuminated Durrell's own "Dark Path" as it wound through ancient Egypt.

VII. The Book of Death and the Ladder of Blue

If one can read Lawrence Durrell's life like a book, then that book might be called *The Book of Death*. As previously noted, Durrell's preliminary title for *The Alexandria Quartet* was *The Book of the Dead*, which in turn refers to the title of the ancient Egyptian funerary texts officially known as *Spells Coming Forth by Day*.[180] It hardly needs to be said that the Egyptian obsession with death, mummies, and tombs has an obvious reflex in Durrell's literary and personal life.

His autobiographical poem at the end of *Caesar's Vast Ghost* emphasizes death. One may question its title, "Le cercle refermé", and ask just what kind of circle is being closed? The poem begins in Benares on the sacred River Ganges — "Boom of the sunset gun / In the old fortress at Benares" (ll. 1-2) — and ends in Provence with the poet uttering his "last goodbye / Goodbye" (ll. 30-31). In this final poem, Durrell's India is not the India of his nostalgic boyhood. That memory he cherished throughout his life and associated with Kipling's India, with *Kim* and, probably, the *Jungle Books* (*EB* 2). No, this is the India of Holy Benares — a city which Durrell probably imagined and never visited[181] — an ancient city with its burning *ghats* for the dead. Nor is Durrell's Provence the sunny Provence of vacationers and tourists seeking a warmer climate.[182] This Provence belongs

---

[179] L. Durrell, "Art of Fiction", p. 36.

[180] T. Wilkinson, *Dictionary*, p. 43.

[181] In his definitive biography of Lawrence Durrell, Ian MacNiven does not record that he visited Benares. In a private correspondence, Michael Haag, an authority on Durrell, did not believe he had ever been to Benares.

[182] *New York Times*, 21 November 1990, Letters to Editor. Heading: Durrell Gave

to "Caesar's vast ghost" and the day when "they are coming to measure me for a coffin" (l. 14). Death begins and closes the circle of Durrell's life.

Ancient Egyptian notions of the afterlife were not Durrell's. Tombs were entrances to another world. The Egyptian afterlife was largely a continuation of the pleasant experiences of peoples' daily lives. Durrell saw those scenes depicted when George Reisner gave him a tour of Mersyankh III's tomb. An Egyptian term for the afterlife was the "Field of Reeds" or the "Field of Rushes".[183] It was a marshy landscape, abundant in wildlife and agricultural produce, and similar to the scene depicted in the painting of Nebamun on his skiff.

In contrast, Durrell's notion of an afterlife has a Buddhist flavour, either as some final stage of enlightenment or as a type of reincarnation. Reincarnation or transmigration is a basic tenet of Buddhism,[184] and it applies to Durrell in its broadest sense, as a radical change in form. Gordon Bowker, Durrell's first biographer, relates an anecdote that after his death "a lama has reported him already reincarnated and living as a keeper of a vineyard in Burgundy".[185] Given Durrell's acute sense of humour and capacity for self-deprecation, perhaps it would be equally befitting for him to be reincarnated as a French "onion-seller". He even posed as that comic figure in a photograph Bowker obtained from Neil Libbert and the *Observer*.[186] The lama's story is apt and pleasing, but Durrell's death-wish is much closer to the Buddhist idea of self-extinction. In Buddhism,

---

Landlords a Good Name. "To the Editor: [¶] Lawrence Durrell (obituary, Nov. 9) possessed a rare talent and a rare sweetness in dealing with people, even strangers. [¶] In the spring of 1976, we were living in Ireland and were feeling a strong need for sunshine. I spotted a notice in the rentals section of *The Herald Tribune*, and my wife picked up the receiver to telephone the number in France. She asked whether August was still available, and we have never forgotten the answer. [¶] 'Madam,' the man said in English after a strange pause, 'you must come then, for the plums will be falling into the pool, the swallows will be darting through the garden, and the white owls will hoot from the stone tower late into the night.' [¶] It was Lawrence Durrell. We could not resist the poet's sales pitch, and so we agree with alacrity to come in the summer. [¶] When we met Mr. Durrell, he proved to be a short, ruddy man with more than a landlord's allotment of hospitable feeling. He lived with his senses always on the alert, and he never disappointed us during that magical month by being anything less than liberal with his wine, his warmth and his observations on the smells, sights and tastes of his adopted Provençal countryside. We will miss him. [¶] C. Webster Wheelock [¶] New York, Nov. 10, 1990 [.]"

[183] T. Wilkinson, *Dictionary*, p. 13; Lichtheim, *Ancient Egyptian Literature*, p. 33.
[184] E. Wood, *Zen Dictionary*, p. 109.
[185] Bowker, *Through the Dark Labyrinth*, p. 424.
[186] Bowker, *Through the Dark Labyrinth*, illus. between pp. 304-05.

enlightenment is associated with pure emptiness, the void, Sanskrit *śūnyatā*.[187] For Durrell, its most severe form appears as a suicidal impulse, and I do believe he had suicidal tendencies.

I take Campion's leap in *The Dark Labyrinth* (1947) as the paradigm for Durrell's trope of self-extinction. Campion jumps naked into the sea and vanishes into nothingness. Variants of the trope also occur in *The Black Book* (*BB* 130), *The Magnetic Island* (*MI* 111), *White Eagles over Serbia* (*WES* 170, 192-93), *Mountolive* (*Quartet* 464-70), and *Sicilian Carousel* (*SC* 217). All these examples differ, but all point in the same direction — at death or reincarnation. Richard Pine also eloquently comments on this process. He emphasizes it as a return to the "womb" which ultimately involves "the pursuit of self by self". He cites Durrell's unpublished notebooks, where one passage reads:

> What I have written before has been an attempt to escape the womb: now, I accept it: I did not realise fully that escape is the involuntary manouvre [sic] which ends in madness — or suicide. You cannot escape.[188]

We have here, of course, an allusion to the proverbial play of *womb* on *tomb*.

One of Durrell's favourite authors was D. H. Lawrence (1885-1930). In *Etruscan Places* (1932), Lawrence visits the Etrurian tombs at Tarquinia. The site is 70 kilometres northwest of Rome and dates to the sixth century BC. There he sees the fresco of "the diver" in the Tomb of Hunting and Fishing[189] and subsequently interprets the figure as representing a return to the watery womb.[190] The topos of the diver appears again about fifty years later in a Greek tomb at Paestum, 80 kilometers southeast of Naples. The fresco depicts a naked man diving off a cliff into a body of water (**Plate 7**).[191]

Campion's leap and the topos of the diver are striking in similarity. Durrell may or may not have been familiar with the discovery of the Tomb

---

[187] *Shambhala Dictionary of Buddhism*, p. 203.
[188] Pine, "Lawrence Durrell's 'Heraldic Universe'", p. 229.
[189] Lawrence, *Etruscan Places*, p. 44.
[190] Lawrence, *Etruscan Places*, p. 60: "In the tombs we see it; throes of wonder and vivid feeling throbbing over death. Man moves naked and glowing through the universe. Then comes death: he dives into the sea, he departs into the underworld. [¶] The sea is that vast primordial creature that has a soul also, whose inwardness is womb of all things, out of which all things emerged, and into which they are devoured back". For an illustration of "the diver" in the Etrurian Tomb of Hunting and Fishing, see Steingräber, *Etruscan Wall Painting*, p. 105.
[191] On the theme of "the diver" in a Greek tomb at Paestum, see Holloway, "Tomb of the Diver", pp. 365-88, esp. 381-85.

of the Diver at Paestum in June of 1968, but he was certainly aware of the legend of Sappho's leap to her watery death on the Ionian island of Lefkas (*GI* 38), and he was most probably aware of Lawrence's posthumous publication on Etruscan tombs. The play on *womb* and *tomb* is one interpretation of Campion's leap. I shall, however, emphasize the Buddhist implications of the return to origins.

The Dewford Mallows episode in *Mountolive* (*Quartet* 464-70) illustrates one kind of self-extinction, although it is the least obvious of these examples. The episode is not a "jump" per se — it is neither sudden nor precipitous — but it describes David Mountolive's father abandoning one identity as husband, father, and judge in colonial India and "gradually" assuming another as a Buddhist monk in Madras, India. There he translates Pali texts of Theravada Buddhism into English. Thus, in broad outline, he reprises the story of Siddhartha Gautama (c. 566-c. 486 BC), who abandons his wife and family, undertakes a spiritual journey, and eventually becomes the Buddha.

A rare gem of storytelling, Durrell's episode neatly depicts in miniature some of his basic ideas about space and time. The story unfolds like a fairytale. Madras is a real place; Dewford Mallows is not. The Mallows is a timeless, unmapped refuge in the English countryside. The fictive name sounds pastoral and idyllic — an aquatic and floral hybrid. While the father chooses to remain in India, his wife and young son return to England and take residence at a retreat mirroring the "Lodge" or monastery in Madras. The parallel abodes hint at, but do not fully develop, Einsteinian "simultaneity", which essentially rejects two events separated in space as occurring at the same time.[192] Instead, Durrell's focus is on time. Space separates the family but not time.

In Dewford Mallows, time has stopped. Indeed, it is frozen — so the episode occurs in the dead of winter. Every time David returns to the Mallows as an adult, he inexplicably suffers from a mysterious childhood illness, a "crushing ear-ache". He then becomes a child again, nursed by his mother. Back in India, Mountolive the monk sends his family copies of his published translations, signed and inscribed. In England, his wife keeps them in a study, a shrine unseen by her husband, which is full of his memorabilia from the East. There his old self as colonial administrator remains frozen in time and stands alongside his new self as Buddhist monk. In Buddhist terminology, one might call what has happened to Mountolive's father as a kind of reincarnation. The old Mountolive Sr. dies, and a new person is reborn.

---

[192] Canales, *Physicist & Philosopher*, pp. 11-12.

Death and self-extinction are the simplest ways to describe the fates of Mountolive's father in the *Quartet* and Campion's in *The Dark Labyrinth*. Durrell the poet probably named Campion the fictional character after Thomas Campion (1567-1620), a poet of the English Renaissance. The English writers of the Renaissance were one of Durrell's great literary passions.[193] Campion is another of Durrell's *alter ego*s.

Durrell's Campion enters the novel mysteriously and exits mysteriously. He is an artist, a painter, undertaking an allegorical journey by sea. He is another "seeker of truth". His ship, the *Europa*, sails to Crete but has no record of his passage on board (*DL* 13). On Crete, Campion becomes trapped in a labyrinth with Virginia Dale, a fellow passenger from the ship. They escape together by stripping off their clothes, holding hands, and jumping off a high ledge and falling into the sea. They tumble down a "ladder of blueness" (*DL* 215).

The colour blue had special meaning for Durrell. *Blue* represented the Mediterranean, the sky, and some vast unknown (*PC* 11, 60; *Quartet* 833). For the ancient Egyptians, it symbolized "life and rebirth".[194] The two notions weren't far apart, but Durrell goes further. Clothes define the social being. When husband and wife Nebamun and Hatshepsut go punting in the Field of Reeds, they wear their finest clothes. They are dressed for the occasion. But, when Durrell or one of his *alter ego*s bathes or swims in the sea, either alone or with female companionship, he strips and goes into blue water naked (*MI* 109; *PC* 16, 23; *Quartet* 829). And so too Campion and his companion. Nakedness strips away the social self with all its trappings and contradictions.

Virginia Dale is observed jumping and surviving the fall, but Campion himself vanishes from the story. He jumps — the reader experiences him jumping — yet a distant observer of the leap sees the woman jumping alone (*DL* 261-62). No Campion alongside. It is as though he never existed, anticipating the mysterious absence of his name on the manifest of the *Europa*. "It's very confusing", says a character (*DL* 13), referring to Campion's fate and origins. Durrell's aim is deliberate confusion.

Confusion has a spiritual objective. In terms of Zen Buddhism, Campion "dissolves into the Infinite", which is a common trope for a form of enlightenment. The social self disappears. Then the entire self disappears completely and becomes, as the Zen master Yamada Mumon Roshi explains, absorbed into nothingness: "This is the completeness of vast emptiness, realm of the perfect circle where all has been swept away" and

---

[193] Pine, *Mindscape*, pp. 119-20.
[194] R. Wilkinson, *Symbol & Magic*, p. 107.

the self then turns into "an empty mirror, honed and polished".[195] The traditional depiction of this process is the brush drawing of the Japanese *ensō*, the enclosed circle (**Figure 14**), which is another kind of *cercle refermé*. Durrell definitely knew of this representation as depicted in the famous "ten ox-herding" drawings of Zen instructional literature. He mentions it in *A Smile in the Mind's Eye* (*SME* 94, n. 4). Death in this context means self-extinction, the ultimate expression of oneness.

The impulse behind Durrell's Heraldic Universe is similar to the impulse that generates Plato's Theory of Forms — the desire to transcend the mundane world of mutability and multiplicity and to reach some timeless realm of permanence and oneness. A. E. Taylor calls Plato's "starting point" as philosopher "an intellectual emotion, a passion for insight into truth".[196] With respect to Lawrence Durrell the thinker, I would emphasize "intellectual emotion". Passions defined his being, as he wrote to Henry Miller in 1944, when he was in Egypt and raised a "toast" to "great passions, short lives" (*DML* 167). The juxtaposition of passion and death is odd but revealing. "Seeker of truth" was also one of Durrell's passions. I would call that perhaps his greatest passion, but it drove him into strange territories. His Heraldic Universe and his denial of time, memory, and even his own extraordinary talents and abilities may in fact be an expression of a deep-seated yearning for death, one which he toasted when he was only thirty-two. That consciousness, if not its ultimate conclusion, is surely one which the ancient Egyptians could understand and sympathize with. And, for both of them, death was not necessarily a bad thing. It was a kind of solution. It was the door of a tomb — or the ladder of blue — leading elsewhere.

---

[195] Mumon, *Ten Oxherding Pictures*, pp. 84, 85.
[196] Taylor, *Mind of Plato*, p. 35.

Figure 14: *Ensō*, c. 2000, calligraphy by Kanjuro Shibata XX, from the personal collection of Jordan Langelier (Wikimedia Commons)

CODA:

DURRELL AND RILKE

CHAPTER TEN

SHORES AND PLAINS, CAVES AND CASTLES

I. Introduction

Shores and plains, caves and castles — these broad features define and separate two great poets. In many ways, Lawrence Durrell and Rainer Maria Rilke mirrored one another. They were both religious writers and philosophically similar. Both delighted in paradoxes and contradictions. Durrell's idea of "truth" is "what most contradicts itself" (*Quartet* 216, 277), and Rilke apostrophizes his symbolic rose as a "*reiner Widerspruch*" (pure contradiction).[1] Moreover, both poets shared views about space and psychology. And both wandered from place to place and had many affairs with women in those places. But they differed greatly as human beings. Their preferred landscapes separated them, and so did their chosen domiciles. Their temperaments were vastly different.

      Putting aside divergent temperaments, the lives of Rilke and Durrell had several similarities which were essential aspects of their personalities. Both poets felt estranged from the countries associated with their native languages. Rilke had an "innate aversion to Germany";[2] Durrell felt "he must escape England".[3] Rilke's spiritual home was Russia, Durrell's was Greece. But in neither country could either poet find a home, either permanent (in Durrell's case) or temporary (in Rilke's case). Both men were essentially homeless and spent much of their lives wandering like vagabonds. Rilke was born in Bohemia and died in Switzerland; Durrell was born in India and died in France.

      These similarities are illustrative, perhaps symptomatic, of a condition which Erich Heller calls "the disinherited mind" in his influential book of the same title, which is devoted to a study of modern German literature, as embodied in the works of Goethe, Burckhardt, Nietzsche, Rilke, Spengler, Kafka, and Kraus. He describes those artists as being dispossessed by modern culture and history, and he takes both his title and

---

[1] Rilke, *Sämtliche Werke*, vol. II, p. 185.
[2] Prater, *Rainer Maria Rilke*, p. 358.
[3] MacNiven, *Lawrence Durrell*, p. 106.

part of his epigraph from a passage near the end of the "Seventh Elegy" of Rilke's *Duino Elegies* (1923). Heller uses J. B. Leishman and Stephen Spender's translation of the following two lines: "Each torpid turn of the world has such disinherited children, / to whom no longer what's been, and not yet what's coming, belongs".[4] Both Rilke and Durrell were disinherited or dispossessed poets. They did not belong anywhere; they were perpetual exiles. This is the spirit of the note provided in the Appendix. So, when Durrell ends his brief essay on Rilke with a cryptic appeal — "The poet cries out through his silence. We need not ask him why we are calling out. We know all too well". — the poet (either Rilke or possibly Durrell himself) is surely calling out to all those who share his sense of alienation.

Their differences, however, were striking, even visually striking. Look at the photographs of the two men. In some photographs, Durrell poses in a pea jacket and resembles a seaman returning home from the seas. But here he is relaxed and dressed casually (**Figure 15**). A plaid shirt suits an occasion for a visit to the zoo in Jersey, which was founded and directed by his brother, the zoologist Gerald Durrell. He could be a common workman, perhaps a stonemason who's just finished building a wall, as he was in the habit of doing at Mazet Michel.[5]

---

[4] Heller, *Disinherited Mind*, p. ii; trans. Leishman and Spender, *Duino Elegies*, p. 63.

[5] MacNiven, *Lawrence Durrell*, p. 489.

Figure 15: Gerald Durrell (left) and Lawrence Durrell (right) at the Jersey Zoo, 1960 (courtesy of Estate of Gerald Durrell – photographer unknown)

He occasionally smiles at the camera. Then look at Rilke, who is always impeccably attired. He looks very much like the major poet he most definitely was (**Figure 16**). He's aristocratic. He's dour and does not smile. And he's much too self-conscious about being photographed. Posing stiffly in three-piece coat and tie, he could be the castellan of a castle, which he indeed was once called.[6] These differences could be attributed to different cultural attitudes in the art of taking photographs and being photographed, but more likely they suggest fundamental differences in two poetic identities, however idealized: Durrell the poet pursuing Everyman's path, much like a Taoist monk, Rilke the poet pursuing his high calling, much like a Catholic prelate.

---

[6] Freedman, *Rainer Maria Rilke*, pp. 474-75.

Figure 16: R. M. Rilke at Château de Muzot, c. 1922 (licenced by Alamy on 24 June 2021)

II. Dying as ripening

Rainer Maria Rilke (1875-1926) was a great poet of the German language. Born in Prague, a major city of the Austro-Hungarian Empire, he was an Austrian citizen until 1918, when he chose Czech citizenship.[7] He is often called a "Bohemian-Austrian poet". Lawrence Durrell did not know German. He read Rilke in translation, and the poet made a deep impression on him. In 1940, he wrote a perceptive review of Rilke's landmark *Duino Elegies*,[8] and in 1942 he tried to persuade T. S. Eliot at Faber and Faber to publish translations of Rilke's work.[9] In a 1959 interview, Durrell said, "I would like to have written only one thing, but it was written by Rainer Maria Rilke: *The Notebooks of M. L. Brigge*".[10]

In 1962, Durrell published a note, translated into German, on Rilke's novel, *Die Aufzeichnungen des Malte Laurids Brigge* (1910). The note was titled "Alle Uhren stehen Still" (All Clocks Stop) (see Appendix). Durrell's imaginative depiction of Rilke's study — an isolated and timeless place with drawn curtains and stopped clock — is memorable and undoubtedly reflects his own work habits. In 1960, two interviewers noted that "[Durrell] writes in a room without windows, with notices of his work in foreign languages he cannot understand pinned to the bookcase".[11] Durrell's study at that time seems to have been a confined space, windowless, and cutoff from the outside world. It was dedicated to the powers of his own imagination.

Lawrence Durrell and Rainer Maria Rilke had much in common. In their own unique ways, both were seekers or pilgrims: Durrell the "seeker of truth",[12] Rilke "the God-seeker" (*der Gottsucher*).[13] They also shared a common imagery and a fondness for mirrors. Durrell's epigraph to *Balthazar* is a quotation from the Marquis de Sade on the ambiguity of mirrors (*Quartet* 208), and Rilke's "Sonnet 3" of the *Sonnets to Orpheus*, Part 2, is a paean to mirrors.[14] Chief among these commonalities, however, is death. Both poets had an acute and instinctive awareness of death.[15] In his

[7] Tavis, *Rilke's Russia*, p. 147, n. 24.
[8] L. Durrell, *Endpapers and Inklings*, vol. 2, pp. 279-80.
[9] MacNiven, *Lawrence Durrell*, p. 259, n. 96.
[10] L. Durrell, *Conversations*, p. 40.
[11] L. Durrell, "Art of Fiction", p. 33.
[12] Morton-Saner, "Conversations with Anthea", p. 5.
[13] Tavis, *Rilke's Russia*, p. 88.
[14] Rilke, *Sämtliche Werke*, vol. I, p. 752.
[15] For a good discussion of Rilke's awareness of death, see Rose, "Rilke and Conception of Death", pp. 41-84.

review of Rilke's *Duino Elegies*, Durrell retells a story that was most likely apocryphal and quite possibly embellished:

> They say that when Rilke was dying, and the doctors wanted to give him morphia to help him away, he would not let them do so. *"Because,"* he said, *"I want to feel my death ripening inside me."*[16]

I cannot find Durrell's source, but there are problems with the accuracy of this anecdote. J. R. von Salis knew Rilke and those attending his death, and he wrote a highly regarded account of Rilke dying of leukemia. Von Salis's version is much less poetic than Durrell's. It portrays a man who, enduring tremendous pain, did not want to face the seriousness of his illness until a few days before he died. He did, however, seek to retain his consciousness. In this account, Dr. Theodor Haemmerli-Schindler, the attending physician, says, "[Rilke's] only wish was not to see anyone who might make him realise the gravity of his condition, which he deliberately concealed from himself". That apparently occurred during the early stage of a three-week illness. The doctor then administered drugs "in accordance with [Rilke's] wish, to relieve his pain by the use of sedatives (*calmants*) without making him lose consciousness". Von Salis also reports Rilke as saying to a close friend, "Help me to my death — I don't want the doctor's death — I want my freedom". Then von Salis adds, "The truth of this report by his most intimate friend cannot be doubted".[17]

Rilke's profound awareness of death led to an unusual incident leading to the advent of his illness. It became part of the Rilkean myth — a mixture of fact and poetry. Rilke's favourite symbol was the rose, and he wrote a short poem on the flower which later served as his epitaph:

> Rose, oh reiner Widerspruch, Lust,
> Niemandes Schalf zu sein unter soviel
> Lidern.
>
> (Rose, O pure contradiction, joy
> to be no one's sleep beneath so many
> eyelids.)[18]

"Lidern" (eyelids) is Rilke's famous pun on *Lieder* (songs). After his death, the story circulated that he pricked his finger on a thorn while picking a rose

---

[16] L. Durrell, *Endpapers and Inklings*, vol. 2, p. 279. Original italics.

[17] Salis, *Rainer Maria Rilke*, pp. 283-86. Here p. 285.

[18] Rilke, *Sämtliche Werke*, vol. II, p. 185. My translation.

for a female admirer, "an exotic Egyptian beauty, Madame Eloui Bey".[19] That small wound did not heal, became infected, and marked the onset of his leukemia. Because the story is undoubtedly true, Egypt as fact and metaphor had an influence on both Rilke and Durrell. Coincidences are sometimes not coincidences.

H. F. Peters's retelling of the anecdote is the stuff of legends, often repeated, and almost too "passing strange" to be believable. Unlikely as it seems, the rose as symbol becomes the instrument of death, much as Durrell's "harpoon gun" in *Clea* symbolizes the lethal aspects of the ancient Egyptian Narmer Palette. But "Madame Eloui Bey" was not a myth. She was indeed an exotic and beautiful young Egyptian, who did in fact meet Rilke in Switzerland in 1926. The Bohemian poet and the Egyptian beauty had a close but brief relationship. Her full name was spelled as either "Nimet Elwi Bey" or "Nimet Bey Eloui". Fluent in French and possessing a "profile seen on Pharaohs in Egyptian royal statuary",[20] she was very rich, a lover of fast cars, and could have been one of Durrell's rare Alexandrians, those "inquisitors of pleasure and pain" (*Quartet* 350). Nimet Eloui resembles Justine. Both women are aggressors who seek out poets (*Quartet* 31-32).[21] In his biography of Rilke, Donald Prater repeats the story of Rilke pricking his finger on the thorn of a rose bush,[22] and Ralph Freedman in his biography also repeats the anecdote, although he finds it "unlikely that the thorn itself caused Rilke's death, as is romantically assumed".[23] That assumption may be unlikely, though not Romantically improbable. Lawrence Durrell was finely tuned to Romantic sensibilities.

Durrell's dubious quotation of Rilke saying, "*I want to feel my death ripening inside me*", recalls two famous quotations from Shakespeare's *Hamlet* and *King Lear*, both of which anticipate death or dying. In *Hamlet*, the Prince of Denmark says, "The readiness is all" (5.2.194); in *Lear*, Edgar says, "Ripeness is all" (5.2.11). *Readiness* and *ripeness* are essentially Shakespearean synonyms and approximate homonyms. As previously noted, *Hamlet* was one of Durrell's favourite plays, and he might have conflated "readiness" and "ripeness" with Rilke's supposed "ripening".

---

[19] Peters, *Rainer Maria Rilke*, p. 184.
[20] Freedman, *Rainer Maria Rilke*, pp. 543 and 617. Freedman quotes a description taken from Jaloux, *Rainer Maria Rilke*, p. 62. The original source is Edmond Jaloux's *La Dernière Amité de Rainer Maria Rilke* (1949). Jaloux's account is primarily a "study" of Rilke, which includes ten of Rilke's short letters to Eloui Bey (pp. 101-10).
[21] Freedman, *Rainer Maria Rilke*, p. 543.
[22] Prater, *Rainer Maria Rilke*, p. 400.
[23] Prater, *Rainer Maria Rilke*, p. 546.

Whatever the truth of Rilke's dying words — and Durrell's account may be true in some poetic sense — the first sentence of *Malte Laurids Brigge* reads: "So, also hierher kommen die Leute, um zu leben, ich würde eher meinen, es stürbe sich hier" (So, then people come here to live; I would rather think it would be to die here).[24] And so near the beginning of *The Black Book*, Durrell writes: "This is the day I have chosen to begin this writing, because today we are dead among the dead; and this is an agon for the dead, a chronicle for the living" (*BB* 22). Durrell began writing *The Black Book* in 1936 when he was twenty-three.[25] It would be interesting to know when he first started reading Rilke.

III. Landscapes

Although possessing vastly different characteristics, landscapes and domiciles were two of Durrell's and Rilke's chief similarities, as dissimilar and contradictory as they appear to be. They pertain to artistic, spiritual, and psychological development. I will treat landscapes first.

For both poets, landscapes were not simply a matter of geography — they also stimulated a psychic response which resonated in their spiritual beings. Durrell's and Rilke's ideal landscapes, however, were divergent experiences — shores versus plains. What they have in common is an appreciation of limitless space, which accounts for Durrell's habit of standing on a precipice, a headland, or a shore and staring into the void. There he confronts "the ladder of blue". So Durrell had his Mediterranean shores. Those are the landscapes he praises at the very end of *Sicilian Carousel* (1977), as he watches the sun rise over the Ionian Sea. Durrell stares into deep space. He looks east in the direction of the island of Corfu set in the Ionian Sea — the places where, some forty years before, he had his first revelation of Mediterranean life. Then his imagination drifts to the moon and beyond:

> I reflected how lucky I was to have spent so much of my life in the Mediterranean—to have so frequently seen these incomparable dawns, to have so often had sun and moon both in the sky together. (*SC* 218)

This ideal landscape will change as Durrell changes. It will be become much darker and will be replaced by the Gothic atmosphere of both Languedoc and the novels of *The Avignon Quintet*. Nevertheless, the idealization of Mediterranean shores remains Durrell's distinctive "spirit of place".

---

[24] Rilke, *Sämtliche Werke*, vol. VI, p. 709. My translation.
[25] Chamberlin, *Durrell Log*, p. 27.

Rilke, on the other hand, found his ideal landscape in the Volga region of Russia, characterized by its boundless horizons and its flat expanses of land. During Rilke's second journey to Russia in 1900, in a letter of 31 July 1900, he wrote of his experiences on the Volga steppes:

> One learns all dimensions here; one discovers: the land is huge, water is something tremendous and the biggest of them all is the sky. What I have seen so far was a single picture of the land, the river, and the world. Here, however, everything is by itself. It seems to me that I have witnessed creation here.[26]

As H. F. Peters points out, a "concomitant" of Rilke's experiences of "vast uninterrupted space" was "loneliness".[27] Loneliness or solitude (*Einsamkeit*) is an essential part of the Rilkean ethic. Here, solitude combines with space to form a psychic environment. The poem "Einsamkeit" (1906) is short, only twelve lines, but it expands into space like the Russian steppes. It describes the state of aloneness as rain, a spatial and purifying activity, which rises, falls, and circulates over vast areas of land and sea and which contrasts with the claustrophobia, confinement, and dissatisfaction of narrow streets and sexual relationships. Like Durrell and his shorelines, Rilke favours the psychology of space, although within a very different geographical context.

Ultimately, Durrellian and Rilkean solitude is an intensely inward state. In his 1973 introduction to a selection of Wordsworth's poetry, Durrell refers to the poet's "real inner poetic life" (*EB* 138). The "real" for Durrell is the private, interior self. He praises that same inner state in his note on Rilke's *Notebooks of Malte Laurids Brigge*. The idea appeared earlier in a book of his poetry. In 1943, when he was living in Alexandria, Faber and Faber published Durrell's first major collection of poetry. The thin book of twenty-nine poems was titled, *A Private Country*. I would put the emphasis on *private*. The publication is public, obviously, but the poems and their genesis are private. So, Durrell dedicates his book: "To Nancy / and / To Ping-Kû / *for her second birthday out of Greece*".[28] Nancy is Durrell's first wife; Ping-Kû is his daughter, Penelope. Following "Ping-Kû" are eight lines of poetry addressed to a "sweet self", who is ostensibly the two-year-old Penelope.

---

[26] Tavis, *Rilke's Russia*, pp. 51 and 158, n. 2. This quotation is Anna A. Tavis's English translation of Rilke's letter.
[27] Peters, *Rainer Maria Rilke*, p. 51.
[28] L. Durrell, *Private Country*, p. [2]. Original italics.

Dedications are highly personal acts intended either as a tribute to some person or as an inscription to be understood and appreciated by the dedicatee(s). Dedications often contain an image or pithy description, such as the one in *Sicilian Carousel*: "*For Diana and Yehudi, fixed stars*" (*SC* 7; original italics).[29] The one in *A Private Country*, however, is more elaborate and also contains what appears to be a personal note to Durrell's first daughter:

> Nothing is lost, sweet self,
> Nothing is ever lost.
> The spoken word
> Is not exhausted but can be heard.
> Music that stains
> The silence remains
> O echo is everywhere, the
>   unbeckonable bird!

The note alludes to Durrell's Heraldic Universe and some imperishable realm. His "unbeckonable bird" may refer to Keats's "Ode to a Nightingale" and his "immortal Bird" (l. 61). *Unbeckonable*, an odd word, is not in the *OED* 3rd edition and suggests a special usage. Durrell's bird is "unbeckonable", presumably, because it is unresponsive. It keeps its secrets. Only a mature reader could unravel these allusions.

Dedications, however, need not be for the living. Durrell dedicated *Clea* (1960) to "My Father", who was Lawrence Samuel Durrell. He died in 1928 in India and in 1960 received his son's belated honour. But this was certainly not the case with Nancy and Penelope. They were both very much alive, although separated from Durrell and probably living in Jerusalem or Beirut. Penelope Berengaria Durrell was born in Athens on 4 June 1940. On 3 July 1942, mother and daughter departed for Jerusalem under orders of the British government for "non-essential personnel" to evacuate Egypt. They never returned. The marriage had been troubled and eventually ended in divorce. Durrell did not see Penelope again until 1949.[30] She was, in a sense, his "lost" child. At the end of his life, she returned and kept her vigil during his wake.[31] The dual dedication is odd, for this one contains a cryptic message — one in which Nancy, an adult, is capable of understanding, whereas Penelope, a child, is incapable of comprehending.

---

[29] Diana Gould was a dancer whom Durrell had befriended in Cairo. She later married the great violinist Yehudi Menuhin. The couple visited Durrell in Cyprus and later in Sommières.

[30] Chamberlin, *Durrell Log*, pp. 13, 55-56, 84.

[31] MacNiven, *Lawrence Durrell*, p. 688.

Odd but not unusual. The dedication is rhetorical. Its purpose is to reflect Durrell's purpose and to project it onto some "sweet self" posing as Penelope, his lost child. In this regard, the dedication resembles the unmailed letter to Tschup-Tschick, whose name, like Ping-Kû's, was another nickname for his daughter (see Chapter Eight above). Durrell's rhetorical devices appear throughout his oeuvre. He often addresses simultaneously a knowing and an unknowing audience. He wants it both ways, as Michael Haag has observed (see Chapter Six above). He both reveals and conceals his privacy. Hence, the odd line in the dedication: "The silence remains". It recalls Hamlet's last words ("The rest is silence" [5.2.336]) and anticipates the epigraph in *Prospero's Cell* ("No tongue: all eyes: be silent") taken from Shakespeare's *Tempest* (4.1.59). If we ignore the enjambment following "Music that stains", the line, "The silence remains", can be read as a solitary sentence. Silence haunts Durrell's world. It is akin to the Void.

Poets guard their privacy. They cannot have it disturbed or overwhelmed. Their psychology is delicate, easily disrupted, and must be protected. So Rilke writes in a letter of 12 September 1919 that he cannot endure seeing the grandeur of the Swiss Alps. Unlike Goethe in the *Italian Journey*, who is awed at the sight of the Alps,[32] Rilke's inner nature rejects the "Romantic sublime" of majestic but terrifying mountains:

> Too bad that in Switzerland Nature seems to me to occur only in exaggerations; what demands these lakes and mountains make, how there is always something too much about them, they have been broken of the habit of simple moments. [...] I remember the lovely times when, traveling through here, I used to draw to [sic] the curtains of the coupé, whereupon the rest of the travelers in the corridors greedily devoured my share of [the] view [of the Alpine scenery] with theirs—I am sure there was none left over.[33]

Durrell had a wistful fondness for the Himalayas of his childhood in India, but those memories of towering mountains and what lay beyond them remained a Tibetan fantasy. He never returned to India — and never

---

[32] "It grew darker and darker; individual objects faded out and the masses ["*die Massen*"] became even larger and more majestic. Finally everything moved before my eyes like some mysterious dream picture and all of a sudden I saw the lofty snow peaks again, lit up by the moon". Cf. the conclusion to the *Italian Journey*: "Any gigantic mass ["*Alles Massenhafte*"] has a peculiar effect on me; it has something about it which is at once fascinating and awe-inspiring" (Goethe, *Italian Journey*, pp. 13, 497; Goethe, *Italienische Reise*, pp. 17, 653).

[33] Rilke, *Wartime Letters*, pp. 140-41.

returning was a way to protect and preserve a dream. To paraphrase Michael Haag once again, it was another way to reveal and yet conceal. More to the point, Rilke's phrase of "simple moments" recalls Durrell's essay, "Egyptian Moments", when he visited the Great Pyramid of Giza, avoided the famous attraction, and preferred the private experience of listening to "the haunting call of rock doves" (*EB* 372).

IV. Domiciles

In terms of the creative process, the actual places where creativity occurs, Durrell had houses located throughout the Mediterranean basin, while Rilke, the rootless poet, lived sporadically in castles scattered throughout central Europe. Durrell's main dwellings were on Corfu, Alexandria, Rhodes, Cyprus, and Languedoc, and each house became associated with particular publications.[34] His primary dwellings had names and personalities. In a sense, they became *alter egos*. They acted like persons and produced one or more major works: "The White House" at Kalami, Corfu (*The Black Book*); "The Ambron Villa" in Alexandria, Egypt (*Prospero's Cell*); "Villa Cleobolus" on Rhodes, Greece (*Reflections on a Marine Venus*); the Turkish house in Bellapaix, Cyprus (*Bitter Lemons* and *Justine*); "Mazet Michel" near Nîmes, Languedoc (*The Alexandria Quartet*); and "Vampire House" in Sommières, Languedoc (*The Avignon Quintet*). These places represent different periods in Durrell's life: from the struggles of finding his *métier* on Corfu, to the success of the *Quartet* on sunny Cyprus and in the bright countryside of Languedoc, and finally to the gloom of the *Quintet* and medieval Sommières.

"Vampire House" was the name Durrell bestowed on his last home (*DML* 454). Madame Tarte's house at 15 route de Saussine was a French three-storey mansion with an acre of land and located just outside the old town of Sommières (**Figure 17**). The house sat "broodingly under a dark grey slate mansard roof" and had a "rampant, overgrown garden".[35] Its walled backyard hid a swimming pool, which Durrell refers to in *Sicilian Carousel* (*SC* 21).

---

[34] I am deeply indebted to David Green of Sydney, Australia, for our discussions on the importance of Durrell's houses. David's essay, "Lawrence Durrell's Houses: Domiciles of Creativity", awaits publication.

[35] MacNiven, *Lawrence Durrell*, p. 546.

Figure 17: "Vampire House" – Lawrence Durrell's house in Sommières (photo: ©
Denise Tart, 2015)

Pools of water and shadow recur throughout Durrell's oeuvre.
They come near the beginning and the end of his career: from *Prospero's
Cell* to *Caesar's Vast Ghost*. The most famous pool of water is located at
the shrine of Saint Arsenius in *Prospero's Cell* (*PC* 16). Durrell later said
that the shrine and pool commemorated his "second birthplace" (*BT* 24). Of
the swimming pool at Vampire House, Durrell also said, "The plums [in
August] will be falling into the pool".[36] Plums fall from trees when they are
ripe and ready to die. The pool may also recall those pools of shadow at the
beginning of *Caesar's Vast Ghost*, as the poet is "diving from penumbra to
penumbra of shadow" (*CVG* 1).

Virgilian shadows hung over Vampire House. Claude-Marie
Vincendon, the third wife, bought Madame Tarte's mansion in the spring of
1966 and soon afterwards died of cancer on the first day of 1967. Her death
had a devastating effect on Durrell. For almost nine years, he clung to her
ashes, kept them in his bedroom, and did not bury them until December

---

[36] Wheelock, "Letter to Editor of *New York Times*", 21 November 1990.

1975.[37] To a lesser degree, Sappho Jane, Durrell's younger daughter, was also affected by Claude's death. Sappho spent time with him in Languedoc and would later refer to "the wreck of my father". Her *Granta* diaries open with an eerie description of their visit to Claude's grave. "In the strange light", she begins with a clear reference to twilight, "he began to improvise a Poe-like story" about Languedoc and its Gothic ambience.[38] Vampire House resembles Poe's "melancholy House of Usher", as first seen in "the shades of the evening".[39] Which is also a reminder of Virgil, the poet who "'discovered' the evening".[40]

In *Sicilian Carousel*, Durrell's narrator speaks of "my old bat-haunted house in Provence" (*SC* 20). Well, we may ask, just where are the bats? In the attic, the belfry? The remark may be another bit of fabulation. As is often the case with Durrell's picturesque statements, an ostensible claim is highly questionable, for he also notes in the same passage that a family of "barn-owls" lived in a nearby "water-tower" (*SC* 21). Which was undoubtedly true.[41] But owls eat bats. It seems unlikely that the two mammals would cohabit the same property in close proximity. He presumably found the obvious connection between bats and vampires irresistible. This is yet another example of what Durrell calls "truth" contradicting itself, or, in another context, of what Rilke praises as a "pure contradiction".

Vampire House and its supposed bats have another connection. Bats live in caves, and caves have symbolic importance for Durrell. *The Dark Labyrinth* (1947) involves a journey through a cave; *Quinx* (1985), the last novel of *Quintet*, ends with a return to a cave; and Durrell's "Heraldic Universe" may owe something to Plato's "Allegory of the Cave" in *The Republic*. Vampire House could be looked upon as a metaphorical cave in its most dreary aspect. In 1990, the year of his death, Durrell publishes his last work, *Caesar's Vast Ghost*. The book contains the poem, "Route Saussine 15", which bemoans a "poisoned" house suffering from a "lack of sun". The grounds have an "abandoned garden" and "a stagnant fountain full of tiny frogs". The poet's companion is "an old blind dog", without bladder control, which sprays urine "everywhere" (*CVG* 8). The poem has the stench of decay. It reeks of a dank cave.

Durrell's and Rilke's dwellings were catalysts. They inspired or enhanced particular forms of creativity. But unlike Durrell's relatively

[37] Chamberlin, *Durrell Log*, p. 171.
[38] S. Durrell, "Journals and Letters", pp. 77, 58.
[39] "The Fall of the House of Usher" in Poe, *Poetry and Tales*, p. 317.
[40] Panofsky, *Meaning in the Visual Arts*, p. 300.
[41] Wheelock, "Letter to Editor of *New York Times*", 21 November 1990.

modest homes, two of Rilke's major dwellings were castles, where he was either a guest or had been given free access. Medieval castles are by definition "Gothic", but Rilke's experiences in them, unlike Durrell's in Vampire House, were not Gothic in terms of the Gothic horror associated with Romanticism. Instead, they provided shelter and seclusion at a highly refined level of accommodation.

Rilke moved easily within the rarified world of the European aristocracy. *The Duino Elegies* were named after Castle Duino (*Schloß Duino*) at the northern tip of the Adriatic Sea on the Istrian peninsula. The fourteenth-century castle sat high on cliffs overlooking the Adriatic and belonged to an old family of German nobility, in particular the Princess Marie von Thurn und Taxis (1855-1934), who invited the poet to visit the castle in October 1912. She was one of Rilke's patrons; in gratitude, he later dedicated the elegies to her. In December 1912, Marie Taxis left Duino, and Rilke stayed alone at the castle. His life had reached a marital and spiritual crisis. Then, during a winter storm, while pacing outside the walls of the fortress, he heard a voice call out from the wind, almost biblical in origin, and was suddenly inspired to begin writing the first two of ten elegies.[42]

The cycle of poems was not completed until 1922 at yet another castle, the medieval Château de Muzot, near the Swiss municipality of Veyras, in the canton of Valais (**Figure 18**). The château was a small manor house in Switzerland's Rhone Valley: "a square, step-gabled tower set in a small garden". Nearby was a chapel with "two arches of roses".[43] Veyras is situated among low mountains and does not have the monumental Alpine views Rilke found so repugnant. In July 1921, Werner Reinhart (1884-1951), a wealthy Swiss merchant and patron of the arts, leased the castle and then subleased it to Rilke, rent-free. He jokingly referred to Rilke as his "castellan", the governor of his castle.[44]

---

[42] Prater, *Rainer Maria Rilke*, pp. 193-204; Freedman, *Rainer Maria Rilke*, p. 323.

[43] Prater, *Rainer Maria Rilke*, p. 337.

[44] Freedman, *Rainer Maria Rilke*, pp. 474-75.

Figure 18: Château de Muzot, c. 1922 (Wikimedia Commons)

The voice in the wind at Castle Duino was Rilke's own cry of desperation: "Wer, wenn ich schriee, hörte mich denn aus der Engel / Ordnungen?" (Who, if I cried, would hear me among the angelic / orders?).[45] The answer came ten years later at Muzot during another wintry setting. In an extraordinary burst of creativity in February 1922, Rilke would complete the remaining ten *Duino Elegies* and also compose the fifty-five poems of the *Sonnets to Orpheus* (1923). On 9 February 1922, after finishing these two sets of poems, Rilke describes the creative process in a letter to his lover Baladine Klossowska:

> That which weighed upon and tortured me is accomplished, and, I believe, gloriously so. It took but a few days, but never within my heart and mind have I borne such a hurricane. I am still trembling from it—tonight I was afraid of collapsing; but no, I overcame ... And I went out to caress this old Muzot, just now, in the moonlight.[46]

Then on 11 February 1922, Rilke repeated part of the story in a letter to his former lover, who later became his close friend, Lou Andreas-Salomé:

> I went outside and put my hand on the little Muzot that had guarded and finally entrusted all this to me, I touched its wall and stroked it like a big old animal.[47]

---

[45] Rilke, *Sämtliche Werke*, vol. I, p. 685; trans. Leishman and Spender, *Duino Elegies*, p. 21.
[46] Rilke, *Letters to Merline*, p. 145.
[47] Rilke, *Rilke and Andreas-Salomé*, p. 332.

The circumstances surrounding the completion of these poems became legendary. W. H. Auden memorialized the event in his "Sonnet XIX" of "Sonnets from China" (1938):

> Awed, grateful, tired, content to die, completed,
> He went out in the winter night to stroke
> That tower as one pets an animal.[48]

So, Rilke treats Muzot like a pet or an old friend. It was a living thing.

The act also characterized some of his relationships with women. He treated them as useful pets — they provided comfort and companionship (but not too much). Muzot was a thing made animate; the reverse happened to many of his lovers. They ultimately became useful artifacts in the service of his art. Rilke's many residences and accommodations had served him well. They had never been permanent places, which was the way he wanted it. Rilke did not want a home, a fixed abode, and, as Freedman comments, he had a "morbid anxiety about being tied down".[49] The fear of being "tied down" could apply to female relationships as well as to domiciles. Rilke had many lovers and epistolary affairs. Some endured, such as his friendships with Lou Andreas-Salomé and Princess Marie von Thurn und Taxis, but the intimate affairs were usually temporary, which he either deliberately or unconsciously kept that way and made sure that they did not interfere with his great need for privacy and independence.

Lawrence Durrell's temperament was completely different. He too had many affairs over the years, but he had one great love — Claude-Marie Vincendon, who far surpassed all the others. Greater than any lover or companion, she was the nonpareil "helpmeet" praised in *Balthazar* (*Quartet* 296). After many years of travel and dislocation, Durrell clearly sought a home, a permanent residence, and he found it in the Provençal mansion which Claude purchased in 1966. The big house — with its enclosed garden, blue pool, and shady trees — had the potential to provide a bit of pleasance, a little peace in a rural refuge. After all, it was in fact a *hortus conclusus*, a walled enclosure concealing a private preserve (**Figure 19**). But Claude died in 1967. Durrell was almost fifty-five, and the house became haunted with his various ghosts. It transformed itself into "Vampire House". The inertia of old age does not explain why he was, in effect, chained to such an unpleasant place full of disquieting memories. Durrell could have moved elsewhere at anytime, but he remained there for another twenty-three years until he died on 7 November 1990.

---

[48] Auden, *Collected Poems*, p. 194.

[49] Freedman, *Rainer Maria Rilke*, p. 475.

Figure 19: "Vampire House" and its *hortus conclusus* (photo: ©Denise Tart, 2015)

V. Requiescant in pace

Rainer Maria Rilke died on 29 December 1926. He was not buried near Château de Muzot. Following the detailed instructions of his will — which even requested a particular type of headstone[50] — he was buried alone in Raron, another village in the canton of Valais. Rilke preached aloneness. He married once and later left his wife and child to pursue his all-important "work" in "solitude".[51] He had subsequent affairs but remained alone until he died ("O pure contradiction"). So he lies buried alone. His only company is a prominent gravesite and headstone, on which are written three lines of his own poetry.

Lawrence Durrell was simply lonely. He endured an "ancient loneliness", as his last poem mentions. He married four times. Near his end, he pursued a fifth marriage. Throughout his life, he sought and needed female companionship. No monument marks Durrell's grave. Nothing. He has no grave. He was cremated. He dies, disappears, and remains silent. Ian

---

[50] Prater, *Rainer Maria Rilke*, p. 383.
[51] Prater, *Rainer Maria Rilke*, p. 136.

MacNiven concludes his biography with a moving account of the last rites. Seven of Durrell's friends gathered at the cemetery of La chapelle Saint-Julien de Montredon, Salinelles. At the site, some of his ashes were buried in Claude's unmarked plot. Beyond that — nothing — emptiness — *śūnyatā*. His ending circles back to India and invokes the burning ghats of Benares. The words on Durrell's Heraldic headstone, wherever it may be and in whatever mysterious realm of Platonic Forms, could be taken from the last words of *Justine* (1957): "Does not everything depend on our interpretation of the silence around us?"[52]

---

[52] L. Durrell, *Justine*, p. 245.

APPENDIX[1]

I. Introduction

The following is my free translation of a note by Lawrence Durrell appearing in *Die Zeit* (Hamburg) on 27 July 1962. Title of headline: "Alle Uhren stehen" (All Clocks Stop or Time Stops). Sub-headline: "Lawrence Durrell über einen deutschen Roman, der ihm wichtig wurde" (Lawrence Durrell on the personal importance of a German novel). Dieter E. Zimmer translated Durrell's English into German. The whereabouts of Durrell's original note is unknown.

According to Alan G. Thomas and James A. Brigham, Lawrence Durrell's note on Rainer Maria Rilke's *Die Aufzeichnungen des Malte Laurids Brigge* was originally titled: "Alle Uhren stehen Still" (All Clocks Are Still), which emphasizes that time has stopped.[2] Dieter E. Zimmer interviewed Durrell for *Die Zeit* (Hamburg) on 27 November 1959.[3]

II. Translation

There are few works in the prose of great poets, whose readings are as stimulating and exacting as the slim notebooks of Malte Laurids Brigge. Although they have roughly the form of a novel and pretend to be the diary of a Danish poet living in Paris, they are fictitious, in the usual meaning of the word. They are a long prose-poem, which borrows the tone of prose, in order to weave a poetical reality with deceptive accuracy and austerity. I am aware of few books that are filled with the same amount of poetical observation and few books in which each line carries so heavily a weight. Moreover, the style of poetry is flawless in its clarity. It presents itself to the reader as reserved, almost surgical, so that one hesitates — even to use one word — a word that to the reader could evoke the joy of de Nerval's "Aurelia" or the gnomic irony of [Paul Valéry's] M. Teste. No, this is

---

[1] Originally published as "Lawrence Durrell on Rainer Maria Rilke's *The Notebooks of Malte Laurids Brigge*" in *C.20: an international journal*, Issue 4 (2021). https://durrelllibrarycorfu.wordpress.com.

[2] Thomas and Brigham, *Illustrated Checklist*, p. 89.

[3] L. Durrell, *Conversations*, pp. 37-38.

something entirely different — the tracing of ephemeral reality, under which lies those illusionary appearances which we call time, history, and memory.

The fact that the material is occasionally autobiographical, that Rilke occasionally borrows the tone of the novel — in order to oppose reality and to serve as a counterpoint to the daily reality of mankind — all that does not, on the whole, impair the importance of poetry. Of course, there are a couple of sketches of people, of places and events, but they all have a dream-like dimension and appear to the reader like visions. Cautiously, they are neither fixed temporally, nor are they provided with a chronology. One has the feeling that, in the room where Rilke earnestly wrote down these words, the clocks stopped and the window-curtains were drawn shut. What does it matter whether it was day or night, spring or autumn, past or future? Only the poetic vision was important — the unintelligible, metaphysical germ of time, its inner mainspring — the still, agonizing search for a concrete, spiritual reality, which conceals the superficiality of daily reality.

So it happens that the sentences — which are as simple as clear, as spare as long and elliptical—are laden with a kind of kinetic beauty, which is a function of their poetic truth. Our poet does not assume a posture, nor does he allow the intensity of his language to appear "poetical", in the bad sense of the word. On the contrary, he faces his inner vision and quietly fills his notebook with his precise transcriptions of what he factually sees: how to play billiards, how to analyze statistics, or how to catalogue stamps. This almost scientific dissociation gives poetry a singular resonance. It conjures the past without sadness, it depicts the present without pity or contempt, and it peers into the future without fear.

Rilke's vision appears to us in an age, which is full of the recurrent quarrels of heretics, clamorous in its theories, and biased in its appeal to our basest hopes of special importance. His vision is free of all private matters. It is too pure to fall into any system, be it aesthetic, social, or religious. It reminds us that his pure vision is like a clear spring. It allows no pollution through time and history.

It is simple — eternal and changeable.[4]

---

[4] The German reads: "Sie ist einfach — ewig und verändlich". *Verändlich* (changeable) does not go well with *ewig* (eternal). I wonder if Durrell originally wrote *unchangeable*, which would be *unveränlich* in German. The eternal is normally associated with immutability, as in the phrase "unvaryingly eternal" from Durrell's 1961 essay, "Women of the Mediterranean": "They [famous women] are all children of this mysterious sea, occupying its landscapes in human forms which seem as unvaryingly eternal as the olive, the asphodel, the cypress, the laurel, and

And the poet's task is this — in the silence of his room, to respect and honour where clocks stop. In front of the window, the story takes place; yet, from the paper the raw material rises slowly, out of which the story can be set and built. This is the task of the poet — it is not for him to rationalize order amid chaos. This task is something else — to show through his mere existence that the poet of mankind is not dead and cannot die, so long as from time to time at least one of his great representatives is born, who takes up the threads of his inner life and weaves them into a poem. The poet cries out through his silence. We need not ask him why we are calling out. We know all too well.

---

above all the sacred vine" (*SP* 369).

BIBLIOGRAPHY

1. Works by Lawrence Durrell cited in the text

The Alexandria Quartet: Justine, Balthazar, Mountolive, Clea (London: Faber and Faber, 1962).

"Alle Uhren stehen [Still] [All Clocks Stopped]." [A short note on Rainer Maria Rilke's *Die Aufzeichnungen des Malte Laurids Brigge*. Translated from English to German by Dieter E. Zimmer] *Die Zeit* [Hamburg] 27 July 1962. [See Appendix for a translation of the German.]

The Avignon Quintet: Monsieur, Livia, Constance, Sebastian, Quinx (London: Faber and Faber, 1992).

Balthazar: a novel (London: Faber and Faber, 1958).

The Big Supposer: A Dialogue with Marc Alyn translated by Francine Barker, illustrated with paintings by Lawrence Durrell (New York: Grove Press, 1974).

Bitter Lemons (New York: E. P. Dutton, 1957).

The Black Book ([1938] New York: E. P. Dutton, 1960).

Blue Thirst (Santa Barbara, CA: Capra Press, 1975).

Caesar's Vast Ghost: Aspects of Provence with photographs by Harry Peccinotti (New York: Arcade Publishing, 1990).

The Dark Labyrinth ([1947] New York: E. P. Dutton, 1962).

The Durrell-Miller Letters: 1935-80 edited by Ian S. MacNiven (New York: New Directions, 1988).

From the Elephant's Back: Collected Essays & Travel Writings edited by James Gifford (Edmonton, AB: University of Alberta Press, 2015).

The Greek Islands (New York: Viking Press, 1978).

Justine: a novel (London: Faber and Faber, 1957).

A Key to Modern British Poetry (Norman, OK: University of Oklahoma Press, 1952).

"Lawrence Durrell: The Art of Fiction XXIII", interviewed by Julian Mitchell and Gene Andrewski, *The Paris Review* 22 (1960): 33-61.

Lawrence Durrell: Collected Poems, 1931-1974 edited by James A. Brigham (London: Faber and Faber, 1980).

Lawrence Durrell: Conversations edited by Earl G. Ingersoll (Teaneck, NJ: Fairleigh Dickinson University Press, 1998).

Lawrence Durrell's Endpapers and Inklings 1933-1988 Vol. 2, *Dramas, Screenplays, Essays, Incorrigibilia* edited by Richard Pine (Newcastle-upon-Tyne: Cambridge Scholars Publishing, 2019).
The Magnetic Island with Greek translation by Vera Konidari (Corfu: Durrell Library of Corfu, 2019).
A Private Country (London: Faber and Faber, 1943).
Prospero's Cell: A guide to the landscape and manners of the island of Corcyra [Corfu] (London: Faber and Faber, 1945).
Reflections on a Marine Venus: a companion to the landscape of Rhodes ([1953] London: Faber and Faber, 1960).
Selected Poems of Lawrence Durrell edited by Peter Porter (London: Faber and Faber, 2006).
Sicilian Carousel (London: Faber and Faber, 1977).
A Smile in the Mind's Eye (New York: Universe Books, 1982).
Spirit of Place: Letters and Essays on Travel edited by Alan G. Thomas (London: Faber and Faber, 1969).
The Tree of Idleness and other poems (London: Faber and Faber, 1955).
White Eagles over Serbia ([1957] Harmondsworth: Penguin/Peacock Books, 1980).

2. Other works cited in the text

Aciman, André, *Out of Egypt: A Memoir* (New York: Farrar, Straus, Giroux, 1994).
Adam, Peter, "Alexandria Revisited", *Twentieth Century Literature* 33.3 (1987): 395-410.
Aldington, Richard, *Literary Lifelines: The Richard Aldington-Lawrence Durrell Correspondence* edited by Ian S. MacNiven and Harry T. Moore (London: Faber and Faber, 1981).
Aldred, Cyril, *Egypt to the End of the Old Kingdom* (London: Thames and Hudson, 1965).
—. *Egyptian Art in the Days of the Pharaohs, 3100-320 BC* (New York: Oxford University Press, 1980).
Allen, James P., *The Art of Medicine in Ancient Egypt* (New York: Metropolitan Museum of Art, 2005).
Allen, Richard Hinckley, *Star Names: Their Lore and Meaning* ([1899] New York: Dover Publications, 1963).
Alpers, Paul, *The Singer of the "Eclogues": A Study of Virgilian Pastoral with a new translation of the "Eclogues"* (Berkeley, CA: University of California Press, 1979).
—. *What Is Pastoral?* (Chicago: University of Chicago Press, 1996).

Alter, Robert, *Imagined Cities: Urban Experience and the Language of the Novel* (New Haven, CT: Yale University Press, 2005).

Anthony, David W., *The Horse, the Wheel, and Language: How Bronze Age Riders from the Eurasian Steppes Shaped the Modern World* (Princeton, NJ: Princeton University Press, 2007).

Arendt, Hannah, "The Achievement of Hermann Broch", *Kenyon Review* 11.3 (Summer 1949): 476-83.

Aristotle, *The Complete Works of Aristotle* Vol. 2 [section on the *Metaphysics*] translated by W. D. Ross, edited by Jonathan Barnes (Princeton, NJ: Princeton University Press, 1984).

Armstrong, Richard H., *A Compulsion for Antiquity: Freud and the Ancient World* (Ithaca, NY: Cornell University Press, 2005).

Assmann, Jan, *The Mind of Egypt: History and Meaning in the Time of the Pharaohs* translated by Andrew Jenkins (New York: Metropolitan Books-Henry Holt, 2002).

Athanassoglou-Kallmyer, Nina Maria, *Cézanne and Provence: The Painter in His Culture* (Chicago: University of Chicago Press, 2003).

Atkinson, Sophie, *An Artist in Corfu* (Boston: Dana Estes, 1911).

Auden, W. H., *Collected Poems* edited by Edward Mendelson (New York: Vintage Books, 1991).

Austin, Norman, *Archery at the Dark of the Moon: Poetic Problems in Homer's "Odyssey"* (Berkeley, CA: University of California Press, 1975).

Awad, Mohamed F., "The House Revisited, the City Remembered", *Deus Loci: The Lawrence Durrell Journal* NS7 (1999-2000): 39-44.

Baines, John, review of *Arrest and Movement: An Essay on Space and Time in the Representational Art of the Ancient Near East*, by H. A. Groenewegen-Frankfort, *Journal of Egyptian Archaeology* 60 (1974): 272-76.

—. "Origins of Egyptian Kingship", in *Ancient Egyptian Kingship* edited by David O'Connor and David P. Silverman (Leiden: E. J. Brill, 1995): 95-156.

—. *Visual and Written Culture in Ancient Egypt* (Oxford: Oxford University Press, 2007).

—. *High Culture and Experience in Ancient Egypt* (Sheffield: Equinox Publishing, 2013).

Bate, W. Jackson, *John Keats* (Cambridge, MA: Belknap Press of Harvard University Press, 1963).

Beddington, Charles, *Venice: Canaletto and His Rivals* (London: National Gallery, 2010).

Benson, Ciarán, "The Metaphor of 'Place-Time' and Lawrence Durrell's 'Heraldic Universe'" in *Islands of the Mind: Psychology, Literature and Biodiversity* edited by Richard Pine and Vera Konidari (Newcastle-upon-Tyne: Cambridge Scholars Publishing, 2020): 244-58.

Beny, Roloff, *Roloff Beny Interprets in Photographs "Pleasure of Ruins" by Rose Macaulay* edited by Constance Babington Smith (London: Thames and Hudson, 1964).

Bergson, Henri, *Time and Free Will: An Essay on the Immediate Data of Consciousness* translated by F. L. Pogson ([1910] New York: Harper & Brothers, 1960).

Berossos and Manetho, Introduced and Translated: Native Traditions in Ancient Mesopotamia and Egypt translated by Gerald P. Verbrugghe and John M. Wickersham (Ann Arbor, MI: University of Michigan Press, 2000).

Biblia Sacra: Iuxta Vulgatam Versionem (Stuttgart: Deutsche Bibelgesellschaft, 1969).

Bierbrier, Morris L., *Who Was Who in Egyptology* 5th edition (London: Egyptian Exploration Society, 2019).

Booth, Stephen, *"King Lear," "Macbeth," Indefinition, and Tragedy* (New Haven, CT: Yale University Press, 1983).

Boswell, James, *Life of Johnson* edited by R. W. Chapman ([1791] Oxford: Oxford University Press, 1980).

Bowker, Gordon, *Through the Dark Labyrinth: A Biography of Lawrence Durrell* revised edition (London: Pimlico, 1998).

Bowra, C. M., *The Greek Experience* (Cleveland, OH: World, 1957).

Breasted, James Henry, *A History of Egypt: From the Earliest Times to the Persian Conquest* 2nd edition (New York: Charles Scribner's Sons, 1909).

Broch, Hermann, *Der Tod des Vergil* Herausgegeben von Paul Michael Lützeler ([1945] Frankfurt am Main: Suhrkamp Verlag, 1976).

—. *The Death of Virgil* translated by Jean Starr Untermeyer (San Francisco: North Point Press, 1983).

Brontë, Emily, *Wuthering Heights: Authoritative Texts, Backgrounds, Criticism* 3rd edition edited by William M. Sale, Jr. and Richard J. Dunn ([1847] New York: W. W. Norton, 1990).

Brown, David Blayney, *Turner in the Tate Collection* (London: Tate Publishing, 2002).

Bryan, Betsy M., "Episodes of Iconoclasm in the Egyptian New Kingdom", in *Iconoclasm and Text Destruction in the Ancient Near East and Beyond* edited by Natalie Naomi May (Chicago: Oriental Institute Seminars, 2012): 363-402.

Budge, E. A. Wallis, *The Book of the Dead: The Papyrus Ani* ([1895] New York: Dover Publications, 1967).

Buford, Bill, "Comment: The Seduction of Storytelling", *The New Yorker,* 24 June and 1 July 1996: 11-12.

Burke, Edmund, *A Philosophical Enquiry into the Origin of Our Ideas of the Sublime and the Beautiful* edited by Adam Phillips ([1757] Oxford: Oxford University Press, 1998).

Canales, Jimena, *The Physicist & the Philosopher: Einstein, Bergson, and the Debate That Changed Our Understanding of Time* (Princeton, NJ: Princeton University Press, 2015).

Carlson, Deborah N., "Seeing the Sea: Ships' Eyes in Classical Greece", *Hesperia* 78.3 (2009): 347-65.

Carson, Anne, *If Not, Winter: Fragments of Sappho* translated by Anne Carson (New York: Alfred A. Knopf, 2002).

—. "The Beat Goes On", *The New York Review of Books* 52.16 (20 October 2005).

Cavafy, C. P., *Collected Poems* revised edition, translated by Edmund Keeley and Philip Sherrard, edited by D. George Savidis (Princeton, NJ: Princeton University Press, 1992).

Chamberlin, Brewster, *The Durrell Log: A Chronology of the Life and Times of Lawrence Durrell* (London: Colenso Books, 2019).

Chaucer, Geoffrey, *The Riverside Chaucer* 3rd edition edited by Larry D. Benson and F. N. Robinson (Boston: Houghton Mifflin, 1987).

Cohen, Roger, "A Daughter's Intimations", *The New York Times* 14 August 1991.

Coleridge, Samuel Taylor, *The Collected Works of Samuel Taylor Coleridge* Vol. 7, *Biographia Literaria or Biographical Sketches of My Literary Life and Opinions* edited by James Engell and W. Jackson Bate (Princeton, NJ: Princeton University Press, 1983).

Collins Robert, *French English, English French Dictionary* 4th edition (New York: Harper Collins, 1995).

Commager, Steele, *The Odes of Horace: A Critical Study* (Bloomington, IN: Indiana University Press, 1967).

Conrad, Joseph, *Lord Jim: A Tale* edited by J. H. Stape and Ernest W. Sullivan II ([1900] Cambridge: Cambridge University Press, 2012).

Cox, Fiona, "Envoi: the death of Virgil" in *The Cambridge Companion to Virgil* edited by Charles Martindale (Cambridge: Cambridge University Press, 1997): 327-36.

Crane, R. S., "The Concept of Plot and the Plot of *Tom Jones*" in *Critics and Criticism: Essays in Method* abridged edition edited by R. S. Crane, (Chicago: Phoenix-University of Chicago Press, 1957): 62-93.

Crews, Frederick, et al., *The Memory Wars: Freud's Legacy in Dispute* (New York: New York Review of Books, 1995).

The Critical Tradition: Classics Texts and Contemporary Trends edited by David H. Richter (New York: St. Martin's Press, 1989).

Curtius, Ernst Robert, *European Literature and the Latin Middle Ages* translated by Willard R. Trask ([1948] New York: Harper & Row, 1953).

Dasen, Véronique, *Dwarfs in Ancient Egypt and Greece* (Oxford: Clarendon Press, 1993).

Daszewski, W. A., "From Hellenistic Polychrome of Sculptures to Roman Mosaics" in *Alexandria and Alexandrianism: Papers Delivered at a Symposium Organized by the J. Paul Getty Museum and The Getty Center for the History of Art and the Humanities and Held at the Museum, April 22-25, 1993* (Malibu, CA: J. Paul Getty Museum, 1996): 141-54.

Davies, Nina M., *Ancient Egyptian Paintings* Vol. 3, *Descriptive Text* (Chicago: University of Chicago Press, 1936).

Davies, Norman de Garis, *The Rock Tombs of El Amarna* Part VI, *Tombs of Parennefer, Tutu, and Aÿ* edited by F. Ll. Griffith ([1908] London: Egypt Exploration Society, 2004).

Davies, Vivian, and Renée Friedman, "The Narmer Palette: An Overlooked Detail" in *Egyptian Museum Collections around the World* Vol. 1 edited by Mamdouh Eldamaty and Mai Trad (Cairo: Supreme Council of Antiquities, 2002): 243-46.

Dawson, Warren R., "Pygmies and Dwarfs in Ancient Egypt", *Journal of Egyptian Archaeology* 24.2 (1938): 185-89.

De Cosson, Anthony, *Mareotis: Being a Short Account of the History and Ancient Monuments of the North-Western Desert of Egypt and of Lake Mareotis* (London: Country Life, 1935).

Diboll, Michael V., *Lawrence Durrell's "Alexandria Quartet" in Its Egyptian Contexts* (Lampeter, UK: Edwin Mellen Press, 2004).

Drews, Robert, *The Coming of the Greeks: Indo-European Conquests in the Aegean and the Near East* (Princeton, NJ: Princeton University Press, 1988).

Dunham, Dows, and William Kelly Simpson, edited by William Kelly Simpson, *The Mastaba of Queen Mersyankh III: G 7530-7540* (Boston: Museum of Fine Arts, 1974). Digital copy.

Durrell, Sappho Jane, "Sappho Durrell: Journals and Letters" edited by Bill Buford, *Granta* 37 (1991): 55-92.

Edwards, I. E. S., *The Pyramids of Egypt* ([1947] London: Penguin Books, 1993).

Eliot, George, *The Mill on the Floss,* 3 vols. (Edinburgh: William Blackwood and Sons, 1860).

Ellmann, Richard, *James Joyce* revised edition ([1959] Oxford: Oxford University Press, 1982).

Empson, William, *Some Versions of Pastoral* ([1935] New York: New Directions, 1974).

—. *Seven Types of Ambiguity* second edition ([1947] Harmondsworth: Pelican Books, 1972).

Enright, D. J., *Collected Poems, 1948-1998* (Oxford: Oxford University Press, 1998).

Fertile, Candace, "The Meaning of Incest in the Fiction of Lawrence Durrell", *Deus Loci: The Lawrence Durrell Journal* NS4 (1995-96): 105-23.

Forster, E. M., *Alexandria: A History and a Guide and Pharos and Pharillon* edited by Miriam Allott ([1922 and 1923] London: André Deutsch, 2004).

Forster, Margaret, *Daphne du Maurier: The Secret Life of the Renowned Storyteller* (New York: Doubleday, 1993).

Frank, Joseph, *The Idea of Spatial Form* ([1945] New Brunswick, NJ: Rutgers University Press, 1991).

Frankfort, Henri, *Kingship and the Gods: A Study of Ancient Near Eastern Religion as the Integration of Society & Nature* (Chicago: University of Chicago Press, 1948).

Fraser, P. M., *Ptolemaic Alexandria* Vol. 1, *Text* (Oxford: Clarendon Press, 1972).

Freedman, Ralph, *Life of a Poet: Rainer Maria Rilke* (New York: Farrar, Straus and Giroux, 1996).

Freud, Sigmund, *Gesammelte Werke* Band 1, *Werke aus den Jahren 1892-1899* (Frankfurt am Main: S. Fischer Verlag, 1952).

—. "Medusa's Head" in *Collected Papers* Vol. 5 edited by James Strachey (London: Hogarth Press, 1953): 105-06.

—. *The Standard Edition of the Complete Psychological Works of Sigmund Freud* translated by James Strachey in collaboration with Anna Freud, 24 vols. (London: Hogarth Press, 1962).

—. *The Complete Letters of Sigmund Freud to Wilhelm Fliess, 1887-1904* edited and translated by Jeffrey Moussaieff Masson (Cambridge, MA: Harvard University Press, 1985).

Fritze, Ronald H., *Egyptomania: A History of Fascination, Obsession and Fantasy* (London: Reaktion Books, 2016).

Gardiner, Alan, *Egypt of the Pharaohs: An Introduction* ([1961] Oxford: Oxford University Press, 1964).

Geertz, Clifford, *Works and Lives: The Anthropologist as Author* (Stanford, CA: Stanford University Press, 1988).

Gere, Cathy, *Knossos & the Prophets of Modernism* (Chicago: University of Chicago Press, 2009).

Gimbutas, Marija, "Proto-Indo-European Culture: The Kurgan Culture of the Fifth, Fourth, and Third Millennia B.C." in *Indo-European and Indo-Europeans: Papers Presented at the Third Indo-European Conference at the University of Pennsylvania* edited by George Cardona, Henry M. Hoenigswald, and Alfred Senn (Philadelphia: University of Pennsylvania Press, 1970): 155-97.

—. *The Goddesses and Gods of Old Europe: 6500-3500 BC, Myths and Cult Images*, new and updated edition ([1974] Berkeley, CA: University of California Press, 1982).

Godshalk, William Leigh, "Some Sources of Durrell's *Alexandria Quartet*" in *Critical Essays on Lawrence Durrell* edited by Alan Warren Friedman (Boston: G. K. Hall, 1987): 158-71.

Goebs, Katja, *Crowns in Egyptian Funerary Literature: Royalty, Rebirth, and Destruction* (Oxford: Griffith Institute, 2008).

Goethe, Johann Wolfgang von, *Italian Journey: 1786-1788* translated by W. H. Auden and Elizabeth Meyer ([1816-17] New York: Schocken Books, 1968).

—. *Italienische Reise* Band 15, Herausgegeben von Andreas Beyer und Norbert Miller in Zusammenarbeit mit Christof Thoenes ([1816 und 1817] München: Carl Hanser Verlag, 1992).

—. *Conversations of Goethe with Johann Peter Eckermann* translated by John Oxenford and edited by J. K. Moorhead ([1930] [N.p.]: Da Capo Press, 1998).

Gogh, Vincent van, *Vincent van Gogh: A Life in Letters* edited by Nienke Bakker, Leo Jansen, and Hans Luijten (New York: Thames & Hudson, 2020).

Goldwasser, Orly, "The Narmer Palette and the 'Triumph of Metaphor'", *Lingua Aegyptia* 2 (1992): 67-85.

Gomme, A. W., "Interpretations of Some Poems of Alkaios and Sappho", *Journal of Hellenic Studies* 77.2 (1957): 255-66.

Greek Lyric I: Sappho and Alcaeus edited and translated by David A. Campbell (Cambridge, MA: Harvard University Press, 1982).

Green, David, "Out in the Midi Sun: Adventures in Lawrence Durrell Country", *A Café in Space: The Anaïs Nin Literary Journal* 14 (2017): 85-95.

—. "Lawrence Durrell's Houses: Domiciles of Creativity" forthcoming.

Green, Martin, "Lawrence Durrell: A Minority Report" in *The World of Lawrence Durrell* edited by Harry T. Moore (Carbondale, IL: Southern Illinois University Press, 1962): 129-45.

Green, Peter, "Alexander's Alexandria" in *Alexandria and Alexandrianism: Papers Delivered at a Symposium Organized by The J. Paul Getty Museum and The Getty Center for the History of Art and the Humanities and Held at the Museum, April 22-25, 1993* (Malibu, CA: J. Paul Getty Museum, 1996): 3-19.

—. "Man of gifts", review of *Patrick Leigh Fermor: An Adventure* by Artemis Cooper, *Times Literary Supplement* no. 5720 (16 November 2012): 14-15.

Groenewegen-Frankfort, H. A. [Henriette Antonia], *Arrest and Movement: An Essay on Space and Time in the Representational Art of the Ancient Near East* ([1951] Cambridge, MA: Belknap Press of Harvard University Press, 1987).

Guerlac, Suzanne, *Thinking in Time: An Introduction to Henri Bergson* (Ithaca, NY: Cornell University Press, 2006).

Guzzoni, Mariella, *Vincent's Books: Van Gogh and the Writers Who Inspired Him* (Chicago: University of Chicago Press, 2020).

Haag, Michael, "The City of Words" in *Alexandria: A History and a Guide by E. M. Forster*, introduction by Lawrence Durrell, revised Afterword and Notes by Michael Haag ([1922 and 1938] New York: Oxford University Press, 1986 and London: Michael Haag, 1986): 237-43.

—. *Egypt* (London: Cadogan Guides, 1993).

—. *Alexandria: City of Memory* (New Haven, CT: Yale University Press, 2004).

—. *Alexandria Illustrated* (Cairo: American University in Cairo Press, 2004).

—. "Only the City Is Real: Lawrence Durrell's Journey to Alexandria", *Alif: Journal of Comparative Poetics* 26 (2006): 39-47.

—. *The Templars: History & Myth* (London: Profile Books, 2008).

—. *Vintage Alexandria: Photographs of the City, 1860-1960* (Cairo: American University in Cairo Press, 2008).

—. "*The Alexandria Quartet*: From One Volume to Four", *Deus Loci: The Lawrence Durrell Journal* NS13 (2012-2013): 64-73.

—. *The Durrells of Corfu* (London: Profile Books, 2017).

Hall, Emma Swan, *The Pharaoh Smites his Enemies: A Comparative Study*, Münchner Ägyptologische Studien 44 (München: Deutscher Kunstverlag, 1986).

Hall, Roland, "Monism and Pluralism" in *Encyclopedia of Philosophy* Vol. 5, editor in Chief, Paul Edwards (New York: Macmillan Publishing &

Free Press, 1967).

Hartwig, Melinda, *Tomb Painting and Identity in Ancient Thebes, 1419-1372 BCE* (Turnhout, BE: Brepols Publishers, 2004).

Hatshepsut: From Queen to Pharaoh edited by Catharine H. Roehrig with Renée Dreyfus and Cathleen A. Keller (New York: Metropolitan Museum of Art, 2005).

Hawkes, Jacquetta, "Art in the Ancient Near East", review of *Arrest and Movement: An Essay on Space and Time in the Representational Art of the Ancient Near East* by H. A. Groenewegen-Frankfort, *Times Literary Supplement* issue 2576 (15 June 1951): 368.

Heller, Erich, *The Disinherited Mind* (Cleveland, OH: Meridian Books/World Publishing, 1959).

Herman, Judith Lewis, with Lisa Hirschman *Father-Daughter Incest* (Cambridge, MA: Harvard University Press, 2000).

Hesiod, *Hesiod: Theogony, Works and Days, Testimonia* edited and translated by Glenn W. Most (Cambridge, MA: Harvard University Press, 2006).

Higgins, Reynold, *Minoan and Mycenaean Art* revised edition (London: Thames & Hudson, 1997).

Hillelson, S., "Nubian Origins", *Sudan Notes and Records* 13.1 (1930): 137-48.

Hodgkin, Joanna, *Amateurs in Eden: The Story of a Bohemian Marriage: Nancy and Lawrence Durrell* (London: Virago Press, 2012).

Hofstadter, Richard, *Anti-Intellectualism in American Life, The Paranoid Style in American Politics, Uncollected Essays* edited by Sean Wilentz (New York: Library of America, 2020).

Hogarth, Paul, *The Mediterranean Shore: Travels in Lawrence Durrell Country*, introduction and commentary by Lawrence Durrell (London: Pavilion Books, 1988).

Hollis, Susan Tower, *The Ancient Egyptian "Tale of Two Brothers": A Mythological, Religious, Literary, and Historico-Political Study* second edition (Oakville, CT: Bannerstone Press, 2008).

Holloway, R. Ross, "The Tomb of the Diver", *American Journal of Archaeology* 110 (July 2006): 365-88.

Homans, Margaret, "Repression and Sublimation of Nature in *Wuthering Heights*", *PMLA* 93.1 (1978): 9-19.

Homer, *The Odyssey*, translation and introduction by Emily Wilson (New York: W. W. Norton, 2018).

Horace (Quintus Horatius Flaccus), *The Odes and Epodes* translated by C. E. Bennett (Cambridge, MA: Harvard University Press, 1927).

An Intermediate Greek-English Lexicon seventh edition, founded on Liddell and Scott's *Greek-English Lexicon* (Oxford: Clarendon Press, 1968).

Jaloux, Edmond, *Rainer Maria Rilke: His Last Friendship [and] Unpublished Letters to Mrs. Eloui Bey* translated by William H. Kennedy (New York: Philosophical Library, 1952).

James, Henry, *Henry James: The Complete Stories, 1898-1910*, notes by Denis Donoghue (New York: Library of America, 1996).

Joho, Tobias, "Burckhardt and Nietzsche on the *Agōn*: the dark luster of ancient Greece" in *Conflict and Competition: Agōn in Western Greece: Selected Essays from the 2019 Symposium on the Heritage of Western Greece* edited by Heather L. Reid, John Serrati and Tim Sorg (Sioux City, IA: Parnassos, 2020): 267-88.

Jonson, Ben, *Ben Jonson and the Cavalier Poets: Authoritative Texts and Criticism* edited by Hugh Maclean (New York: W. W. Norton, 1974).

Kaczvinsky, Donald P., "When Was Darley in Alexandria? A Chronology for *The Alexandria Quartet*", *Journal of Modern Literature* 17.4 (1991): 591-94.

Kant, Immanuel, *Observations on the Feeling of the Beautiful and Sublime* translated by John T. Goldthwait (Berkeley, CA: University of California Press, 2003).

Kazantzakis, Nikos, *Report to Greco* translated by P. A. Bien (London: Faber and Faber, 1973).

Keeley, Edmund, *Cavafy's Alexandria: Study of a Myth in Progress* (Cambridge, MA: Harvard University Press, 1976).

—. *Inventing Paradise: The Greek Journey, 1937-47* (New York: Farrar, Straus and Giroux, 1999).

Keller-Privat, Isabelle, *Lawrence Durrell's Poetry: A Rift in the Fabric of the World* (Teaneck, NJ: Fairleigh Dickinson University, 2019).

Kelly, R. Talbot, *Egypt: Painted and Described* (London: Adam & Charles Black, 1903).

Kemp, Barry, *The City of Akhenaten and Nefertiti: Amarna and Its People* (London: Thames & Hudson, 2012).

Kleist, Heinrich von, *Heinrich von Kleist: Sämtliche Werke und Briefe*, Herausgegeben von Helmut Sembdner, Zweibändige Ausgabe in einem Band (München: Deutscher Taschenbuch Verlag, 2001).

—. *The Marquise of O and Other Stories* translated by David Luke and Nigel Reeves (London: Penguin Books, 2004).

Kline, Morris, *Mathematical Thought from Ancient to Modern Times,* 3 vols. (New York: Oxford University Press, 1972).

Knoepflmacher, U. C., *Emily Brontë: "Wuthering Heights"* (Cambridge: Cambridge University Press, 1989).

Larkin, Philip, *Philip Larkin: The Complete Poems* edited by Archie Burnett (New York: Farrar, Straus and Giroux, 2012).

Lawrence, D. H., *Studies in Classic American Literature* ([1923] New York: Viking Press, 1961).

—. *Sketches of Etruscan Places and Other Italian Essays* edited by Simonetta De Filippis ([1932] Cambridge: Cambridge University Press, 2002).

Leigh Fermor, Patrick, *Mani: Travels in the Southern Peloponnese* (New York: Harper and Brothers, 1958).

Levin, Harry, "The Implication of Explication", *Poetics Today: International Journal for Theory and Analysis of Literature and Communication* 5 (1984): 97-109.

Lewis, Wyndham, *Time and Western Man* ([1927] Boston: Beacon Press, 1957).

Lichtheim, Miriam, *Ancient Egyptian Literature: A Book of Readings* Vol. 1, *The Old and Middle Kingdoms* (Berkeley, CA: University of California Press, 1975).

Lillios, Anna, Anna Lillios to International Lawrence Durrell Society listserv. 5 July 2007.

Loprieno, Antonio, *Ancient Egyptian: A linguistic introduction* (Cambridge: Cambridge University Press, 1995).

Lynn, Kenneth S., *Hemingway* (New York: Simon and Schuster, 1987).

Macaulay, Rose, *Pleasure of Ruins* ([1953] New York: Walker, 1966).

MacKay, Marina, *Ian Watt: The Novel and the Wartime Critic* (Oxford: Oxford University Press, 2018).

MacNiven, Ian S., "Lawrence Durrell and the Nightingales of Sommieres [sic]", *On Miracle Ground II: Second International Lawrence Durrell Conference Proceedings, April 24, 1982* edited by Lawrence W. Markett and Carol Peirce (Baltimore: University of Baltimore Monograph Series, 1984).

—. *Lawrence Durrell: A Biography* (London: Faber and Faber, 1998).

—. "Durrell's Egyptological Sources", Email to author, 29 September 2014.

Major British Writers II, enlarged edition, Reuben A. Brower, [editor of W. B. Yeats] (New York: Harcourt, Brace & World, 1959).

Malek, Jaromir, *In the Shadow of the Pyramids: Egypt during the Old Kingdom*, photographs by Werner Forman (Norman, OK: University of Oklahoma Press, 1986).

Malinowski, Bronisław, *Magic, Science and Religion: And Other Essays* ([1925] Garden City, NY: Doubleday Anchor Books, 1954).

Mann, Michael, "The Contradictions of Continuous Revolution" in *Stalinism and Nazism: Dictatorships in Comparison* edited by Ian

Kershaw and Moshe Lewin (Cambridge: Cambridge University Press, 1997): 135-57.

Mann, Thomas, *Short Stories of Three Decades* translated by H. T. Lowe-Porter (New York: Alfred A. Knopf, 1955).

Manniche, Lise, *Sexual Life in Ancient Egypt* (London: Kegan Paul International, 1987).

Marchand, Leslie A., *Byron: A Biography*, 3 Vols. (New York: Alfred A. Knopf, 1957).

McGann, Jerome, *The Poet Edgar Allan Poe: Alien Angel* (Cambridge, MA: Harvard University Press, 2014).

McPhee, John, *Basin and Range* (New York: Farrar, Straus and Giroux, 1981).

Mendelsohn, Daniel, "Constantine Cavafy: 'As Good as Great Poetry Gets'", *New York Review of Books* 20 November 2008: 55-58.

Meyers, Jeffrey, *The Enemy: A Biography of Wyndham Lewis* (London: Routledge & Kegan Paul, 1980).

Miller, Henry, *The Colossus of Maroussi* (New York: New Directions, 1941).

—. *Big Sur and the Oranges of Hieronymus Bosch* (New York: New Directions, 1957).

Milne, J. Grafton, "Greek and Roman Tourists in Egypt", *Journal of Egyptian Archaeology* 3.2/3 (1916): 76-80.

Morrison, Ray, *A Smile in His Mind's Eye: A Study of the Early Works of Lawrence Durrell* (Toronto: University of Toronto Press, 2005).

—. "The City and its Ontology in Lawrence Durrell's *Alexandria Quartet*", *Mosaic: a journal for the interdisciplinary study of literature* 46.2 (2013): 55-70.

Morton-Saner, Anthea, "Conversations with Anthea", *The Herald: [Newsletter of] the International Lawrence Durrell Society* 45 (November 2020): 2-5.

Muhlestein, Kerry, *Violence in the Service of Order: The Religious Framework for Sanctioned Killing in Ancient Egypt* (Oxford: BAR Publishing [British Archaeological Reports], 2011).

Mumon, Yamada, *Lectures on the Ten Oxherding Pictures* translated by Victor Sōgen Hori (Honolulu, HI: University of Hawai'i Press, 2004).

The New Sappho on Old Age: Textual and Philosophical Issues edited by Ellen Greene and Marilyn B. Skinner (Washington, DC: Center for Hellenic Studies, 2009).

Newberry, Percy E., "The Petty Kingdom of the Harpoon and Egypt's Earliest Mediterranean Port", *Annals of Archaeology and Anthropology* 1 (1908): 17-22.

Nin, Anaïs, *The Diary of Anaïs Nin* Vol. 2, *1934-1939* edited by Gunther Stuhlmann (New York: Harcourt Brace, 1967).

O'Connor, David, "Context, Function and Program: Understanding Ceremonial Slate Palettes", *Journal of the American Research Center in Egypt* 39 (2002): 5-25.

—. "The Narmer Palette: A New Interpretation" in *Before the Pyramids: The Origins of Egyptian Civilization* edited by Emily Teeter (Chicago: Oriental Institute of the University of Chicago, 2011): 145-52.

Onions, C. T., *A Shakespeare Glossary* second edition ([1919] Oxford: Clarendon Press, 1969).

Otis, Brooks, *Virgil: A Study in Civilized Poetry* ([1964] Norman, OK: University of Oklahoma Press, 1995).

The Oxford Book of Greek Verse in Translation edited by T. F. Higham and C. M. Bowra (Oxford: Clarendon Press, 1938).

The Oxford Classical Dictionary fourth edition edited by Simon Hornblower, Antony Spawforth, and Esther Eidinow (Oxford: Oxford University Press, 2012).

The Oxford English Dictionary third edition https://oed.com. Accessed 30 June 2021.

Oxford Latin Dictionary edited by P. G. W. Glare (Oxford: Clarendon Press, 1982).

Page, Denys, "ΔΕΔΥΚΕ ΜΕΝ Ἀ ΣΕΛΑΝΑ", *Journal of Hellenic Studies* 78 (1958): 84-85.

Panofsky, Erwin, "Et in Arcadia Ego: Poussin and the Elegiac Tradition" in *Meaning in the Visual Arts: Papers in and on Art History* ([1955] Chicago: University of Chicago Press, 1982): 295-320.

Parkinson, Richard, *The Painted Tomb-Chapel of Nebamun* photographed by Kevin Lovelock (London: British Museum Press, 2008).

Patch, Diana Craig, *Dawn of Egyptian Art* (New York: Metropolitan Museum of Art, 2011).

Peirce, Carol Marshall, "A Reading of Durrell's Map: John Wain's Oxford Lecture", *Deus Loci: The Lawrence Durrell Newsletter* 3.2 (1979): 3-8.

—. "That 'one book there, a Plutarch': Of *Isis and Osiris* in *The Alexandria Quartet*" in *On Miracle Ground: Essays on the Fiction of Lawrence Durrell* edited by Michael H. Begnal (Lewisburg, PA: Bucknell University Press, 1990): 79-92.

Peirce, Charles Sanders, *The Essential Peirce: Selected Philosophical Writings* Vol. 1, *1867- 1893* edited by Nathan Houser and Christian Kloesel (Bloomington, IN: Indiana University Press, 1992).

Peters, H. F., *Rainer Maria Rilke: Masks and the Man* (New York: McGraw-Hill, 1963).

Pinchin, Jane Lagoudis, *Alexandria Still: Forster, Durrell, and Cavafy* (Princeton, NJ: Princeton University Press, 1977).

Pine, Richard, *Lawrence Durrell: the Mindscape* revised edition (Corfu: Durrell School of Corfu, 2005).

—. *Minor Mythologies as Popular Literature: A Student's Guide to Texts and Films* (Newcastle-upon-Tyne: Cambridge Scholars Publishing, 2018).

—. "The Ancient Egyptian *Book of the Dead*", Email to author, 3 November 2020.

—. "Lawrence Durrell's 'Heraldic Universe': The Magnetic Island of Self-Discovery" in *Islands of the Mind: Psychology, Literature and Biodiversity* edited by Richard Pine and Vera Konidari (Newcastle-upon-Tyne: Cambridge Scholars Publishing, 2020): 219-43.

—. *A Writer in Corfu: an essay on Borderlands, Exile and Metaphor* with a translation into Greek by Vera Konidari (Corfu: Durrell Library of Corfu, 2020).

Plato, *The Republic of Plato* edited by Francis Macdonald Cornford (New York: Oxford University Press, 1945).

—. *Plato: The Complete Works* edited by John M. Cooper (Indianapolis, IN: Hackett Publishing, 1997).

Plutarch, *Plutarch's "De Iside et Osiride"* edited and translated by J. Gwyn Griffiths ([Cardiff]: University of Wales Press, 1970).

Poe, Edgar Allan, *Selected Writings of Edgar Allan Poe* edited by Edward H. Davidson (Boston: Houghton Mifflin, [1956]).

—. "The Philosophy of Composition" in *Edgar Allan Poe: Essays and Reviews*, notes and selection by G. R. Thompson (New York: Library of America, 1984): 13-25.

—. *Poetry and Tales*, notes by Patrick F. Quinn (New York: Library of America, 1984).

Powell, Dilys, *The Traveller's Journey Is Done* (London: Hodder and Stoughton, 1943).

—. *The Villa Ariadne* ([1973] London: Michael Haag, 1985).

Prater, Donald, *A Ringing Glass: The Life of Rainer Maria Rilke* (Oxford: Clarendon Press, 1986).

Quibell, James E., *Hierakonpolis I* (London: Bernard Quaritch, 1900). http://www.etana.org/sites/default/files/coretexts/15249.pdf. Accessed 4 June 2021.

Rader, Ralph W., "Literary Form in Factual Narrative: The Example of Boswell's *Johnson*" in *Essays in Eighteenth-Century Biography* edited by Philip B. Daghlian (Bloomington, IN: Indiana University Press, 1968): 3-42.

Ransome, John Crowe, "A Poem Nearly Anonymous" in *Milton's "Lycidas"*: *The Tradition and the Poem* edited by C. A. Patrides (New York: Holt, Rinehart and Winston, 1961): 64-81.

Redwine, Bruce, "The Melting Mirage of Lawrence Durrell's White City: Impressions of the Durrell Celebration, Alexandria, Egypt, 29-30 November 2017", *Arion: A Journal of the Humanities and the Classics* 16.1 (2008): 19-46.

—. "Haag's Many Alexandrias", review of *Alexandria: City of Memory* and *Vintage Alexandria: Photographs of the City, 1860-1960* by Michael Haag, *Arion: A Journal of the Humanities and the Classics* 17.3 (2010): 133-59.

—. "Nancy and Larry", review of *Amateurs in Eden: The Story of a Bohemian Marriage: Nancy and Lawrence Durrell* by Joanna Hodgkin, *A Café in Space: The Anaïs Nin Literary Journal* 10 (2013): 140-44.

—. "Tales of Incest: The Agony of Saph and Pa Durrell", *A Café in Space: The Anaïs Nin Literary Journal* 11 (2014): 54-68.

—. "Virgil and Durrell in Arcady: *Umbra*, Penumbra, and Dark Pastoral", *C.20: an International Journal,* Issue 2 (December 2019). https://durrelllibrarycorfu.wordpress.com.

—. "Remarks on *Sicilian Carousel* and Its Fabulator" in *Islands of the Mind: Psychology, Literature and Biodiversity* edited by Richard Pine and Vera Konidari (Newcastle-upon-Tyne: Cambridge Scholars Publishing, 2020): 83-98.

—. "Lawrence Durrell on Rainer Maria Rilke's *The Notebooks of Malte Laurids Brigge*", *C.20: an international journal*, Issue 4 (2021). https://durrelllibrarycorfu.wordpress.com.

Rilke, Rainer Maria, *Wartime Letters of Rainer Maria Rilke, 1914-1921* translated by M. D. Herter Norton (New York: Norton Library/W. W. Norton, 1940).

—. *Sonnets to Orpheus* translated by M. D. Herter Norton ([1942] New York: Norton Library/W. W. Norton, 1962).

—. *Duino Elegies: The German Text, with an English Translation, Introduction, and Commentary by J. B. Leishman and Stephen Spender* ([1939] New York: W. W. Norton, 1963).

—. *Sämtliche Werke*, 6 Bände, Herausgegeben vom Rilke-Archiv. In Verbindung mit Ruth Sieber-Rilke besorgt durch Ernst Zinn (Frankfurt am Main: Insel-Verlag, 1966).

—. *Letters to Merline (1919-1922): Rainer Maria Rilke* translated by Jesse Browner (New York: Paragon House, 1989).

—. *Rainer Maria Rilke and Lou Andreas-Salomé: The Correspondence* translated by Edward Snow and Michael Winkler (New York: W. W.

Norton, 2006).

Roberts, Andrew, *Napoleon: A Life* (New York: Viking, 2014).

Robins, Gay, *The Art of Ancient Egypt* (Cambridge, MA: Harvard University Press, 1997).

Romano, James F., "The Origin of the Bes Image", *Bulletin of the Egyptological Seminar* 2 (1980): 39-56.

Romer, John, and Elizabeth Romer, *The Seven Wonders of the World: A History of the Modern Imagination* (New York: Henry Holt, 1995).

Rose, William, "Rilke and the Conception of Death" in *Rainer Maria Rilke: Aspects of his Mind and Poetry* edited by William Rose and G. Craig Houston (London: Sidgwick & Jackson, 1938): 41-84.

Rosenmeyer, Thomas G., *The Green Cabinet: Theocritus and the European Pastoral Lyric* (Berkeley, CA: University of California Press, 1969).

Roth, Ann Macy, and Catherine H. Roehrig, "Magical Bricks and the Bricks of Birth", *Journal of Egyptian Archaeology* 88 (2002): 121-39.

Sabloff, Jeremy A., *The New Archaeology and the Ancient Maya* (New York: Scientific American Library, 1990).

Salinger, J. D., *The Catcher in the Rye* (New York: Little, Brown, 1951).

Salis, J. R. von, *Rainer Maria Rilke: The Years in Switzerland: A Contribution to the Biography of Rilke's Later Life* translated by N. K. Cruickshank ([1936] Berkeley, CA: University of California Press, 1966).

Schäfer, Heinrich, *Principles of Egyptian Art* edited by Emma Brunner-Traut, translated and edited by John Baines ([1919] Oxford: Griffith Institute, 2002).

Schlegel, Friedrich, *"Athenäums" — Fragmente und andere Schriften* (Stuttgart: Philipp Reclam jun., 1978).

—. *Philosophical Fragments* translated by Peter Firchow (Minneapolis, MN: University of Minneapolis Press, 1991).

Sciaretta, Antonio, *Antonio Sciaretta's Toponymy*. http://www.asciatopo.altervista.org/sicilia.html. Accessed 12 October 2018.

Shakespeare, William, *The Norton Shakespeare* third edition, edited by Stephen Greenblatt et al. (New York: W. W. Norton, 2016).

The Shambhala Dictionary of Buddhism and Zen by Ingrid Fischer-Schreiber (Buddhism), Franz-Karl Ehrhard (Tibetan Buddhism) and Michael S. Diener (Zen), translated by Michael H. Kohn (Boston: Shambhala, 1991).

Sherry, Norman, *Conrad's Eastern World* (Cambridge: Cambridge University Press, 1971).

Shipley, Lucy, *The Etruscans: Lost Civilizations* (London: Reaktion Books, 2017).

Silva, Luiza Osorio G., "The Myth of the Mundane: The Symbolism of Mud Brick and Its Architectural Implications", *Journal of the American Research Center in Egypt* 56 (2020): 181-97.

Smith, Helena, "Literary Legend Learning to Type at 92", *Guardian,* 2 March 2007.

Smith, W. Stevenson, *The Art and Architecture of Ancient Egypt* second edition revised by William Kelly Simpson (New Haven, CT: Yale University Press, 1981).

Smyth, Herbert Weir, *Greek Grammar* revised by Gordon M. Messing (Cambridge, MA: Harvard University Press, 1956).

Snell, Bruno, *The Discovery of the Mind in Greek Philosophy and Literature* translated by Thomas G. Rosenmeyer ([1953] New York: Dover Publications, 1982).

Solomon, Eric, "The Incest Theme in *Wuthering Heights*", *Nineteenth-Century Fiction* 14.1 (1959): 80-83.

The Song of Songs: A New Translation with an Introduction and Commentary translated by Ariel Bloch and Chana Bloch (Berkeley, CA: University of California Press, 1995).

Sorensen, Roy, *A Brief History of the Paradox: Philosophy and the Labyrinths of the Mind* (Oxford: Oxford University Press, 2003).

Stanford, W. B., *The Ulysses Theme: A Study in the Adaptability of a Traditional Hero* (Oxford: Basil Blackwell, 1954).

Stein, Gertrude, *Gertrude Stein: Writings 1932-1946* selected and notes by Catharine R. Simpson and Harriet Chessman (New York: Library of America, 1998).

Steiner, George, "The Baroque Novel" in *The World of Lawrence Durrell* edited by Harry T. Moore (Carbondale, IL: University of Southern Illinois Press, 1962): 13-23.

—. "Homer and Virgil and Broch", review of *Oxford Readings in Vergil's "Aeneid"* edited by S. J. Harrison, *London Review of Books* 12, no. 13 (12 July 1990): 10-11.

Steingräber, Stephan, *Abundance of Life: Etruscan Wall Painting* translated by Russell Stockman (Los Angeles: J. Paul Getty Museum, 2006).

Stephanides, Theodore, *Autumn Gleanings: Corfu Memoirs and Poems* edited by Richard Pine et al. (Corfu: Durrell School of Corfu, 2011).

Stevenson, Alice, "Palettes", *UCLA Encyclopedia of Egyptology.* https://escholarship.org/search?q=palettes&searchType=eScholarship&searchUnitType=series. Accessed 6 January 2022.

Stewart, Andrew, "The Alexandrian Style: A Mirage?" in *Alexandria and Alexandrianism: Papers Delivered at a Symposium Organized by the J. Paul Getty Museum and The Getty Center for the History of Art and the Humanities and Held at the Museum, April 22-25, 1993* (Malibu, CA: J. Paul Getty Museum, 1996): 231-46.

Tavis, Anna A., *Rilke's Russia: A Cultural Encounter* (Evanston, IL: Northwestern University Press, 1996).

Taylor, A. E., *The Mind of Plato* (Ann Arbor, MI: University of Michigan Press, 1960).

Thomas, Alan G., and James A. Brigham, *Lawrence Durrell: An Illustrated Checklist* (Carbondale, IL: Southern Illinois University Press, 1983).

Thompson, Elizabeth, "Dwarfs in the Old Kingdom in Egypt", *Bulletin of the Australian Centre for Egyptology* 2 (1991): 91-98.

Tietze-Conrat, E., *Dwarfs and Jesters in Art* translated by Elizabeth Osborn (New York: Phaidon Publishers, 1957).

Veit, Ulrich, "Ethnic Concepts in German Prehistory: A Case Study on the Relationship between Cultural Identity and Archaeological Objectivity" in *Archaeological Approaches to Cultural Identity* edited and translated by Stephen Shennan (London: Unwin Hyman, 1989): 35-56.

Virgil (Publius Vergilius Maro), *Vergil's "Aeneid": Books I-VI*, revised edition, introduction, notes, vocabulary, and grammatical appendix by Clyde Pharr ([1930] Lexington, MA: D. C. Heath, 1964).

—. *Virgil: "Eclogues"* edited by Robert Coleman (Cambridge: Cambridge University Press, 1977).

—. *Virgil: "Eclogues, Georgics, Aeneid I-VI"* translated by H. Rushton Fairclough, revised by G. P. Goold (Cambridge, MA: Harvard University Press, 1999).

The Virgilian Tradition: The First Fifteen Hundred Years edited by Jan M. Ziolkowski and Michael C. J. Putnam (New Haven, CT: Yale University Press, 2008).

Warrell, Ian, *Turner's Sketchbooks* (London: Tate Publishing, 2017).

West, Martin, "A new Sappho poem", *Times Literary Supplement* no. 5334 (24 June 2005): 8.

West, Nancy Martha, *Kodak and the Lens of Nostalgia* (Charlottesville, VA: University Press of Virginia, 2000).

Wheelock, C. Webster, Letter to the editor, "Durrell Gave Landlords a Good Name", *New York Times* 21 November 1990 (Section A, page 22).

Whitehead, Alfred North, *Process and Reality: An Essay in Cosmology*, corrected edition edited by David Ray Griffin and Donald W. Sherburne ([1929] New York: Free Press, 1985).

Whiting, Bartlett Jere, *Modern Proverbs and Proverbial Sayings* (Cambridge, MA: Harvard University Press, 1989).

Wilkinson, Richard H., *Symbol and Magic in Egyptian Art* (London: Thames & Hudson, 1994).

—. *Egyptology Today* edited by Richard H. Wilkinson (Cambridge: Cambridge University Press, 2008).

Wilkinson, Toby, "What a King Is This: Narmer and the Concept of the Ruler", *Journal of Egyptian Archaeology* 86 (2000): 23-32.

—. *The Thames & Hudson Dictionary of Ancient Egypt* (London: Thames & Hudson, 2008).

—. *The Rise and Fall of Ancient Egypt* (New York: Random House, 2010).

Wilson, A. N., *Betjeman: A Life* (New York: Farrar, Straus and Giroux, 2006).

Wilson, Andrew, *Beautiful Shadow: A Life of Patricia Highsmith* (New York: Bloomsbury, 2003).

Wilson, Jeremy, *Lawrence of Arabia: The Authorized Biography of T. E. Lawrence* (New York: Antheneum, 1990).

Wilson, John A., *The Burden of Egypt: An Interpretation of Ancient Egyptian Culture* (Chicago: University of Chicago Press, 1951).

—. *Signs & Wonders upon Pharaoh: A History of American Egyptology* (Chicago: University of Chicago Press, 1964).

Wimsatt, W. K., Jr., *The Verbal Icon: Studies in the Meaning of Poetry* (Lexington, KY: University Press of Kentucky, 1954).

Witemeyer, Hugh, *George Eliot and the Visual Arts* (New Haven, CT: Yale University Press, 1979).

Wood, Ernest, *Zen Dictionary* ([1957] Rutland, VT: Charles E. Tuttle, 1972).

Wood, Michael, "Sink or Skim", *London Review of Books* (1 January 2009): 11-12.

Yeats, W. B., *The Collected Works of W. B. Yeats* Vol. 1, *The Poems* revised edition edited by Richard J. Finneran (New York: Macmillan Publishing, 1989).

Ziolkowski, Theodore, *Virgil and the Moderns* (Princeton, NJ: Princeton University Press, 1993).

INDEX

(Asterisks indicate important topics.)

Index

Loria, Giuseppe Alessandro, 3, 15-16
Lynn, Kenneth S., 22

Macaulay, Rose, 178-79
MacKay, Marina, 103
MacNiven, Ian S., 30, 42-43, 49, 100n.31, 116, 118, 121, 128, 136n.24, 146, 162, 164, 166, 182, 194, 200, 202, 207n.181, 234
madness, xi, 29, 37, 154-55, 209, *see also* schizophrenia
The Magic Mountain (Mann), 51, 115
Malinowski, Bronisław, 97
Mallarmé, Stéphane, 104
mandala, xvi, 195
The Man Who Never Was (Ewen Montagu), 136n.27,
Manetho (Egyptian priest), 199
Mani (Greece), 56, 89-91, 93, 111, 132, 144, 152
Mann, Thomas, 58, 115
"Tonio Kröger", 58
Manzaloui, Mahmoud, 7n.6
Mareotis Lake (Alexandria), 16, 164, 168, 169-70, 172-73, 178, 183-84, 196n.124
Marlowe, Christopher, 140
Matisse, Henri, 138, 165
Mazet Michel (Languedoc), 10-11, 217, 227, and Figure 3
McPhee, John, 170
McPherson, Joseph W., 164
Medusa (Corfu), 154-55, *see also* Gorgon
Meguid, Ibrahim Abdel, 6
*memory, xv-xvi, 7, 11, 33, 51-52, 56, 71, 80, 92, 100, 124-25, 137, 144, 149-50, 157, 166, 172, 182, 194-95, 201, 203, 207, 212, 236
Mendelsohn, Daniel, 52
Menuhin, Diana and Yehudi, 225n.29, *see also* Gould, Diana

metaphor, xvi, 4, 15, 26, 36, 44, 56, 88, 89n.8, 102, 111-12, 117, 121, 130, 136n.23, 142, 157, 177, 182-95, 197, 202, 222, 229
metaphysics, xvii, 125
Milarepa (Tibetan sage), 93
Miller, Henry, xvii, 8, 10, 16, 23-26, 39, 42, 78-79, 85, 95, 101, 106n.45, 132, 140-41, 171, 190, 202, 212
Millington-Drake, Marie, 121, 123
Milton, John, 18, 119, 142
minor mythologies, 111
Minotaur (Crete), 124-25, 127-30
*mirrors, 3, 35-36, 42, 76, 83, 89, 158, 166, 173, 212, and Plate 4
Mitchell, Michael, 118
Mithraism, 128, *see also* Minotaur
Morrell, Lady Ottoline, 60-61
Morrison, Ray, 179, 195, 197
Morton-Saner, Anthea, 160, 194, 220n.12
Mumon, Yamada Roshi, 211-12
Muzot, Château de (Switzerland), 230-33, and Figures 16, 18, *see also* Rilke
Meyers, Jeffrey, 191n.106, 192
Myers, Nancy (LD's first wife), xvii, 1, 17, Chapter Two *passim*, 35, 97, 99, 121, 136n.23, 137, 139-40, 157n.72, 192
*myth/mythos/mythmaking, xvii, 4, 20, 22, 24, 35, 51n.4, 52, 109, 121-25, 127, 130-31, 132n.11, 154-55, 160, 175-77, 184, 186, 195, 221-22

Nabokov, Vladimir, 30
Nag, Sumantra, 44n.69
*"Narmer Palette", 60, 161, 179-207, 222, and Figures 11, 12
Nashe, Thomas, 140
Nasser, Gamal Abdel, 4, 51, 70
Naxos (Sicily and Greece), 123-25

*Nebamun (ancient Egyptian
official), 171-75, 196, 208, 211,
and Plate 5
necrophilia, 46, *see also* incest
*never/nevermore, 91-93, *see also*
"*jamais de la vie*" *and* "The
Raven"
Newberry, Percy Edward, 184-85
New Criticism, 103, 105
Nin, Anaïs, 23-25

O'Connor, David, 182, 196, 199
Octavian/Augustus, 57, 139
Odyssey (Homer), 121, 127
Oedipal complex, 41
*One and Many (Aristotle), 74, 97,
163
orientalism, 177-78
*orphan as literary trope, 107, 136-
37
Osirian themes, 160, 184
Otis, Brooks, 133, 137, 139-40, 147

Page, Denys, 109
Paipeti, Hilary Whitton, 96n.23,
100n.31
Panofsky, Erwin, 119n.13, 133, 135,
229n.40
Paracelsus, 206
paradise, 87, 132, *see also*
Eden/Edenic
paradox, 66, 102, 110, 127-28, 152,
154, 163, 216
Paris, 23-24, 56, 61, 78, 132, 165,
235
Parkinson, Richard, 170n.37, 171-
72, 175
Parthenon Marbles, 161
*pastoral literature/pleasance, xviii,
16-18, 59, 83, 115, 119-21,
Chapter Eight *passim*, 210, *see
also* "*locus amoenus*" *and*
"*hortus conclusus*" *and* "*et in
Arcadia ego*"
Pastroudis café (Alexandria), 70
pedophilia, 39

Personal Landscape, 7-8, 20n.25
Peters, H. F., 222, 224,
Peirce, Carol, 95, 160
Peirce, Charles Sanders, 183
*penumbra, 131n.1, 134-35, 143-45,
152, 156, 159, 228, *see also*
shadow *and* umbra
Picasso, Pablo, 161
Pinchin, Jane Lagoudis, 51n.4, 52
Pine, Richard, 18n.20, 49, 86, 87n.5,
96n.23, 100n.31, 110-11, 116,
136, 144n.47, 155, 171, 189,
209
*plagiarism, 24, 96-99, 134
*Plato and Platonic Forms, xvi-xvii,
xix, 74, 99, 127n.40, 190, 212,
229, 234, *see also* "Allegory of
the Cave" *and The Republic*
Plutarch, 153n.14, 160, 184
Poe, Edgar Allan, 36, 93, 115, 122-
23, 206, 229
"Annabel Lee", 122-23
"The Fall of the House of
Usher", 36, 38, 229
"The Raven", 93, *see also*
never/nevermore
Pollak, Max, 89n.9
Pope, Alexander, 52
Porter, Peter, 6-7, 10
postmodernism, 32
Pound, Ezra, 144, 149
Powell, Dilys, 17n.18, 126
Prater, Donald, 222
*promontories, 54, 71, 91, 152
Proust, Marcel, 78, 100, 191
Provence, 75, 97, 128, 133, 143,
146, 167, 192, 195, 207, 229,
see also Languedoc
pseudonyms, xvii, 138, 165, *see
also* "Charles Norden" *and*
Epfs, Oscar
Purcell, Henry, 140

Quibell, (James) Edward, 182

Rader, Ralph W., 33, 55, 194n.117